Dr. Frank Alabiso is a clinical psychologist with more than 40 years of experience in treating individuals for the psychological effects of trauma on personality development. Over the span of his career, Dr. Alabiso has treated four individuals afflicted with the rare diagnosis of multiple personality disorder. In the course of his private practice, Dr. Alabiso became acquainted with Lillian. Inspired by her personal strength and her triumph over mental illness, Dr. Alabiso joined Jean Baker Reynolds in bringing Lillian's story to light.

Jean Baker Reynolds has had a long and distinguished career as an editor and proofreader of publications for the U.S. Navy. Ms. Baker Reynolds is the recipient of the Distinguished Service Award from the Military Order of the Purple Heart. Unrestrained by the formal training of psychiatrists at the time, Ms. Baker Reynolds did what no psychiatrist could have done. She devoted 10 years of her life to Lillian's triumph over multiple personality disorder. At age 93, Ms. Baker Reynolds is enthusiastically engaged in writing a series of children's books.

Respectfully dedicated to Lillian's loving husband, the extraordinary man who supported and loved her all the way through their ordeal, and to those brave personalities who protected Lillian from the pain of child abuse.

—The authors

Frank Alabiso, Ph.D.

LILLIAN: A TRUE STORY OF MULTIPLE PERSONALITY DISORDER

Based on a memoir by
Jean Baker Reynolds

AUSTIN MACAULEY PUBLISHERS™

LONDON * CAMBRIDGE * NEW YORK * SHARJAH

Ordering Information
Quantity sales: Special discounts are available on quantity purchases by corporations, associations, and others. For details, contact the publisher at the address below.

Publisher's Cataloging-in-Publication data
Alabiso, Ph.D., Frank
Lillian: A True Story of Multiple Personality Disorder

ISBN 9781649792037 (Paperback)
ISBN 9781649792051 (Hardback)
ISBN 9781649792068 (ePub e-book)
ISBN 9781649792044 (Audiobook)

Library of Congress Control Number: 2021900787

www.austinmacauley.com/us

First Published 2023
Austin Macauley Publishers LLC
40 Wall Street, 33rd Floor, Suite 3302
New York, NY 10005
USA

mail-usa@austinmacauley.com
+1 (646) 5125767

This book would have never been updated and produced without Jean Bley's insistence. Fascinated and intrigued by the story, she pushed Jean Baker Reynolds to get it published, convincing her that it is an important book. So, with the help of Dr. Alabiso, Jean reworked it, resulting in: *Lillian: A True Story of Multiple Personality Disorder.*

Kerry Ross and Stephanie Rheinheimer devoted many hours to scanning and formatting. Robert Bonner kept Jean's computer in working order. Robert Goolrick was Jean's legal adviser. Heartfelt gratitude goes to all for their comments and encouragement.

Special recognition is extended to Rev. Christopher Hobgood, whose wisdom, guidance, and spiritual leadership contributed immeasurably to Lillian's healing, and to Laura Hobgood, who was always at the ready to help when needed.

The book has been supported by our attorney and legal adviser, Brendan Lillis, and by our technical assistants Jennifer Kreuzer, Amanda McMullen and Mary Burich.

We are indebted to the following individuals who read the manuscript and generously provided their invaluable feedback: Philip DeVore; John E. Lee Jr.; Trudy Hynes; Dale Beebe; Gina Zali, Psy.D.; Linda Nash, Ph.D.; and Jennifer Kreuzer.

Special recognition is given to Milton Robinson, M.D.; Richard Kluft, M.D., Ph.D.; and Ralph Zannoni, B.S. True pioneers in the treatment of multiple personality disorder at the time, these individuals provided insight and inspiration for the writing of this book.

Finally, the authors acknowledge Lynda Reed, Ph.D., for sharing her memories and heartfelt feelings for Lillian.

Jean Baker Reynolds
Frank Alabiso, Ph.D.

Table of Contents

Foreword

When this story began more than 40 years ago, psychiatrists and other doctors seemed mystified by patients with more than one personality.

The diagnosis at the time was multiple personality disorder. Known today as dissociative identity disorder, this mental condition is characterized by an individual's displaying the behavior of two or more personalities. In more recent times, doctors have successfully treated this complex condition.

When a young child experiences severe trauma that is so unbearable – severe physical, sexual and emotional abuse – the brain locks the memory into a newly created self in the mind like a piece in a jigsaw puzzle. That self-withholds the secret from the host personality's mind and develops an identity of its own. It is the mind's attempt to create a defense mechanism.

Lillian was afflicted with this condition, owing to the severe abuse she experienced as a child and teenager.

Lillian's mind held each trauma separately in the form of a personality. The personalities took over Lillian's body, developing lives and personae of their own.

As Lillian's Aunt Jean, I became friends with 22 personalities over a number of years. I played hide-and-seek with 4-year-old Mary, taught 5-year-old Amy to write and to play the piano, and shopped and communicated endlessly with many of the others by telephone, letters and in person.

In the process, each personality revealed its beginnings to Lillian's psychiatrist, to my pastor and ultimately to me.

The entire basis of each personality consisted of trauma memories. As the personalities exposed their hidden memories, they were somehow able to give those memories back to Lillian, and the personalities were no longer needed. However, Lillian had to experience whatever the horrors were before the integration could take place. One by one, the personalities became integrated, and those "pieces of the puzzle" melded into Lillian herself. She became one.

With integration, I missed each one of them. For I had become a trusted friend. I played with the children, agonized over the teenagers' problems and became privy to the very reason for their existence.

Every handwriting was different and never deviated. Each personality wrote a farewell letter and was gone.

During Lillian's first visit to my house in the late 1970s, I encouraged her to start a journal. Today, my closet holds 26 journals, 14 notebooks, several shoeboxes full of letters from Lillian and videos of the various personalities.

Lillian's story has been documented with incredible detail.

During this same period of time, Dr. Alabiso became a therapist to Lillian's youngest son, James.

As patient and therapist, James and Dr. Alabiso forged a therapeutic bond. A story in itself, James formed separate relationships with each of the personalities.

Jean Baker Reynolds

Preface

In 2019, Jean Baker Reynolds, then 90 years old, contacted me with a request: Would I assist her in bringing Lillian's story to light?

Jean had remembered me from my work with Lillian's 10-year-old son, James, some 40 years earlier.

Over the next 24 months, Jean and I met in person, collaborated by emails and shared memories of key events in the lives of Lillian and her family. In the process, we became friends.

Jean Baker Reynolds is an extraordinary person.

In this book, the reader will meet each of Lillian's personalities and come to understand the intricate relationship between multiple personality disorder, child abuse and the path to healing.

In the opening chapters, the reader experiences the same confusion that initially confronted Aunt Jean.

Can the reader believe that the personalities are real? How does the reader get to know them? How does one distinguish one personality from another? How does one learn to navigate the labyrinth of communication needed to give voice to each personality?

Lillian's personality consisted of separate, fragmented parts, many of whom had never revealed themselves to one another before, much less to others.

For most of us, the parts of our personalities are woven together by our memories. But what happens when we have no memories? What happens when the components of memory (facts, feelings and body states) are split apart and not available to one another?

The challenge for Aunt Jean was to develop a system of communication that connected Lillian's personality parts, ultimately leading to the recovery of Lillian's hidden memories.

Letters, journal entries, telephone conversations with Aunt Jean, disappearances and reappearances; all yielded bits of information about the personalities and their origins.

Jean was not a therapist. Her thinking was original and not constrained by formal training.

Relying on the healing powers of curiosity, acceptance and love, Jean's approach was beautiful in its simplicity: Get to know them, accept them, love them, connect them, and they will heal.

Lillian is an exquisite and beautifully written story of poverty, transgenerational abuse, mental illness, and the healing power of love, science and spirituality.

As one reader put it, "You will laugh, cry, turn away and come back again to its compelling truth."

It has been my privilege to have been befriended by Aunt Jean and to have served as the reader's guide.

Frank Alabiso, Ph.D.

Lillian's Family

Husband	Jimmy
Jimmy's Parents	Grandma, Pap
Children	Keith, Evan, James
Sisters	Rosalind, Letty
Mother	Jessica
Stepfather	Herbert
Foster Brothers	Children for Money
Paternal Aunt/Uncle	Jean, Walter
Maternal Aunts	Pearl, Mary, Gladys

Prologue
Lillian Wanted Her Story Told

Lillian Mason Wrote: Multiple personality disorder (MPD) is a curable illness. It is a dissociative disorder characterized by disruption of memory and identity.

Aunt Jean experienced the many other "selves" she encountered within me. Other family members may have differing versions of the events described here.

In the events described by various personalities, Aunt Jean has made every attempt to be faithful to their truths, as they are no longer present to speak for themselves. Aunt Jean has attempted in her own way to show not only the downside of having multiple personality disorder, but also the mystery, the fun times and the healing involved in our living of this story. In the early months of my therapy, Aunt Jean suggested I keep a diary. Soon, not only I but also the personalities chronicled our daily thoughts in our journals; 26 in all. We wrote of our intimate feelings, fears and experiences, and soon discovered the healing power of words, both spoken and written. We could write when there was no one to talk to. The journals often provided my only form of communication with the "others," since I could not see them.

Lillian is not intended to be a medical history. Any one of you might have been Aunt Jean, but she is unique because she is my aunt.

Lillian Mason, 1994

Part 1

Chapter 1
Six of One

In Chapter 1, we meet Lillian, Aunt Jean, Lillian's husband and Lucy, the first personality to reveal herself. Through Lucy, we are introduced to Julie, Lee, Esther and Amy; all well-formed personalities, each with distinct personality traits and history.

Chapter 1 provides the reader with a glimpse into the complexity of establishing a relationship with personalities who have no mechanism for communicating with one another and who cannot be present at the same time, much less work together.

Imagine the complexity of speaking to each part as a different person – a person who, in reality, does not exist. Yet, Aunt Jean develops a relationship with each one of them, thereby becoming a friend, interpreter and protector; a role no therapist could have fulfilled. Indeed, the psychiatric wisdom at the time taught that therapists should not encourage the development of personality states.

Finally, in the face of accepted theory at the time, Aunt Jean's eagerness to befriend each personality ultimately leads to Lillian's becoming one person.

FA

Jean as Narrator: It was the winter of 1976. Lillian was living in a trailer park in Niagara Falls, New York.

To Lillian, it seemed she could never do anything right. Things appeared in her house that she did not buy: that new coffeepot and a dirty coffee cup in the sink. How? Who? She didn't even like coffee. Food disappeared from the refrigerator. Clothes she had never seen, with price tags still attached, showed up in her closet.

Transfixed by the rushing water, Lillian found Niagara Falls to be calming. She drove there often.

Life was so confusing and unhappy, but the majesty of Niagara Falls was always the same. She could count on it. Its consistency was soothing. The crashing water seemed to draw her. Sometimes she just sat in her car. Sometimes she walked to the edge.

Today was different; she had plans. Ending it all would make it better for everyone else.

Lillian Mason carefully placed her keys in her purse on the front seat and got out of the car. Checking that the passenger door was locked, she depressed the lock button on the driver's side before closing the door. She was satisfied that her keys and purse were locked inside, safe until her husband could unlock the car with his keys. There was money in her purse. She had cashed Jim's paycheck just that morning before the day had begun to deteriorate.

The Falls were calling to her, seducing her, promising peace. She could feel the spray of the water as it rose above the Falls. It was her friend.

Lillian walked calmly around the viewing pavilion to the riverside of the pillar supporting it. There, facing the roaring river, she removed her green winter coat, leaning back against the pillar to brace herself while she folded it. She then reached up and placed it on the pavilion floor. No use wasting a perfectly good coat. She removed her glasses and laid them on the coat.

"This is it. I need to do this for everybody, but I have to be sure." Lillian paused, looking first down into the great whirlpool below and then out over the gorge. She felt no fear, only relief at finally making her decision.

It was the middle of winter. No one was in sight. All was quiet except for the roar of the water – so powerful and beckoning. Beyond it, all lay at peace. Just as she stepped toward the ledge, she heard, "Stop! LILLIAN! Stop!"

His voice startled her. She felt weightless for an instant, expecting to fall. An iron hand gripped her arm. Lillian struggled. The man yelled, "Help me! Losing my grip!"

A second officer grabbed onto the first. They strained to their limits. "Let her go, or we will go over!"

"No! Pull, dammit!" the first officer shouted.

With the realization that she was endangering someone else's life, Lillian reversed her actions and allowed herself to be pulled back onto solid ground. She was shaking and apologetic. She hadn't meant to bother anyone, and she had nearly dragged two innocent men to their deaths.

Cautiously, the officers backed her away from the ledge. Holding her arms behind her back, the Niagara Falls State Park policemen walked her to their patrol car. They were breathing hard. When she asked how they knew her name, they said her husband, Jimmy, had called them. One officer guarded her while the other retrieved her coat and glasses.

On the way to the hospital, their passenger volunteered, "She's been wantin' t' end her life fer a while now. This time we was gonna let 'er."

Who was the "we?" And then a small voice said, "I dis' want somebody t' love me."

Lillian was involuntarily admitted to Memorial Hospital. Her patient chart was marked "Attempted Suicide." She was placed in a psychiatric intensive care room (PIC room), across from the nurses' station, where she could be watched.

Jimmy met them at the hospital. Lillian had always displayed mood swings. He considered them normal for her. But now, he knew she had needs beyond his patience. Lillian was assigned to see Dr. Milton Robinson, chief psychiatrist.

Lillian was sure that her husband's parents would never approve of his spending money on a psychiatrist. So, she was reluctant to ask Dr. Robinson to be her doctor. She knew she needed help, but would it be fair? Lillian thought not, and the doctor refused to accept her as a patient unless she herself asked him. Lillian finally made an appointment for "help in losing weight" and admitted that she had "a few other things to work out."

Dr. Robinson set about collecting a history. Lillian Mason was having difficulty controlling her children. She had been going with her three sons to a $5-per-visit family clinic for several months. The children insisted upon telling things to the therapist that Lillian knew nothing about. She thought they were exaggerating. No, she was sure that they were lying. "If that's what they need to do in order for us to get help, let them talk. That's the least I can do for them," Lillian told Jimmy. The sessions were tape-recorded. Sometimes it was Mom and Keith. Sometimes it was Mom and Evan. At other times, it was James, Evan and Keith. Occasionally the therapist worked with Lillian alone.

The therapist's report said that Evan came home from school to an accusing mom. A whole set of dishes was broken, and the pieces were in a bushelbasket. Lillian asked Evan why he broke her dishes, and Evan denied it.

After all, he had been at school all day, and the dishes were okay in the morning!

One day when Lillian returned to the clinic, the director met her at the door. Ushering her into his office, he proceeded to replay the tape recording from the previous visit. Lillian was shocked to hear, about 10 minutes into the tape, a small child's voice plaintively calling out, "I dis' want somebody t' love me."

The therapist did not conceal his annoyance at what he interpreted to be Lillian's mockery – "We'd better end this session right now!"

After that, she couldn't bring herself to go back to the clinic by herself but continued taking her sons right up till the time of her suicide attempt.

Jimmy told the doctor that he sometimes heard a child's voice in the night. He had no explanation.

Dr. Robinson pored over medical journals and conferred with colleagues in his search for a diagnosis. There was the park policeman's report of a voice saying that she had been wanting to take her life for a long time, and this time "they" were going to let her do it. Then there was the small child's voice and Lillian's accusation about broken dishes. Jimmy had said Lillian was moody – sometimes very up, and other times angry or sad without provocation.

After Lillian was released from the hospital, she began seeing Dr. Robinson at his office. His file grew. Lillian couldn't remember her childhood. Some of what Lillian's sons told the therapist bordered on child abuse. Someone had actually filed a child abuse complaint against her the previous year.

Upon discovering that Keith had become sexually active, Lillian had begun having flashbacks to her own childhood. Lillian described, as a child, being able to "step back" and watch another child. Dr. Robinson knew she was describing one of the symptoms of multiple personality disorder. Lillian said she could make it happen by causing a roaring in her head.

Knowing full well that many, if not most, psychiatrists did not believe in what he was thinking, Dr. Robinson decided not to mention multiple personality disorder to Lillian. Instead, he would wait for further developments. Weeks became months.

One day Lillian told the doctor that a friend had once told her that when she called herself Lucy, she was aggressive and seemed happier.

"I would like to meet that Lucy someday," the doctor said. In a flash, the mousy figure, clutching a large purse in her lap, straightened up, removed her glasses and plopped the purse on the floor. She wore a big smile, and her eyes were shining.

"I'm Lucy, and I'm the one who broke those dishes! Sometimes I just get mad!" Lucy was bouncy and bubbly, just the opposite of Lillian.

Lucy took her name from Lillian's middle name. She said she was 18. Lillian was 37.

Lucy enlightened Dr. Robinson, disregarding if he was ready or not!

"There are five of us. Six countin' Lil. That Julie, she cries all the time. She is named for a doll Lil used to have. Then there is Lee; he protects all of us. But watch out for Esther. She is furious! Lil's mother's name is Jessica but wanted to be named Esther and sometimes called herself that. I don't like Esther."

"That's four, Lucy. Who else?" the doctor asked when he could finally speak. "Amy," Lucy replied. "Lil used to have a pretend playmate when she was in the coal cellar or closet for a long time, and her name is Amy. She is 5 years old."

The doctor's interest grew. The appearance of Lucy seemed to confirm that Lillian Mason was suffering from multiple personality disorder. Dr. Robinson had never treated a patient with multiple personality disorder before; few doctors had.

Lucy vanished as quickly as she had appeared. The glasses were replaced, and the purse came back onto her lap. Lillian was back, slouching in the chair. She looked at her watch. "What happened?" She had lost time again. Her hour was almost up, and she didn't remember saying much to Dr. Robinson.

"Lucy was here, Lillian." Dr. Robinson gave her a copy of the book *Sybil* to read. She read it overnight and returned it to the doctor's office the next day. Lillian wondered why he had given it to her; it had nothing to do with her!

My husband (her Uncle Walter) and I hadn't seen or heard from our niece, Lillian and her husband, Jimmy, for some time, so Jimmy's telephone call was a surprise. We exchanged the usual pleasantries, and then, with no warning, he asked, "Do you believe in multiple personalities?"

I was too stunned to reply. He had to repeat the question. I told him I knew very little but was a believer. I said I had read *Sybil* and had seen the movie twice. I had also seen *The Three Faces of Eve*.

"Lillian is a multiple personality," he said, his voice low. "One of her personalities attempted suicide by going over Niagara Falls. The police rescued her."

Before I could say anything, Lillian began speaking. She had been listening. "Oh, Aunt Jean, there are five of them. There are Julie and Lucy, and then there is Lee, he is male, and a 5-year-old named Amy," she said. Lillian paused and said, as if to herself, "That's only four. Who else, Jimmy?"

"Esther," Jimmy replied. "Oh, yes, Esther," Lillian said, her voice fading. "But the doctor says she is very angry." Jimmy broke in, "Jean, what we are calling about is just this: One of them wants to write you a letter, and we wanted to see if it would be okay with you. Her name is Julie. She says she knows you and wants to be friends. The doctor thinks it would be good for her to have a friend."

I asked about the doctor. Jimmy said he was a psychiatrist named Dr. Robinson. Giving me the doctor's address and telephone number, Jimmy told me I could call him if I wanted to.

My mind was trying to fathom the idea of writing to someone who was Lillian and, I supposed, somehow not quite Lillian.

"How do I answer Julie if she writes?" I asked. "How do I address a letter?"

"You can address it to Lillian and write Julie's name someplace on the envelope," Jimmy said. "Whoever gets it out of the mailbox will put it on her jewelry box. Julie will get it when she's here."

Hanging up, I couldn't really believe the conversation. I had always been quite fond of Lillian, although I had not seen her often. Her father, the brother of my husband, Walter, had died in a tragic shop accident when Lillian was only 7 months old. Lillian and I had met once in a while at family get-togethers, but we didn't really know each other very well.

During the summer before her senior year in high school, Lillian came for a visit with her older sister, Rosalind, who was working in Washington, D.C. We lived nearby, just three miles from Springfield, Virginia. Both nieces spent the weekend with us. Then, on Monday morning, Rosalind went off to work, and Lillian remained with us for the week.

Lillian was an adorable young lady. We talked by the hour and built a warm relationship in the days that followed. I had no hint that anything was wrong with her life. That is until one night, I was awakened by her screaming, "No! No! Oh, no!" she yelled. I hurried to her bedside. "Lillian, Lillian, it's all right," I said, touching her shoulder lightly. "You're okay, Lillian, it's Aunt Jean! Wake up! Are you having a bad dream?"

Lillian opened her eyes and sat up, crying. I held her until her crying subsided, then suggested that we go into the living room for a while. I didn't want her to go back to sleep too soon and get back into that nightmare.

We sat on the sofa, and after we had talked for an hour, she told me that her employer had raped her. She was afraid to go back to work because she didn't know how to keep him from doing it again.

Her mother and her sister had spread the word over the last several years that, "Lillian isn't right. She makes things up. She lies." But holding and listening to her that night, I believed her. I wanted so much to keep her with us, but I knew, somehow, that she would never be permitted to stay. The best I could do was insist, "You need to tell your mother about that employer." She calmed down. The rest of the visit was uneventful. Shortly after Lillian's return to her home in Ohio, we received a telegram from her mother:

> YOU TAKE CARE OF YOUR OWN BUSINESS. STOP.
> I'LL TAKE CARE OF MINE. STOP.
> JESSICA.

We didn't know what to make of it. What could we have done that Jessica thought was so bad? We couldn't figure out any way to deal with Jessica or her telegram. She had effectively shut us out. I wanted to contact Lillian, but Walter convinced me that it was Jessica's prerogative to keep her child from us, and I sadly acquiesced.

The word from Rosalind was vague. "Lillian isn't right. She's giving mother such trouble!"

In the spring, we were surprised to receive a graduation announcement and a photograph of Lillian. She was a beautiful girl, and I could not detect anything out of line in the picture. As I wrapped and sent a small gift, I kept thinking about Lillian. I wondered how she had dealt with her employer.

A few days later, Rosalind called to say that Lillian had made a suicide attempt and was committed to a psychiatric ward. She told us that the doctors there didn't want anyone to contact Lillian. The electric shock treatments didn't seem to help. Rosalind became "too busy" to visit us much, and we were left in the dark about Lillian.

The next time I saw Lillian was about two years later at her wedding. The groom was James Mason, who said he was planning to become a pastor. Lillian called us and asked her Uncle Walter to take photographs of her wedding. She remembered that he had taken some portraits of her when she had visited us.

The bride was radiant in white satin and lace. Her sister looked charming as the maid of honor. Walter took numerous photos. When we inquired where the newlyweds would be spending their honeymoon, Lillian said they didn't know because they didn't have money for a motel. We gave them a key, some money for gas and food, and directions to our house in Virginia. They accepted and stayed at our home until we returned from our visit with relatives in Ohio.

After the honeymoon, they moved to Florida, where Jimmy hoped to enter the seminary but never did. In the following years, we heard from them every Christmas but seldom saw them.

Now I was waiting to hear from Lillian again, a Lillian who had somehow become a person who was living many lives, a Lillian who had tried to kill herself, or was it themselves? I could not understand how one person could be five other persons. I wondered if I would ever hear from Lillian or the "others" but decided to wait awhile before calling the doctor. Two days after Jimmy and Lillian's phone call, the first letter arrived.

My heart beat a little faster when I saw Julie's handwriting. It was totally different from Lillian's smooth, flowing, near-perfect penmanship. In place of a return address on the envelope was written "Julie." I opened the envelope and withdrew a letter. The delicate handwriting captivated me. Each word ended with an upward and backward swirl. I smiled to myself. My hands held proof of multiplicity, yet I remained skeptical. I couldn't read fast enough. Mystery and fascination flooded my mind.

Julie's letter said that she was 30 years old, and she had green eyes and short brown hair. Lillian was 37 now, and as I remembered, her eyes were blue, and her hair was brown and short. Julie said she was a friend of Lil, and that she occasionally wrote a little poetry and liked classical music. She wrote that she was afraid of men and preferred being alone.

Then I came to a paragraph that shocked me. Julie wrote that she was worried about Lee. He had some pot. "That's marijuana, isn't it? Isn't that dangerous?" she wrote.

I answered her the same day, addressing it to Lillian and writing "For Julie" on the envelope. I asked where Lee got the pot and agreed with her that pot was indeed dangerous. I said I would worry too if I had a friend using pot. I closed my letter by inviting any of the others (the only word I could think of) to write to me.

In what seemed the shortest turnaround time in postal history, I received a letter from Lee. "Hey, Ms. Jean. I know you've been talkin' to Julie and likewise. You shouldn't ask Julie where I get my grass or stuff. It puts her on the spot, and she knows these things, but it wouldn't be proper to betray any confidences. Okay? I forgot to tell right off; I am Lee Marvin. The grass can be got. I usually get a nickel bag for $12.50 from guys here in the park. That's where the gun came from too. I got a Browning semi-automatic pistol, but it's not registered, so we aren't saying too much about it. I don't have any bullets yet, so don't get hyper. That doctor of ours knows. He is an all-right guy. I gave him the grass, and the pills were a bad scene. I don't need them anyway. You want to ask me something, go ahead. Ask in Julie's letters, but she don't do my answers for me. You got a good guy for a husband. Lee Marvin."

In the same mail was a letter in a yellow envelope bearing the return address of Lucy. Her handwriting was really poor. She described herself as being 18 years old, right-handed (Lillian and Julie were left-handed), taller than Julie and Lillian, and having long brown hair and blue eyes. She wrote, "I completed the eighth grade, consider myself religious, like people, clothes and jewelry, and sometimes get angry and break things. I like to paint."

On the bottom of the page and beginning at the opposite side of the page was printed, in childlike fashion, "YMA," Amy spelled backward. What a puzzle!

For reasons I could not understand, I found myself instantly treating all three names as separate people. I answered each letter carefully, hoping to retain communication with Lee, Julie and Lucy. For Amy, I printed the words "I love you" and drew a heart, a smiling face and a cat. Under the cat, I printed "CAT" and added, "by Jean to Amy." I thought she might color the page and send it back to me.

I tried to keep the letters in the back of my mind while going about my business. As a theater organist and music teacher, I gave private organ lessons in my home, four afternoons and three evenings a week. I had about 25 students, ranging in age from 6 to 70.

Our daughter had married and moved to the West Coast. Walter worked late most evenings. Our two sons were grown and away from home. I had time to do a lot of thinking about my new friends.

The next day, I suddenly felt the need to talk to somebody. I realized I was in over my head. After all, I had not even gone to college. Walter had not been too pleased with my intense interest in his niece's plight, so I decided against talking to him. Instead, I talked to my friend Rev. Chris Hobgood, who was the minister at my church and a man easy to talk with.

After reading their letters and copies of my answers, Rev. Chris said he would like to meet her (or them), if Lillian ever came to visit me. Rev. Chris, too, was fascinated by the different handwritings. We discussed, at length, the power of the human mind and decided that while we could not understand what was happening to Lillian, we had to believe it and help her. He concurred with my approach to their letters. We couldn't decide whether to refer to Lillian as "her" or "them."

Lillian wrote to me next.

The real Lillian, I thought, writing a real letter about her family. Their eldest son, Keith, had recently joined the Navy and was in basic training. Middle son Evan starred in a recent little-theater production. Six-year-old James was visiting his paternal grandparents, Pap and Grandma, in Ohio.

Just before signing off, Lillian wrote, "I did a dumb thing and burned my arm, but it doesn't amount to much." One of those kitchen accidents, I assumed. They happen to everyone.

Also in my mailbox that day was another letter from Julie. She told me of her visit to a museum and asked some questions about a Mozart record she had borrowed from the library. Then she broke off and began writing about Lil as if Lillian were someone else. Julie wrote that Lil had received a letter from her sister Rosalind, who said how bad Lil was. Julie added, "So, Lil bought a bottle of drain cleaner and poured it on her wrist. The burning helped Lil not to feel so bad," Julie wrote. "It helps Lil because she knows she had been born a bad seed. I am learning from the doctor that I should not cut her anymore, to bleed out the bad, so the badness was relieved by the drain cleaner. It's a bad burn. She had to go to the doctor."

I had barely recovered from Julie's chilling words when I opened the third letter. It was from Lucy, who wrote of going to an aquarium with the two younger boys, Evan and James, and with Lillian's husband.

I wondered where Lillian was when Lucy was with Lillian's husband and sons. And what did Lillian think about Lucy taking her place?

Included in Lucy's envelope was a response from Amy. She had drawn a heart, a smiling face and a cat – like mine but in reverse order. The cat's tail curved to the right; my cat's tail curved to the left.

Under the cat were the letters "tac" and at the top of the page, "uoyevoli" – "I love you," backward.

From the letters that followed, I kept trying to comprehend the working of her mind. For instance, when Julie wrote, "Lil has a headache and is lying down right now," I wondered how Julie could have been writing to me while Lillian was lying down. How could this be? Was it not the same body? And why did Julie keep calling her Lil?

Julie seemed to have given herself the role of an interpreter for me. To try to explain it all to me, Julie wrote a poem:

Six of One

Six people live together, in a commune, you might say,
   (that's side-by-side all night and all day)
Though each other's faults are as clear as can be,
They are so different in their ways, you will see.

There is Amy,
Who is just a babe in the woods,
She can't read or write,
Nor would she if she could.

Then Lucy is there, as always, I guess,
Trying to spread happiness to all the rest.
Oh, she can get angry; we all have seen that!
Then her mood will change at the drop of a hat.

And Lee is just the opposite, lonely and cool,
But believe you me, he is nobody's fool!
He helped us through a dark time somehow,
Our bad times are over, and his have come now,

Julie (that's me) is changing her ways,
Hurt is receding, and good are her days.
She has felt shame and degradation,
But the doctor has helped her learn not to run.

Lillian, we see as quiet as a mouse.
Never fear, her inner strength, one day, will win out,
Don't let the good front she shows put you off,
She fought through a life of hell: she is not soft.

Esther is last as usual. She is a square,
Pretending, pretending, no therapy needs there!
Who is to say, but if she lets down her mask,
her road's the hardest, if she is to come back.

Well, now you have met us. That's all I would hope,
And when I say that I'm not making a joke,
Six people, six lives, each precious to them,
We hope you won't say we're the same one again.

Another letter from Julie focused on Lee, who she said was having a hard time with his sexuality. He wanted to talk to Dr. Robinson, but Lil, Julie and Lucy were taking up the whole appointment hour. Finally, in desperation, Lee wrote a note to Dr. Robinson and put it in Lil's purse, hoping she would simply hand it to the doctor. Lillian saw the note in Lee's inimitable handwriting and decided that she could not give the doctor a piece of paper signed "Lee Marvin." Wasn't Lee Marvin a movie star? What would the doctor think? Lee phoned Dr. Robinson the next day and asked for an appointment for himself. He spent the whole hour.

Julie's letter continued, "Whenever Lee can't stand Mr. Mason's bossiness, he takes Lil's car keys and drives around. It's cramped sometimes, for so many of us to live in a house trailer: Keith, Evan, Mr. Mason, James, Lil and us others. Lee likes to be alone."

"One time when Lee tried to leave, Mr. Mason said, 'No, you are not leaving. Give me those car keys!' When Lee insisted, Mr. Mason – he is a really big person, you know – he got Lee down on the floor and sat on him, so he couldn't leave in the car. So, Lee left, and Lil was there. Her husband was sitting on her!

"She said, 'Jimmy, you're hurting me! Let me up. What's going on?' And Mr. Mason got off her. He never wants to hurt his wife, but he was really frustrated with Lee.

"Another time, Lee was smoking, and Mr. Mason grabbed his cigarettes away. 'You can't smoke! Stop it. Put that cigarette out!' Mr. Mason shouted.

"Lee said, 'You smoke, and so does your kid Evan. I will smoke if I want to.' Mr. Mason was really mad. Mr. Mason thinks Lee is just trying to aggravate him. He keeps saying, 'I don't want my wife leaving here!' But Jean, Lil doesn't want to leave, Lee does. Mr. Mason gets even more angry because every time he and Lee get into an argument, Lee can just give the body back to Lil. Lil has blank times, and she never knows what's been happening, so she just keeps quiet.

"Lee is smoking grass and popping pills, and Lil wonders where he got the stuff. He did a dumb thing by letting her come back before the effects of the pills wore off, and she wasn't sure what was going on. I think Lil is afraid to say anything to anyone."

Julie kept calling Jimmy "Mr. Mason" and Lillian, "Lil." The whole scenario, as she described it, mystified me. She seemed to see Lee and Lillian as separate entities. I answered Julie's letter the same day and mailed it at the post office to save a day's time. I urged Julie to tell Dr. Robinson about Lee and to do it quickly.

Chapter 2
A Bad Seed

Chapters 2-6 paint a picture of each personality, not only by name but also by mannerisms, attitudes, dialect and voice – all telltale signs of a presence other than Lillian.

Each personality has a history of abuse. Each has a role in protecting Lillian from what she ultimately must face if she hopes to get well.

Chapter 2 provides a glimpse into the inner workings of the mind of a person afflicted with multiple personality disorder – insight into the interrelationships between personality parts and insight into each part's role, leading to an understanding that each part, no matter how dangerous or self-destructive, exists to protect Lillian from an unthinkable past.

As the chapters progress, Jean develops separate relationships with each of the personalities, and in doing so, earns each one's trust.

Indeed, Jean becomes a trusted participant in Lillian's multiplicity as interpreter, go-between and most importantly, as the source of unconditional love and acceptance.

FA

Jean as Narrator: The events leading up to Lillian's first visit to Virginia were not what I had expected. The day had begun with a phone call from Jimmy. He said Lee had written a letter to Dr. Robinson, saying he was depressed and feeling trapped. In the phone call, Jimmy explained, "He said that I was lording over him." Jimmy went on, "And he decided to kill himself. He was going to take Lillian to a motel, swallow pills and send Lillian back to me."

When the doctor received Lee's letter, he called Lillian and said that she and Jimmy should come to see him at once. Meanwhile, Jimmy, in disbelief, called the motel, which confirmed a reservation for two in the name of Lee

Marvin. Jimmy canceled the reservation and took Lillian to Dr. Robinson, knowing by now that he had also taken Lee.

Dr. Robinson talked Lee out of going to the motel, but Lee insisted that he had to leave town. "Go away, split." The doctor helped Jimmy and Lee negotiate. Would a trip to Jean's help? Lee conceded that it might, and that was how Jimmy and Lee agreed to keep Lillian alive.

"Will 'they' come along too?" I asked Jimmy when he called. How crazy that sounded! Jimmy chuckled.

Obviously, he understood much more than I did – "Yes, don't you get it? Wherever Lillian is, they are. What I mean is that they can be there if they want to be. They are all different and real, and each must be dealt with separately," he explained.

"Will I know which is which? I mean, who is who?" I had to ask.

"Part of the time, you will, but sometimes it's hard to tell. Lillian will always let you know when *she* is there. Julie and Lee are introverts. Lucy is an extrovert. Lucy talks a lot, and she will be there a lot of the time. Also, neither Lillian nor Julie can eat. Lucy likes to eat, so if you see someone eating, you can identify Lucy. If you see anyone smoking, that will be Lee. None of the others smoke. Julie calls me 'Mr. Mason,' and so does Lee. Julie reads with a dictionary on her lap. She likes to type too. Lee doesn't like me, because I represent authority to him."

When I expressed my concern that I might do or say something to upset one of them or interfere with what the doctor was doing, Jimmy said, "I don't think you will, but don't worry about it. There have been suicide attempts before, and there will be again. We are trying to save her life, and all we can do is keep trying. Jean, if she self-destructs, she self-destructs. We have to accept that possibility without feeling we let it happen. Otherwise, we don't have a chance of helping her. I don't think anybody will try anything at your house, because they know Uncle Walter would never let them come back."

He added, "Don't be surprised to see a bandage on her wrist. She, or somebody, burned her wrist with drain cleaner again."

I prepared for Lillian's visit by purchasing five various-colored notebooks and setting up a table in my studio for all of the personalities. I showed it to her soon after I picked her up at the airport and drove her to our home. "Here are some books, a dictionary and a typewriter for Julie, and here is some sketch paper for Lucy," I said. "There is an ashtray for Lee, and crayons and primary writing paper for Amy if she comes and wants them. I didn't know what to do for Esther."

Whom was I talking to? What made me think this was the right way to treat "them"? What would I do if one of them actually appeared? I could feel my stomach thumping – or was that my heart? I decided to approach the whole idea with a let's-pretend attitude and plunged ahead.

Lillian and I sat down at the dining room table, which was destined to become the location for many intense discussions with the many parts of this dear lady.

"Aunt Jean, this whole thing just can't be right," she began. "How can it possibly be? Dr. Robinson believes that when I 'lose time,' one of the 'others' uses that time. What do they look like? Why are they there? How did they get there in the first place? Will they ever go away? The doctor is sure that they will give their memories back to me, and then I will know why they 'are,' and when I remember certain things, I will understand why and when they came. He says when they give their memories back to me, they will no longer be needed, and they will go away. I wish it was not true, but I know I have lost time for as long as I can remember. Oh, Aunt Jean, what are we going to do?"

Lillian kept pouring her heart out to me. It was as if she had never talked to anyone about this before. In fact, she never had.

"Dr. Robinson even says one of them is male," she went on. "How does anyone expect me to believe that?! One of them is *5 years old!* I was told that their handwriting is different from mine. I wonder if they really can do that."

"Here, let me show you, Lillian," I said, spreading out three of the envelopes I had received: one each from Julie, Lucy and Lee on the table. "Do you want to see the picture Amy sent me?"

"No!" she said sharply.

At dinnertime, I was a little shaken when she said, "Did you get a letter from me today?"

I thought that might be Lucy because she was eating. "No, did you send me a letter? Are you Lucy?"

"Yes," she said. "I wrote you a letter before I knew we'd be coming here. You will probably get it tomorrow."

She continued eating while carrying on an animated conversation with Walter and me. She was so happy and completely at ease. Neither Walter nor

I could believe that we were laughing and joking with one of the personalities and not our niece Lillian.

After dinner, a new conversation started, and I realized that it was Lillian who, again, was talking with me. Her voice was softer than Lucy's. "Jean, I don't remember my childhood," she said. "Dr. Robinson says that's not normal. Do you remember yours?"

"I remember a lot but certainly not everything that happened every day," I told her. "I can recall many of my young years, and I have scads of memories; some good, some not quite so good."

"I thought of maybe starting a diary," she said vaguely. "What do you think? It would probably be dull."

"Oh, Lillian, I think that would be great," I replied. "And I doubt it would be dull. If you feel like going, we can drive up to the bookstore right now. They have nice hardbound books for people to write their own stories in. I would like to give it to you as a gift." She agreed, and at the bookstore, we selected a red book with gold designs. I saw it being written in several times during the visit.

The next morning, I heard the front door open and close. Peeking out the bedroom window, I saw Lillian sitting on the front steps, smoking. Our cat, Fluffy, was sitting beside her. "No, not Lillian," I thought. "This must be him – Lee." Later, while I was in my bedroom dressing, I heard Lee come back inside and go into what I began thinking of as "their" bedroom.

My head was in a whirl. Do I buy into this fantasy? Should I keep my bedroom door closed when dressing? I usually left it open when I had female houseguests. I pushed the door partway shut and stood behind it to finish dressing. Dr. Robinson and Jimmy had bought into what I thought of as a facade, and they knew a lot more than I.

As I passed "their" open door, whoever was sitting on the edge of the neatly made bed said, "Good morning." I went to her? Him? Them? And gave her (it turned out to be Lillian) a hug and greeted her.

Someone drank juice for breakfast while I had toast and tea. We talked for a long time, then decided to run some errands. In the car, chatting as any two friends would, I complimented her on the outfit she was wearing.

"I don't know who decided what to wear today," she said. "I guess I packed so fast that I forgot to bring any dresses. But one thing I found out is if I lay a dress out to wear and it gets put back, and a pants outfit appears on me, that means Lee is going to be out."

"It might have been Lee who selected your outfit today," I said. "He sat on the front of the porch this morning and smoked a cigarette."

She didn't respond to that. Instead, she said she had a headache and asked if we could go to a drugstore. Lillian asked at the counter for water to wash the pills down. I wanted lunch by that time but didn't know how to approach the subject. I sat on one of the counter stools and opened a menu in front of us. "Does anything look good?" I asked.

"Yes! Everything does!"

It was then that I caught on to Lucy's way of appearing when food was mentioned. She talked about Lil, about money, ate a bacon-lettuce-tomato sandwich and drank lemonade. "Lil only drinks diet cola, and I don't like it," she said.

Lucy told me she had a dime bank. "I have an agreement with everybody that I get all the dimes that come in change from buying things," she explained. "I always pay with bills so I can get more dimes. But we shouldn't spend so much of Lil's money."

When I paid for our lunches, I handed her the two dimes in change. She thanked me and cheerfully put them away in her own little dime bag inside Lillian's purse.

We continued shopping, and I made another purchase. My change included a dime, which I handed to her. She looked at me questioningly. "Have you been talking to Lucy?" she asked. "Jimmy told me she has a dime bank and takes all the dimes."

"Yes, Lucy had lunch with me," I said, as if this was all becoming quite reasonable. "Just drop the dime in your purse. She can get it later." Aha! Lillian was back.

Lillian still had a headache. I suggested returning home, but she suddenly became bouncy and happy. "No, let's not go home," she insisted. "Didn't you say you wanted to go to the delicatessen?"

I was confused, but then I realized Lucy was with me again, and Lucy did not have a headache. Lucy told me about talking Evan into going to Lil's sister Rosalind's house with just Julie, Lee and Lucy. "After all, Dr. Robinson calls us by our own names, so we thought it was time for Rosalind to meet us."

But Rosalind insisted on calling all of them Lillian and scolding, "Stop this nonsense!"

Julie was allergic to animal fur and plants. Rosalind had animals, including a guinea pig, running loose in the house. And she had lots of plants. Julie became nauseous, and Evan decided they better leave.

A few miles down the road, Evan had to stop the car for Julie to get out and vomit. The whole trip was a disaster. Lucy said they should never have gone, and they would never go back. I couldn't begin to picture the scene Lucy described.

During a lull in my conversation with Lucy, Lillian reappeared. She was feeling clammy, and her headache was worse. The minute we got in the house, I heard Lillian vomiting in the bathroom. Had she picked up Julie's feelings from the trip three weeks previously? Was that the way a memory came crashing back, accompanied by long-past physical sensations? Lillian took two more pills, and finding no relief, took a tranquilizer prescribed by Dr. Robinson. Lillian went to bed; at least I thought she was going to bed. Being an organ teacher, it was time for me to tend to my students.

I returned from the studio two hours later to find Lucy chatting with my aged mother, who lived with Walter and me. Apparently Julie had talked with Mom too. Lucy asked if it would be okay for them to call my mother "Grandma Baker" and to use their own names. I agreed. I had been showing Mom their letters and telling her about my multiple friends in one body.

The next day, when lunchtime came, I suggested going out to a steak place. Her eyes brightened, and Lucy said, "Oh, yes, let's!"

We each ordered a steak, french fries, a hot roll and salad. Lucy and I had what I considered a normal conversation. Her letter had arrived that morning. I thanked her, adding, "It was nice of you to leave the envelope unsealed for Amy. I liked the picture she sent me."

"I think she sounds her words out. She is only 5," Lucy said.

"I would like to write to Amy," I said. "But since she can't read, would you read her letter to her?"

Lucy hesitated and then replied, "No. I don't think I want to do that." "That's okay. I will send her a picture. You know, I think you are right. Amy does sound her words out. I believe Amy can learn to write." I was intentionally planting what I thought was a positive idea, hoping Amy was listening.

"Jean, this integration thing bothers me," Lucy interrupted. "I don't like it no way."

"I don't understand it, Lucy. All I can do is trust Dr. Robinson." We didn't talk about Amy anymore that day.

In the afternoon, Julie spoke with me. She answered many of my questions even before I asked them.

I was completely at ease with Julie and felt free to ask anything. However, I didn't know what to ask. So, I merely listened and tried to believe all I was seeing and hearing.

Julie continued, "After Lil and Mr. Mason were married, they moved to Florida. Lil thought her husband had money saved to go to the seminary there, but she discovered that he did not. Since he was having no success at finding work, Lil and I were lucky enough to land a nice secretarial position with a lawyer. Lil worked part of the day, and I did some of the work too. I did most of the typing. Lil hadn't been able to go to school much of her senior year. She kept falling down stairs, and they thought it was intentional. It was, since Lil's mother kept pushing Lil down the stairs. So, Lil did it before her mother could. I was the one who took the second year of typing and shorthand. I still remember some of my shorthand. In less than a year, Lil got pregnant. We went back to Ohio to live at her mother's to have the baby. Her husband got a job driving a truck. We lived in a little house for a while; then bought a mobile home. We all still live in a mobile home now in New York. We moved a lot to go where Mr. Mason got work. He still drives a truck, but right now, he is home almost every evening."

I was due to teach my afternoon organ lessons. Julie asked to try out my typewriter. I had some work ready to be typed for a book of organ instruction I was writing, and Julie offered to type it for me.

Suddenly, I sensed that Lillian had reappeared. Looking at her watch, she wondered aloud where the last two hours had gone.

"Julie was here, and she is going to do some typing for me while I go out to teach," I said. "Oh," was her reply.

I was really tense about the whole concept. I wish I knew how to treat them. When my teaching was done, Julie showed me what she had typed. Then, with a change so subtle I could not detect it, Lillian was with me. "Did Julie get her typing done, Jean?"

"Yes, she did. Are you Lillian?"

"Yes. May I see what Julie typed?"

Scanning the typed pages, she commented, "Julie is a better typist than I am." "That's because she took the second year of typing for you. She said you couldn't go to school most of your senior year," I relayed.

"Jean, I never saw what Julie typed before. I am having a hard time believing there is a Julie. Did you see her? How do you know she typed this? Am I crazy? What do they look like?"

"I do see them, Lillian. I have seen Lucy and Julie. They are nice, and they are real. THEY LOOK JUST LIKE YOU. I can't explain. But if you're crazy, so am I!"

Lucy had dinner and exchanged jokes with Walter. She played with Fluffy and watched some television while I was with my evening students.

After Walter went to bed, I learned more about Julie.

Lucy explained, "She first came to help Lillian when Lillian was 5. That would have been soon after Lillian's mother, Jessica, married Herbert, who came with two older boys – foster children for money, he called them."

Julie took over the conversation. "Lil already knew by that time that she was a bad seed, and she didn't know how to be good," Julie said. "She wanted to overcome the bad and was willing to try anything. Her new 'dad' offered to spend lots of time with this 'bad' child and teach her. One of the first lessons was how to cut herself and get the evil out by bleeding. At first, the very thought of cutting herself intentionally was repulsive and frightening to Lil, but Dad said, "It's because Dad loves his little girl, and he wants to make her good." When she hesitated, he said, "You do it, or I will!"

"Lil couldn't." She cried. He slapped her and said, "Stop your blubbering, brat, and do it!"

"She was not allowed to cry out loud, but she was hysterical inside. So she went away in her head, and I was there. I was scared to cut, but I was more scared of him. I knew I had to do that for Lil. Besides, he was watching to make sure I got enough blood out. After a few times, I got used to doing the cutting. It wasn't so hard, and when Dad agreed that it was only a small bad day, just a small amount of blood was required. The worse Lillian was, the more blood I had to get out. We always felt better after bleedings, just like Dad said we would. But lots of times, neither Lil nor I knew what we had done that was bad. Lil's mother said to do whatever Dad says, without question. And he would say, 'Tell me to make you be good. Say it!' And Lil would do anything he said. She wanted to be good like her sister Rosalind was.

"When I got a little older, Dad bought me my own pocketknife and even showed me where to hide it inside myself, so it would be handy whenever I needed it. He checked every so often to make sure it was still there."

Julie seemed to drift away for a moment, and then Lucy came back. "I've learned from Dr. Robinson how wrong that was, and I'm trying not to do it anymore. I get so scared, Jean, all I can think of is to run. Doctor helps me to get my mind straightened out. When I finally get it right, though, and give Lil the memory of that bleeding, she still gets the feeling and wants to run."

Changing the subject, I told Lucy, "I'm trying to find a way to keep all of you separate and not mix you up. I bought five notebooks and five stick-on labels. I would like each of you to put your name on a label and choose a notebook to put your letters in. We can put Julie's poems in hers too and your drawings in yours. Anything sent to me can go in a notebook. What do you think?"

I had actually begun thinking about writing a book someday but also needed a file for each personality.

"Since I am here now, can I have the red one?" Lucy asked.

"Sure, just put your name on it. You have the first choice." As Lucy picked up the red notebook, I left the room for a few minutes.

When I returned, Julie was writing her label. "I think I'd like the blue notebook, if that's okay, Jean?"

"Good, Julie." I felt good to be able to recognize them by their writing or by what they were doing.

While Julie labeled her notebook, I went to get my three-hole punch. When I got back, Lee had the green notebook already labeled and was writing "Lee Marvin" on the label. "I don't write much. You sure you want a whole notebook for me? I could maybe share Julie's," Lee said.

"No, Lee, I want you to have your own. We can take pictures of your carvings, and I can make copies of my letters to you. We don't have to fill it up." I had been told that Lee liked to carve.

"Okay." Lee was gone before I had time to acknowledge him!

"Do I get one too?" A little voice asked.

"Amy?"

"Mmm hmm."

"Sure, you get one, Amy. Yellow or orange? What? We already have some of your pictures to put in your notebook. Here's a label. Can you make your name on it?" I was pleased, to say the least.

Amy carefully printed her name backward and stuck the label, crooked, on the orange notebook. "What we goin' put in?"

"The nice pictures you sent me. Here is the heart, cat and smiling face picture, and here's the page from the coloring book." I punched them and opened Amy's notebook. Together we slipped the pages over the rings, and Amy snapped the rings shut.

"There!" she said. "You got one for Esther?"

"Yes, Amy."

"What we doin' with hers? She mad. You like her?"

Amy's voice and mannerisms were so beguiling. She could have had anything under the sun within my power to provide.

"I don't know Esther yet, but when I meet her, I bet I will like her. Is she mad at me?" I had been warned by Jimmy not to ask for Esther – "She's too angry."

"Not you," Amy replied.

"Good. This will be her notebook. I hope she likes yellow!"

Amy was gone, and Lillian was there. "What's all this, Jean?" she asked, noticing the notebooks. When I caught her up on what had just occurred, she looked at all the names and commented that Esther was missing.

"I have the yellow one for Esther whenever she wants it."

"Oh," Lillian said.

***

Jean as Narrator: I noticed that someone had gone to their table, so I went to see. She looked up all bright-eyed and smiling.

"Hi, Jean," a small voice said.

"Amy? Is that you, Amy?" I took my cue from the fact that she was sitting where the crayons were.

She nodded her head. I hadn't planned what I might do or say. Where the words and the ideas came from, I couldn't tell you. But I said, "Hi, sweetheart, I've been waiting so long to see you!"

43

"I seed you b'fore, but you cou'n't see me." She was only a little shy. I was the shy one at that moment! What did she expect?

"Amy, I got you a pencil – a big fat one for your little hands." What am I saying? These hands are the same as Lillian's. "Can you make your name?"

"Mmm hmm," was her "yes," and she reached for the pencil with her left hand. But then she looked at me, frightened, and jerked her hand back. Reaching tentatively with her right hand, she finally picked up the pencil. She was having trouble figuring out exactly how to hold the pencil. At that moment, it hit me like a ton of bricks – Lillian was left-handed. Was Amy?

"Amy, honey, you can use either hand. Which hand can write better?"

Her confusion confirmed my suspicion. With her right hand, she painstakingly made the right leg of the capital 'A' first, drawing from the bottom to the top backward. "Amy, try the other hand. See if it works better."

"You won't hit my hand?"

"No, sweetie, I won't hit your hand, and I won't let anyone else hit your hand either."

The poor child was only 5 years old. I remember that Lillian's birthday was in November. So Amy had experienced a young start to first grade.

She switched hands, made a capital "A," and with shaking hands, passed the pencil back into her right hand.

"It's okay to use the other hand, Amy. Isn't it easier to write with your left hand?"

"Don't hit my hand!" she pleaded.

"No, no, never," I reassured her.

"You tie my hand b'hind the chair?"

"No, no, Amy. I don't tie hands."

Amy jumped up off the chair. "Amy not sit on chair. Amy bad, dirty girl!"

"Oh, Amy, you are not bad or dirty. You are clean and beautiful."

She sat back down. I had to think of something to prove to her that it was okay to write left-handed. I continued, "Wait a minute, Amy. Will you wait right there for me? I want to get something nice for you. I will be right back."

If I leave for a minute, will she be gone when I return? Oh, I hope not! I can't believe what is happening! Hurrying into my bedroom, I took a red wraparound bracelet from my jewelry box. When I got back, it was obvious from the childish expression on her face that Amy was still there.

"Look what I have for you – a pretty bracelet. Let's put it on the good arm. This is the pretty and good hand. I like this hand."

Patting her left hand, I wrapped the bracelet around her left wrist. She said, "It's pretty. How long can I keep it?"

"It's yours. You can take it home with you to help you remember which arm it belongs on – the left one, the one Jean wants Amy to write with. Okay?"

She nodded, and we did some more printing. Then we got the crayons out and colored a picture together. As soon as the picture was colored, Amy printed her name correctly on it and said, "Go now."

"Okay, Amy. I'm glad I got to see you."

"Me too." And she was gone.

But who was with me when next we talked? I didn't know. For the most part, I was unable to discern "who" it was: Lillian, Julie or Lucy. Julie and Lucy were sure that they looked different, and they were confused when I approached Lucy with a "Julie" conversation or vice versa.

To save myself from the embarrassment, I decided to ask whenever it appeared that "she" had become "someone else." "Who are you?" and "What's your name?" I asked repeatedly.

One day Lucy said to me, "Jean, you know me. Why do you always ask? Don't you remember me?" Clearly, there was something wrong with *my* mind. Lucy had, after all, told me what she looked like in her very first letter to me. But what I saw was that she looked exactly like Lillian. Her upbeat attitude, her actions and her quick wit certainly were different, but her physical appearance was identical to Lillian's. I wondered how to convince her of that. She thought she was a trim 18-year-old, and she acted like it. I still saw her as a grossly overweight 37-year-old. She would soon be 38.

"Lucy, dear Lucy, to me, you look just like Julie and Lillian. I am sorry, but I can't tell you apart. I have to ask."

"Why do you need to know?" She dodged any discussion of looking like Lillian.

Remembering Julie telling me how important it was to have her name used, I fumbled my way through, "I like to call you by name when I talk to you, and I don't want to offend you by calling you the wrong name."

Lucy didn't buy my explanation, but after all, she was a guest in my house, and I was insistent, so she reluctantly complied.

Seemingly out of context, Lucy started a new conversation. "Jean, you should've seen Lee in the hospital. We are all afraid of being locked up, but Lee escaped through the emergency exit about every day and ran down the stairs. Buzzers and alarms went off, and he was usually caught before he could get out of the hospital."

Lucy described the scene with great animation.

"The staff there was afraid of us. I guess they didn't appreciate it when I broke the glass out of a picture hanging out in the hall. They thought the place was safe. I just wanted to show them it was not safe. They never saw a multiple before. They called us all Lillian.

"One day a patient escaped and jumped from the roof. I guess he figured he'd be better off dead than in there. Here's the newspaper article about the dead man." Lucy handed me a clipping from the Niagara Gazette. The man had jumped to his death.

Lucy continued, "Everybody was waiting to see what happened. Lee went too, and so did all the security officers, nurses, staff and patients. At first, they couldn't tell what happened, but when they heard someone escaped, they thought it was us. Without asking any questions, they grabbed Lee and locked him in a PIC room. He is really strong, but there were too many of them."

"What is the PIC room?" I asked. I knew I had asked before, but I couldn't remember.

"That's where they lock up patients they think are dangerous. I'm not sure what the right word is but maybe patient-isolation control. No, it might be psychiatric intensive care. Anyway, there is no window, no bathroom; just bare room, one chair and a mattress on the floor. No sheets or pillow either. But sometimes they will let you have a pillow after the first day. They take your clothes, all except your underwear, and make you wear one of those stupid hospital gowns. After they put Lee in there, he thought, 'No way will anyone see a bra on me!' So he let Lillian back, and she didn't know where she was or why she was there. Staff wouldn't tell her. They kept saying she knew why. Finally, Lil begged for a paper and pencil so she could write a note and one of us could write back and tell her what happened.

"After a long time, they gave her a piece of paper, but nothing to write with. Lil just knew one of us had killed somebody or done something awful to be locked up like that. So, she crumbled the piece of paper up and stuffed it into her throat as far down as she could reach.

"It's a good thing they checked on her when they did, 'cause she stopped breathing and passed out on the floor. It took them a long time to finally look in her throat and get the paper out. They had to give her CPR to get her breathing again. She was in the hospital, 'cause she was suicidal, but she was working with the doctor to try to get past it."

"Is Lillian okay now?" I asked Lucy.

"I guess so," she replied.

Sitting at the dining room table late that evening, she said, "Jean, it's me, Lillian. When I was in the PIC room at the hospital, I had what I think was an 'out-of-body' experience. I knew the police said that someone had been killed, but I didn't know how or why. So I thought maybe I had killed someone. Why else would they separate me from the other patients? I asked for a pencil and paper. The staff would only give me paper! How could I write to another personality and ask what happened with just *paper*?"

Lillian continued, "Out of frustration, I stuffed the paper down my throat, cutting off my air supply. I think I passed out, and I seemed to be hovering over myself, watching me on the floor. I saw a male nurse rush in and kneel beside me on the floor. I saw his back. I could feel what he was doing from above and behind him. The body on the floor seemed separate from me. That body was inert and lifeless, and I, above, was full of energy. I watched that young man working on that body and felt myself being drawn down into it against my will. I felt free and didn't want to go back into the body lying there. Somehow I knew the body on the floor was me but didn't wonder why I was also above. It seemed natural. I was dismayed to find myself going back into the body and throwing up."

My head was spinning. It was a lot for me to process. I am not at all sure I did process it at the time. Before the visit was over, I had a lot more to process. I felt like I was on a roller coaster that was racing out of control.

Lucy had told it so matter-of-factly. "When Dr. Robinson came in, he asked to talk to whoever knew what happened. We told him, and then he told Lil. I was scared! I thought Lil was a goner!"

I had to ask, "Is Lee okay now, Lucy? Does he have any problems about talking to me?"

"No. He will talk to you whenever he gets ready."

Julie appeared. "Since I don't cut her now, Lil has to hurt herself some other way to relieve the evil."

"How does she do that, Julie?" I asked, my voice barely above a whisper.

"By pouring drain cleaner on her arm. Do you want to see where she burned herself last time?" Julie removed the bandage on Lillian's (and her) wrist, exposing a deep burn.

"I will dress this tonight," Julie explained.

"It looks better than it did. We used this cream her family doctor gave her," Julie said, gently placing a sterile pad over the wound and wrapping it heavily with protective soft gauze.

"Why would Lillian burn herself, Julie? I don't understand."

"You remember, don't you, Jean, that Herbert and Jessica had a baby when Lil was 10 years old? Her name is Letty. She is grown up and married now and has kids of her own."

"That's right. I never saw Letty more than one or two times in all those 20-some years I've been married to your (and her) Uncle Walter. It seemed that Jessica didn't want us to be around her family," I injected.

Julie continued, "Every time one of her sisters or her mother writes her a letter, they put her down, and Lil can't stand the pain. The feelings of bad seem to get stronger and stronger each time she thinks about how much she wants them to accept her.

"Lil feels that she is worse than worthless. She compares herself to a toilet. Since toilets and sinks need to be purged with a strong cleaner like drain cleaner, she tries to cleanse or purify herself the same way. Burn out the bad, so she can stand to keep alive one more day. Lil doesn't even feel it while it's happening. She doesn't seem to have any feelings. Doctor says she will feel it as she begins to get better. She is really sick, Jean!"

I hoped Dr. Robinson knew what he was doing.

I watched the plane take off, wondering whether I would ever see any of them again. What a four days!

On the way back from the airport, it dawned on me that I had spent very little time with Lillian. Most of the time, she was Julie or Lucy. Lillian was there for less than three hours of the whole four days. Amy was there twice.

The morning after they departed, I smiled when I saw that the yellow notebook was neatly labeled "Esther Winslow." When Lillian told Dr. Robinson about the notebooks, he asked why I didn't get one for Lillian. I didn't think Lillian was a personality. I thought she was my niece!

I stopped in to see my pastor, Rev. Chris Hobgood. He was intrigued. "The next time she comes, see if you can get her to come and see me, or I will come to your house to see her, if that's okay," he offered. I was so relieved to be able to talk freely about the mystical world I had entered. Rev. Chris was a good listener, and he believed me.

Back home again, I stood in awe, looking around "their" bedroom to see if anything had been overlooked in the packing.

My eyes lit on an envelope with my name on it, leaning against the bedside lamp. It was a thank you card signed by Julie, Lucy and Lee. Lee had written, "Thanks for making it okay to be here." The yellow notebook labeled "Esther Winslow" was proof to my eyes that she (they) had been there.

Two days later, I got a letter of appreciation from Lucy. She added a P.S. "That little girl was bad. She stole your crayons."

I picked up the phone and called. Lillian answered. At least she sounded like Lillian – "I need to talk to Lucy. Is she there?" I asked.

"Yeah, I'm here, Jean. What'd I do?"

"Lucy, you didn't do anything wrong. I loved having you here. I got your letter today, and I wanted to tell you that Amy was supposed to have the crayons. Don't you remember when you first arrived that I said that those crayons were for Amy if she wanted them? I am glad that she took them home."

But the next day, a letter came from Lillian pleading with me to forgive her. Somehow my box of crayons got put in her luggage, and she found them. She was afraid I wouldn't want her to come back.

"Lillian, those are Amy's crayons. I gave them to her. I want her to use them. Please put them down low where she can reach them."

What had I just said? Where Amy can reach them! She was the same size as Lillian!

The letters kept coming from Lucy and Julie.

Between the two of them, I discerned the depth of Lillian's need for her sisters' acceptance.

Julie and Lucy reached out to make friends with Letty, Lillian's younger half-sister. Julie wrote a letter to Letty, signing her own name. Julie, Jimmy and Lillian went to Ohio to see Letty to explain her multiplicity. A few weeks later, Letty told Lillian that she caused Letty to have a nervous breakdown by telling her she had multiple personalities. Letty thought Lillian didn't want to be there whenever Julie or Lucy showed herself. The final blow came with

Letty's saying she just couldn't stand to be around Lillian anymore. Then Lillian got a letter from Rosalind. "Sometimes, it's necessary for families to sacrifice one for the good of the rest. Mother knew Dad needed someone to try his various ideas and experiments on, and I believed her then and still do that he could never have actually hurt you beyond a certain point."

The letter went on about how lucky they were to have a father while growing up, and if Lillian would just keep that in mind and forget the rest, her problems would be reduced to the proper size. Rosalind went on to write, "None of us enjoyed seeing you being used or punished, but everyone needs an outlet, and Dad really needed to do the things he did. Have you ever considered having electroshock again? Mother says that will go a long way in helping you forget any unpleasant memories."

Finally, the letter stated that Rosalind could not allow our families to visit together again. "Until you are committed to an institution for treatment or are cured, it makes no sense to go on with that mental function of yours in front of my healthy, sane children. I will simply deny I wrote this if you show it to anyone, and you are fully aware of who would be believed."

Chapter 3
Julie

In Chapter 3, we begin to experience the chaos of multiplicity – part against part, amnesia, mutilation, attempted suicide and a system of communication between parts that is split within itself, with each part desperately attempting to communicate with the others and with each part desperately trying to hold back the flood of memories of unthinkable abuse.

At the same time, Jean's struggle to communicate with each personality becomes more complex.

In this chapter, Jean speaks both as narrator and in the first person, interchangeably, almost as if she has two parts of herself.

As the personalities become more open to one another, each personality is out more often; each communicates by letter, journal entry, note and through Aunt Jean, who serves as a link between Lillian's parts. For the first time, Lucy communicates with Lillian directly – a milestone in the healing process.

With this process comes memories of cruelty and abuse. Chaos ensues as Lillian's desire to die becomes more intense and more dangerous.

Having entered the world of multiplicity, the reader begins to be able to decipher who is "out," who is talking to whom, who is safe and who is dangerous.

Indeed, the reader comes to accept the personalities as if they are living people.

In service of easing any difficulty the reader may encounter in following the communication between the parts, the personalities are labeled when they speak or offer a journal entry. To further aid the reader, Jean's comments are labeled either as Jean as a character in the story, or as Jean the narrator.

FA

Jean as Narrator: Julie and Lucy wrote, begging me to stay friends with them and Lillian. They also tried to explain how Lillian's sisters' rejections affected her. Lillian was overwhelmed with feelings of how bad she was. In the past, relief for Lillian had been achieved by Julie's bleeding her, but now Julie knew that was wrong. Lillian was becoming suicidal. Julie gave in and made two small cuts on Lillian, but then Julie realized that Mr. Mason would be mad at her, and she panicked.

Taking one of their cars, Julie took off. She was going to drive to my house to get help but got lost. Stopping at a motel, Julie wrote me a postcard, saying how frightened she was. She was there for two nights and finally called Dr. Robinson. He was out of town, but his associate Ralph Zannoni took Julie's call and told her it was okay to return home. He would call Jimmy. Julie was crying too much, so Lee took over and drove to the hospital, where she was given a strong sedative. Lillian told Dr. Robinson on the phone that it seemed like the minute people find out that she is a "multiple," she is treated like a freak, and they don't want anything to do with her. The doctor suggested that she let someone else take over until he got back to his office in three days. Julie took over.

Julie thought, "Mr. Zannoni was very kind."

A few weeks later, Julie discussed religion with Mr. Zannoni, and he suggested a class. When she went to sign up for it, she was required to have a last name. She didn't have a last name! How could she get into the class? Thinking hard, Julie came up with a solution. She would take Mr. Zannoni's name. She became Julie Zannoni. It was later okayed by him.

Julie's Journal: "Lil is really feeling low, and I hate that. I wish her family wasn't there. Lee maybe was right when he talked of killing himself or all of them. Everything is so bad that we just should have never come home where people can get to Lil and hurt her. I am so glad that Jean is my friend and Lil's friend too!

"Jean, when someone else takes over, it doesn't mean Lil couldn't stand to be there at that moment. I hope you understand that we take over when we want to do something sometimes. We all have our lives to run and things to do. I hope you know that! I'm going to cry. I will write you more later. I'm sure Lil will as soon as she is able.

"It is really great to have a couple of people talk to me and use my own name, instead of having to answer to Lillian. Lil's stepdad called her Lee instead of Lil. Her mother even called her Esther for a little while. The doctor says that helped make Lil into all the rest of us; only I don't believe that. Besides, I am willing to go by the name of Lillian if that is the only way I can still exist.

"Lee is really mixed up now. Lil found another gun. Lee had gotten bullets for it. For a while there, I was worried, but then Lil tossed it into the Niagara River. I am glad it's gone because I don't think Lee can get hold of more money to buy another one now. He is taking some purple pills he calls 'speed' in the morning and afternoon and then at night; it's a real letdown. Lil suspects but didn't say anything to the doctor today, but I wanted her to. Lee told the doctor today that if he had a gun, he would have used it on himself. I am glad, a little bit, to hear that." Lee said, "Julie doesn't need me anymore, and I feel useless." Wish he'd get things together again. Mr. Mason talked to him once and said he would help Lee find some wood for his carving, but he didn't.

"There was a time when I felt suicidal, and Lee kept me from carrying out my intentions. So I wish I could help him now. Only I don't know what to do. At least Dr. Robinson knows how he is feeling. So I will leave it up to him. There is a phone number where any of us can call the doctor at any time and get in touch with him. It's nice to know it's there."

Jean as Narrator: Julie had some time for herself. She went to the library and listened to stereo records of one of the samples available there. Chopin, Bach, Mendelssohn and Mozart were her favorite composers. Each time she relinquished the body to Lillian, I heard from Lillian. She told me Julie was writing in the journal now too, and when Lil saw classical records, she questioned who borrowed them from the library. Julie enjoyed studying the jacket notes.

Lillian found tickets to the ballet and to an opera. Julie told me she planned to go with a friend she had met at the library. Lillian didn't care. She had no interest in classical music, ballet or opera. She was jealous that I wrote to her personalities, although I wrote to her too. I told her I could think of no reason she couldn't read their letters. That introduced another worry. "I can read what you write to them, but I wonder what they tell you! Is any part of my life private?"

Lillian also wondered how many people knew her as Julie or Lucy. She was constantly on the verge of tears, but I noticed Julie wasn't crying so much anymore. She used to cry all the time. Julie's letters to me became more and more "normal" and loving. She had given the ability to cry to Lillian.

Julie Wrote: "Do you have a favorite composer? Bach? I said him because of your playing the organ so beautifully yourself. I will keep this letter short. It's time for Mr. Mason to come home, and I want to leave before he gets here. Love from your friend, Julie."

Jean as Narrator: Lucy was also taking more time. She really liked to paint. Someone asked Lillian to paint a picture for a grandchild, and while she was trying to think of what kind of picture would appeal to a little girl, Lucy went to the blank easel in the art studio and painted an animal. Julie wrote that Lil would be surprised to see that it's already finished next time she goes to the studio.

Lillian's strong feelings about being bad, her passionate wish to be accepted by Letty and Rosalind, and her refusal to bleed herself resulted in self-inflicted burns and a plan to kill herself.

I received an urgent call from Julie, "Jean, I don't know what to do." From her voice, I thought she was crying.

"Why, Julie? What's happening?"

"Lil is going to take pills. She just wants to not be."

"Do you know where the pills are, Julie?"

"Yes."

"I need you to stay and help me. Do you think you can stay?"

"I think so. What should I do?"

It was a relief that Julie was willing to help. I sensed that there was no time for thinking out a game plan. I could only think one step at a time. Dealing with someone who was suicidal was not something I had ever done before.

Upon learning that the pills were in Lillian's dresser drawer, I asked Julie to bring them to the phone. I had no way of knowing whether Lillian might come back into the body. While Julie was retrieving them, I thought of what to do with them. Julie returned with the pills. I kept using her name. I needed her!

"Julie, take the telephone and the pills and go into the bathroom. Tell me when you are there," I insisted.

"I am in the bathroom."

"Are you still Julie?"

"Yes."

"Julie, open the bottle, dump the pills in the commode, then flush it. I want to hear the flush." And I did, in fact, hear the toilet flush.

"Thank you, Julie. I am so glad you called. I don't want anything to happen to my Lillian. I love her." What a relief!

Julie heaved a sigh, "I'm so glad you were there when I called. Dr. Robinson said if Lil dies, we all die. Do you believe that?"

"Yes, Julie, I am positive of it. Are you okay now?"

"I am fine. I hope Lillian feels better soon."

"Thanks again, Julie. I love you!" And we hung up.

Lucy Wrote: "Dear Jean, we are in the hospital because Lil needed to be in here. Her mother told her she never wants to see her again, and Rosalind says that there is no such thing as us. I don't know why Lil is so emotional about this. I'm not. We don't have to see her mom anymore. I wish Lil would decide to let go of them and get on with living her own life. I am glad Lil has you for a friend (and me as your friend too). I'm not going to eat for Lil anymore. I cheat too much. This way, I won't get in trouble, and Lil can be the one that gets fat. From your friend, Lucy."

Jean Wrote: "Lucy, you told me just a little bit about Esther. Does she know me? Do you think she would like to be my friend? Was she here when you were here?"

***

Jean as Narrator: Friday at 4 o'clock was Lillian's regular appointment time with Dr. Robinson. I expressed so much interest in his methods that Lillian began calling me every Friday night, shortly after 11 when the rates went down, and telling me what she learned that day. Our calls gave her some much-needed stability. I looked forward to the calls, and if she didn't call by 11:05, I called her. This particular Friday, Lillian had seen a note Julie had written to Jimmy and stuck on the refrigerator with a magnet. It said, "Mr. Mason, don't come home from work and crawl into bed with me. Sleep on the couch, or I will!" Lillian didn't think that was funny, but I did! I began to visualize Jimmy's life from a new perspective.

Lillian Wrote: "Julie wrote to Aunt Jean, I guess. There is an envelope on the TV addressed to her. I feel very alone. How funny to write that when there are supposed to be six of me. I feel like I am on a tightrope. I am sick, severe headache. Blacked out again."

Julie Wrote: "Well, Jean, I sure did it this time. Lil has had a pretty bad week, and yesterday the doctor who was supposed to see her son James called and canceled the appointment that Lil had made 30 days ago and made another appointment a month later, and Lil got mad. Really! Lil called Dr. Alabiso and then felt so bad because she thought he said all of James' problems were because of her.

"She said if James' problem was her, she could take care of that fast. She is always too down on herself, and I got scared because I don't want to die. Not yet! And I took off in the car, away from Niagara Falls and the gorge, and Lee decided he'd fix it all by going to your house and borrowing a gun from Lil's Uncle Walter.

"Anyway, I was crying and driving and wanted to call the doctor but was afraid to get out of the car at the telephone booth, and a state trooper, a couple of them, said I was going over 100 miles an hour, and I told them I was trying to get help for Lil and Lee, and my name was Julie, and the officer started to get mad because I wasn't Lillian Mason, but I had her license. The officer asked what kind of pills I was on and if I was a diabetic. I told him Lil was, and the pills were hers, not mine, and I couldn't let him talk to Lillian because she didn't want to live. He just didn't seem to understand what I was saying. So I asked him to please call our doctor. It was a real mess.

"He finally understood enough to want to call Mr. Mason, but I told him he wasn't my husband and just call the doctor, so he said, 'Damn Mr. Mason' and 'Hell, I don't care. I will call the doctor!'

"He wrote Lillian a ticket for going so fast, but it was before he realized I (Julie) was driving and not Lillian. So he said he couldn't tear up the ticket, but he'd talk to the judge and try and explain the situation.

"He called Mr. Mason anyway and asked him if he had a wife with five or six names and started to take us (me, Lillian, etc.) to the hospital in Syracuse. I got scared, so Lucy took over, and she told him her name, and he kept shaking his head and talking to himself. I don't know why it took the state police so long to stop me. I just put the gas pedal to the floor as soon as I got on the thruway, about 5:30, and it was 7 before someone got in front of the car, so I saw them and stopped. All I was trying to do was to get some help.

"The people at the hospital were nice to Lucy, and then Lil got control of the body before Mr. Mason got there, and she was scared they were going to keep her, but after she found it was still the same day, and that her husband was on his way, she was okay.

"Lil has never even gotten a parking ticket, so I don't know what will happen. She is supposed to go to court, but if Lil loses her license to drive, she won't even be able to see the doctor. I hope nothing else bad happens this week.

"The state trooper says he believes in multiple personalities, so why can't Lil's family? Lillian says if anything else can happen, she just knows it will, and I am sure I am not doing the right things when I try to help. Are you sorry you met me?

"It's time for Lil's kid to get ready for some party, so I will have to quit and let her get him ready. I hope we are still friends. Julie."

***

Jean as Narrator: Too much was going on. Lillian was gaining a pound a week, and she was already overweight. She complained to Dr. Robinson that she wasn't even driving and got a ticket, and it wasn't fair. She just wanted to not be. So Lee took over again. He got a haircut. When Lillian started to brush her hair the next morning, the brush flew out of her hand, clattering to the floor. She had expected more resistance to her brushing. Where was her hair? She didn't like that kind of surprise.

Julie's left arm and two fingers got "numb" all the time. Julie wrote in her journal, "Is it a punishment for being such a bad person? If I ask anyone, they will know I'm bad, so I can't tell anyone. Dr. Robinson said he wasn't mad at me, but I must still be a bad person. That's why Lil falls. She doesn't want to be, so she's being punished. Maybe I could ask the doctor or Jean?"

Lucy Wrote: "I hope you will still want to see us. Does your silent husband think we are all just a bunch of 'sickies' like Esther does?"

Jean as Narrator: I mailed a block of walnut to Lee, hoping he could use it for carving. He answered me every time I sent him a letter. He had been spending hours and hours carving.

Lee Wrote: "Some guys wanted me to buy some pot or speed today. I told them not to come to this house no more. Thank you for the wood, Mrs. Jean. I need better carving tools, but I did finish the doctor's elephant by coating it with an oil finish."

Jean as Narrator: I thought Julie's left arm and finger numbness came from Lee's gripping carving tools he was working on.

Lillian stopped referring to Jessica as "Mother." She called her "Jessica" and nearly spat out the name. A new memory had been given to her: that of Jessica beating her over and over with both hands and always on her head. The only way to stop Jessica was to throw herself down some stairs.

Jean Wrote: "That is the first time you told me that your mother did anything to you, Lillian."

Lillian Wrote: "Doesn't every mother beat a bad teenager? Only I had forgotten what bad thing I did for her to keep hitting me like that. I wonder if that's why I have been falling on steps lately."

Jean as Narrator: I was trying to convince her that the beatings were not normal. She insisted that she had been a bad teenager. My words fell on deaf ears.

Weeks later, Jimmy called to say that Dr. Robinson was going to a medical convention, and Lillian was suicidal. Could she come and stay with us for a few days? Without hesitation, I replied, "Of course."

***

Jean as Narrator: Lucy could hardly wait to give me her version of Julie's wild drive.

Lucy: "Jean, you should have seen her! When Lil just gave up and didn't want to live anymore after talking to James' Dr. Alabiso, she was going to end her life. Julie drove so Lil wouldn't try to kill herself. But Julie was upset too. She turned the radio on, loud. Driving along the thruway, she was hysterical. The more she cried, the faster she drove. After a long time, a state police car turned on the siren and blinking lights. But Julie didn't hear or see anything. I never knew she was such a good driver. She finally saw a snowplow that they put across the road to stop her. She jammed on the brakes, and the car screeched to a halt."

Jean: "Lucy, that must have been some experience for everybody concerned!" I exclaimed.

Lucy: "I wonder if we will all go to jail. Julie was just scared."

Jean as Narrator: Lucy disappeared, and Julie was with me again.

"Jean, what will happen to us? Do you think we will be put in jail?" Julie began crying.

"No, Julie. They don't put people in jail for one speeding ticket. You didn't hurt anyone, and you didn't destroy any property or even wreck the car. I know you feel bad, but please stop worrying about jail," I pleaded.

Julie: "Driving is so important to Lil. Almost every Friday, when she leaves Dr. Robinson's office, she drives around for a couple of hours thinking about whatever they discussed. That's when she works things out. Sometimes, she goes to the Falls and watches the water. There is so much power there. Lots of nights, after James is in bed and Evan is home to watch him, Lil drives around all night long and gets home just in time to get James up and ready for school. I think she will just die if she can't drive."

Jean: "Julie, you must not let Lillian die, no matter what! I know the car is important to her and to all of you, but life is more important. Please, please, Julie, help me keep her safe. You help me so much when you write or tell me on the telephone what Lillian is thinking. I care about you and Lillian more than I know how to tell you." I could feel Julie's pain.

***

Jean as Narrator: Walter decided to take some vacation time and suggested I fly to New York and visit Lillian for a few days. He would drive up the following weekend and join me for some quality time enjoying Niagara Falls again.

Julie Wrote: "Lil, I am so very sorry about the driver's license. Please forgive me. I feel bad. Please don't feel so bad."

Lillian Wrote: "It's okay. I know you feel bad about the ticket, but you probably saved my life, and that's something! I felt bad, but I can learn to live with it, and if it is hard sometimes, well, that's how it has always been. It's okay, Julie. Aunt Jean is coming next Sunday, and she is going to bring a cassette recording of classical music for you."

Jean as Narrator: I had Julie's cassette, and I had a little gift for Amy, so I needed some small item for each of the others. Knowing Lillian was trying to watch her weight, I purchased an inexpensive bathroom scale for her. One of my organ students had given me another block of walnut for Lee. That left

Esther. I found a needlepoint kit and took a chance that she might like to do needlepoint. Lucy had asked for photos of Fluffy, and I had those for her.

Upon my arrival at Lillian and Jimmy's mobile home, I distributed the gifts. Unsure of Esther, I merely stated, "Here is a little something I bought for Esther," and placed it on the TV.

One by one, the others received their mementos and graciously thanked me. Evan was staying at a friend's house, so I could sleep in his room, which was located at one end of the trailer. Lillian and Jimmy's bedroom was at the opposite end, and James' room was next to theirs. The central area served as kitchen, dining room and living room.

Lillian was glad to see me but was having tremendous difficulty trying to remain herself, especially in the last week. She was trying to be responsive to James' needs. Dr. Alabiso wanted James placed in another school. Lillian showed me a note that Julie had typed to her.

Julie Wrote: "Lillian, you saw the people at the school meeting. They taped it, and I didn't say I was you. The multiple personalities were mentioned but not too much. They are in agreement that James would be in a class for emotionally disturbed children and in a class of about eight kids. They review it each year. One of the men talked yesterday with Dr. Alabiso, James' doctor, so the doctor knew ahead of time about what they needed to know. They have transportation provided for the kids in the class.

"Taking James out of school last year was mentioned; also, your need to be away from James for a while. They also mentioned that you were having trouble controlling your feelings and that maybe your being in a hospital ward had something to do with James not wanting to go to school for fear you wouldn't be home when he got home after school. You will be notified in 10 days about the decision, but there is no problem about him being placed in that class with a woman teacher. James' soiling was mentioned. That's all I remember right now. Your husband can fill you in if you have any questions. I don't want to do this anymore. I was shaking and forgot what I was saying once. They seemed like nice people and seemed concerned about doing what is right for James."

Lillian: "Aunt Jean, I couldn't talk, so Julie took over. I really messed things up in trying to be a mother. I can't do much of anything right, which really doesn't matter except in being a mother. When I do everything wrong, it's not me but my kids who have to pay for it. I tried, but I don't think anyone else would understand the way I feel sometimes. I love James, but I can see things he does wrong, and I want to really hurt him just once, so he'd know he had to listen, but I don't dare. What if I hit him and then can't stop?! That can happen for real!"

Jean: "What do you mean, Lillian?"

Lillian: "Everyone sees nice, calm, quiet Lillian. That's on the outside. Nobody sees the inside that gets confused and wants to do something violent, so someone else will know what I'm really like. The next time I feel like hurting James, maybe if I hurt myself instead, that will cure the problem.

"When I saw Dr. Robinson on Friday, I couldn't talk at first. He said I was replacing going away in my head with being unable to speak. He also said maybe Jimmy is too easy with me when I say I can't speak, and when he doesn't insist that I talk anyway. I don't think much of that!

"Dr. Robinson said Esther was in his office for a little bit, but he didn't say what they talked about. I have to ask."

Jean as Narrator: Later, Lucy called me over to the table and showed me what was written in the journal.

Lillian's Journal: "Lee cut his (my) hand again tonight carving. The knife always slips at the wrong place. It is always deep. If it's going to hurt, why not make it worthwhile, and let it be my wrist. I'd never have the nerve, but if it happened, it would be okay with me. I don't want there to be any family therapy. I've tried suggestions before. It doesn't help. It's just me that's wrong, as always."

Esther's Journal: "Tell Dr. Robinson to go to hell. How is that for your entry from Esther?! Poor Lillian, can't do it, can you? You don't swear! You may think you are fooling others, but don't forget what you really are. Your mother knew. It wasn't HERBERT she hit when she came across him French kissing you in the kitchen! Would you like me to tell Jimmy (your husband) since you told him you couldn't? What's the matter, Lucy? Can't take it when it isn't your anger that's making waves? Dear, dear Julie, my how you have grown! YOU ALL MAKE ME SICK! Forget what made you afraid before? What short memories you have! Life is still the same. You are still all to blame. No one wants you around except as a curiosity. You aren't anyone's real friends. Just a bunch of freaks! All Dr. Robinson wants is someone to make money from. He doesn't believe anything you say, Lillian. Dear Jim (your husband) doesn't care if you are around or not. Lucy makes a much better bed partner! Shall I sign my entry 'love'? Esther."

Jean as Narrator: I continued reading. I felt like an eavesdropper. "Lucy showed it to me," I justified to myself.

Lillian Wrote: "What am I supposed to think of what's written above? Who is taking me someplace and making me find my own way back? At the mall, without even my purse along with money to call someone to come and get me! I felt stupid just standing there wondering what to do. Not even a dime to call home. I had to walk. Couldn't mention it to Jimmy. He was sleeping, but that meant James was home without me for a long time. And why was I at the mall? No one had bought anything.

"I asked Jimmy last night about that new sign out front with our house number on it. He said, 'I put it up so Uncle Walter could find the house better.' I am glad it is done. I tried to cash a check, and they wouldn't accept it without a driver's license!"

Jean as Narrator: When I closed the journal and returned to the sofa, Lucy had more to tell me. "Esther left home around 2 o'clock the other day. She was going for a walk. The next thing Lil knew, she was walking along the expressway. It was getting dark, and she couldn't make out the time or day on her watch. She couldn't figure out if she was in Niagara Falls or what day it was. There was a fence along the road, and a couple of kids were riding bikes. Lil called to them and asked if they could call the police for her. She knew they would take her home. The kids got off their bikes, jumped the fence, came up the hill and asked if she had any money. Lil said she didn't even have a dime for a phone call, and one said, 'Hey, lady, you got a watch?' Lil put her hand on her watch, but they knocked her down and took her watch. They took off. Lil sat a minute, then got up and started walking. Finally she just sat down on a curb until a police car came by and asked if she needed help.

"Lil asked what town and what day it was. She explained she has blackouts and sometimes ends up in other towns on other days. He asked her name, address and phone number, and then he took Lil home.

"Lillian told him she had multiple personality disorder, and he wanted to know if there had been a movie about her on TV. She said it was not her, but there are more of us around than anyone talks about. He said, 'Jesus, you must be something to live with!' He made out a larceny report. Jimmy went right out and bought Lil another watch. He knows how important it is to her."

Jean as Narrator: Julie informed me that Lillian doesn't want to live right now. She thinks she would be doing everybody a favor by killing herself. Lil thinks she should be dead before anybody ever gets to see Esther. Also, Esther's repressed memories are beginning to seep into Lil's consciousness. They are memories of brutality equaled only by the resulting anger that Esther, as the keeper of those memories, has been forced to carry in order for Lillian to survive.

Lillian caught me up on James' therapy. Dr. Alabiso had seen James twice so far, and James was anxious to go back to see the doctor again. Although Lillian readily admitted that she knew James talked to Dr. Alabiso about her, she had no reservations about James' great need for help. She blamed herself.

The evening passed quickly, and the next morning, when I got up, Jimmy was pacing nervously while James kept asking questions. "Where is she? Will she come back? Who left?"

Someone had walked away early in the morning. Jimmy told me that Esther had been acting out, so he suspected she was the culprit this time. Jimmy explained, "She takes just enough money to take a bus somewhere, then leaves, and Lil is there but doesn't know where she is. As soon as she can, she calls me, and I go get her. This is nothing new. The others have done it too but never this bad. I just hope she's all right."

All we could do was wait by the telephone. Nearly two hours later, a park policeman called to say that Lillian was with him at Niagara Falls park police headquarters. He had found her wandering around and questioned her. Jimmy thanked him, and we left to pick her up. On the way, Jimmy explained, "The park police know her, and they try to watch out for her whenever Lillian or any of the others go there. They never forgot her! She nearly pulled two of them in with her when she made that suicide attempt last winter." And he added, "By the way, I wrote them a thank you letter, and those officers were given commendations for bravery in saving her life."

Upon our return to their home, Lillian expressed her embarrassment and distress that whoever took off and went to Niagara Falls was trying to be mean to her. It was degrading to have to beg a dime for a phone call or have the park police involved.

James was relieved to see her and asked, "Are you my mom now?"

"Yes, James, I am Mom. How is my big boy? Come here. I want to hold you for a minute."

"I missed you, Mom," James said.

"I missed my James too."

They were affectionate, and I was pleased to see that. Later in the day, Lucy talked to me about the morning's events: "Esther has been doing that, Jean; taking off, walking until she gets tired, and her feet get sore, then leaving, so Lil has to find her way back on hurting feet. Esther doesn't take Lil's purse or even a dime. Do you have any ideas about what we could do to help Lil?"

Jean: "Lucy, when my daughter used to go out on dates, I always made sure she had money to call home if she wanted to. When she went roller skating, we taped a dime to the inside of her boot. Maybe we could fasten one inside your bra or something."

Lucy: "But Esther could be watching, and she would know that the dime was there too!"

Jean: "Oh, yes, I forgot about that, Lucy. She knows everything we know, doesn't she?" I was thinking, "The plot thickens."

We drove Jimmy to work that day and kept the car so we could go shopping. Since Lillian's license had been surrendered, I did the driving. Julie and Lucy kept me entertained most of the afternoon.

As I prepared for bed later, I heard heavy steps and someone muttering. Without a doubt, someone was angry. Esther? I heard a crashing sound. Then something was thrown. Was I scared? Yes, I was scared! I thought of escape. But I couldn't get out the door without going right past her. Even if I did get out, I didn't have my car. Walter was already on his way here, so I couldn't call him. I didn't know where he was. He was due about noon the next day.

"Don't panic, old girl," I told myself. I put my clothes back on and made sure all of my belongings were in my suitcase in the event I had to make a hasty exit.

Just then, "she" appeared at my bedroom door. "Jean, I'm Julie. May I come in?"

I hesitated momentarily but really had no choice.

"Please do. Julie, what's going on?" I tried to conceal my fear.

Julie: "Esther was here for a few minutes, but she is gone now. I am so worried, Jean. Did she frighten you? Are you going to leave? She won't be back. I promise you. Oh, Jean, please don't go!"

Jean: "I am glad it's you, Julie. Is everything all right now? Tomorrow morning, I think we should call Mr. Zannoni, since Dr. Robinson is out of town. He needs to know what happened, and we have to find out if it's dangerous for me to be here." I tried to act like it was nothing, but when Julie left my room, I locked the door and slept with my clothes on. Esther had scared the bejabbers out of me!

The next morning, Lucy told me, "We thought we were all strong enough to keep Esther from being nasty when you were here, but we couldn't. Look what she did. My pictures of Fluffy are ripped. She broke the plastic cover off the cassette you bought for Julie, and the cassette is gone. She threw the wood you bought for Lee, but just look at the bathroom scale!"

Jean: "Let me see it, Lucy. Something is written on it!"

Jean as Narrator: We stared, unbelieving at the words written with lipstick: "Lillian is a whore bitch." Julie again appeared. She was always so soft-spoken. "Oh, Jean, I tried to clean that all off before you got up, but I couldn't." She began crying, "Please don't stop being my friend. I am so sorry. I am afraid you won't ever come back. I can't find my cassette, and she broke the cover."

I comforted Julie as best I could and asked her to call Mr. Zannoni. She did and made an appointment to see him at noon. I drove the car and waited in Mr. Zannoni's outer office. He was able to diffuse Esther, at least until we left.

Then the most extraordinary thing happened. Lucy spoke to Lillian as if Lillian were there.

Lucy: "Lil, you shouldn't have been so scared. It wasn't so bad. Esther says her body is separate from yours. When you or Julie hurt yourself, it doesn't hurt her, and it would if it was the same body.

"I don't want integration. A girl in the doctor's office said sometimes she doesn't want to get well because then she wouldn't have her doctor anymore. I guess you heard that part. If our getting well or whatever means I won't be anymore, I don't want to. I hope, Lil, you don't want to get well either. Just don't think like you are now. I want to live."

Jean as Narrator: When we left the doctor's office, Lillian asked that I take her to the police station to inquire about her driver's license. I never imagined anybody could be so hung up on a driver's license as Lillian was. It was as if she had lost her right arm; pardon me, her left arm. I also ordered a medical alert tag for her to wear around her neck. It was to be inscribed with the words "multiple personality, call Dr. Robinson" and his phone number.

Then we went shopping. Lucy told me Esther had agreed on a truce until noon the following day. I was relieved.

Julie gave me some books she had finished reading. Among them were *The Thorn Birds* and two books by Taylor Caldwell. I looked forward to reading them.

Julie: "Jean, I think I should tell you something."

Jean: "What's that?"

Julie: "This afternoon, while we were shopping, Esther bought a can of drain cleaner. She expects Lil to use it after you go home. What should I do?"

Jean as Narrator: Bizarre, things seem to be thrown at me each time I became complacent. Again, there was little time for thought. I had to act now!

Jean: "If you know where it is, Julie, will you get it for me? Can you do that without creating a problem?" I asked, thinking Esther might reappear and object to my interference.

Julie: "She hid it here in the cupboard, behind some other things," Julie said, reaching up into the kitchen cabinet.

Jean: "Do you have any ideas about what I can do with it? Pour it down the drain?"

Julie: "Maybe, but I will bet this is the cleanest drain in the whole trailer park! It gets a treatment every time Lil burns herself!"

Jean: "That's true. Why don't I put it in my suitcase to take it with me? I will find a safe way to dispose of it at home."

Jean as Narrator: Lucy found Julie's cassette on top of the refrigerator. Lucy's Fluffy photos were ripped in half. Lucy carefully taped them together again. Lee's wood was found and returned to its basket, and Esther's gift was gone. Amy's gift had not been touched.

I was glad to see Walter when he arrived shortly before noon. In the afternoon, Walter invited Lillian and James to accompany us on a trip to the Maid of Mist boat ride at the base of Niagara Falls.

Lillian: "I would like to go. I have lived here for several years now and have always wanted to go on that ride. That would be fun!"

Jean as Narrator: Donning our yellow slickers and hats at the Falls, the lady with us chattered away. She was explaining things to James and savoring everything about the trip. When we returned home that evening, Lillian looked at her watch and lamented, "How can it be that late? Did we go yet?"

Lucy had gone with us, and Lillian had neither seen nor felt a thing. Lillian was disgusted with Lucy, but in her usual manner, she said no more about it.

On our way back to Virginia, I tried to tell Walter about Esther frightening me, but he didn't want to hear. "This is a vacation," he said. "Can't you talk about anything else?"

Chapter 4
Lee

Building on Lucy's newly formed ability to communicate directly with Lil, Jean goes on to engage Lee in helping her to foster a trusting relationship with Amy.

In the process, Lee freely speaks of the sexual abuse that resulted in Julie's completing Lil's senior year of high school for her.

The abuse itself was repetitive, ritualistic and at times sadistic. Even with the help of Julie and Lee, Lillian was unable to fend off the repeated attacks of her employer.

Chapter 4 further reveals Jessica's disdain for Lillian, her emotional cruelty and above all, her belief that Lillian was born "a bad seed."

FA

Jean as Narrator: Even as Lee became more comfortable around me, my strong feeling that I was playing a game persisted. I had expected Lee's voice to be deeper. I watched for other ways to recognize Lee. He walked with his shoulders back and took longer strides. He sat with his knees apart and his right ankle across his left knee. Lee had purchased a pair of black jogging shoes, and he fiddled with the string of the shoe resting on his knee as he sat chatting with me.

Lee noticed me looking at his new haircut. A conversation soon ensued. "I went to a regular barbershop and got a real man's haircut. I have been to those so-called 'beauty shops,' but they always just cut it the way they want it to look, and that's usually like a girl's."

Cigarettes were a part of Lee's identity. He kept track of the ashtray that I had offered on his first visit, but he only smoked outside. His hobby was woodcarving, and his work was beautifully detailed. My favorite piece was a miniature man's high-top work shoe with wrinkles and eyelets. The tongue of the shoe rolled forward with the abandon of a well-worn shoe. It was exquisite. He also carved animals.

Lee: "Do you know anything about different woods?"

Jean: "Not a whole lot. My father was a skilled cabinetmaker, and the smell of freshly sawed lumber brings on a rush of warm memories. He made some of the walnut furniture in my home."

Lee: "Warm memories, Jean? Did you actually like your father?"

Jean: "Yes, Lee, I loved him very much, and I miss him. He was a good and loving man."

Lee: "We don't like that word 'love.' None of us do. Lil's stepdad used to say, 'Let me love you.' But love hurt."

Jean: "You were asking about wood, Lee. Do you have wood? I would really like you to make one of those little shoes for me."

Jean as Narrator: I found myself changing the subject when the conversation got heavy. I did not, at the time, have any experience with the healing power of words. And I had no idea that caring and gentle questioning was the sure and only path to healing. I believed that the listener was required to do something or, at the very least, offer advice.

Lee: "I need some more wood, but I don't know where to get any. Do you?"

Jean: "Let's go to the lumberyard and see what we can find."

Lee: "You sure you have time? I could ask Mr. Mason if we could go looking when he gets back home."

Jean: "I think it will be fun. We can go as soon as I do these dishes and change my clothes."

Jean as Narrator: Riding together in the car offered a great opportunity for a conversation. Lee was much more at ease than I was.

Jean: "I have so many questions, Lee, and I am not at all sure I have any right to ask them."

Lee: "Ask away. If I don't want to answer, I will tell you so. You know I can."

Jean: "Yes, your letter made that very clear to me."

Lee: "Are you mad about the letter?"

Jean: "No, no, not at all, but I will admit you got my attention immediately!"

Jean as Narrator: We both laughed.

Jean: "When did you first come to help Lillian, Lee?"

Lee: "You know, don't you, that Lil's real father died when Lil was only about 7 months old?"

Jean: "Yes, Lee, I do know that."

Lee: "When Lil was 5 years old, her stepfather married her mother. He was tongue-tied, so he couldn't say Lillian, just 'Lee-Yun' He nicknamed her 'Lee.' When he brought friends from work to the house, and they saw her, they were surprised that Lee was a girl. They expected to see a boy. So I decided to be a boy and named myself Lee. I have always been stronger than Lil or Julie. I took my second name from a man I admired. He was a deputy sheriff and carried a gun."

Jean as Narrator: The words spilled out. I wondered for how many painful years these words and feelings had been locked inside him. He went on.

Lee: "I wasn't out much for a long time, but sometimes I watched. Things were different after the other man came to live there. I thought he had some right to do the things he did to Lil because she was so bad, and now he was 'family.' The summer before Lil's senior year in high school, she worked for a man named Mr. Sampson at a truck patch near home. It was a roadside market, and she mostly waited on customers, but sometimes helped to unload the wagons. One day she was unloadin' watermelons, and the last one was so big, she came off the wagon right with it, and that man was standing on the ground where she fell. He caught her in his arms and hugged her too long and too tight. Then he forced her into the shed and started pullin' off her clothes. Lil couldn't take it, and Julie took over. Next thing I know, he's rapin' her. I tried to help Julie, and I fought like a maniac, but he said, 'So you are one of them that likes it fighting! Well, I like it that way too!' It was a fierce fight, but he was too strong for me. He kept saying, 'Stop fighting! Stop it right now! Stop fightin', or people will see the bruises and think you don't want it, and I know that you do!' That made me even madder, but I still couldn't stop him. When Julie got home and told Lil's mother, she was asked, 'Did you cry rape like the Bible says to?'"

Jean as Narrator: Lee was telling the story in a calm voice, but I pictured Lillian/Julie in a panic.

Lee: "When Julie shook her head no, Lil's mother yelled, 'Then you asked for it! I am raisin' my kids decently, and you are not going to ruin my reputation!' She was really mad. Julie begged not to have to go back there to work, but Lil's mother insisted, 'It's all your fault. What would the neighbors think if you quit?' We couldn't figure out what the neighbors had to do with it. Julie had no choice. She kept workin', and he kept rapin' her. She cried, and I fought every time. Once I took his gun and shot at him, but I missed. Lil couldn't be around, and Julie took most of the senior year of high school and worked for that son of a bitch. I helped Julie all I could. Julie would get cryin' at school and couldn't stop, but she couldn't tell anybody."

Jean: "Oh, Lee, how awful! And I remember she told me about that, and I had said, 'You need to tell your mother!' And you say her mother knew it! I am so sorry! Sorry is not a strong enough word! But I didn't know exactly whom I was talking to. What happened when you got back home?"

Lee: "Lil got put in the mental hospital. They said she tried to commit suicide, but she didn't. They gave her electric shock treatments."

Jean as Narrator: I was stunned when it all hit me. So that's why we didn't hear from her after she returned home after visiting us in 1957! And I had failed to grasp the extent of the rape Julie told me about then, thinking it was a one-time occurrence, when in fact, it went on for months.

Arriving at the lumberyard, Lee made his selection. At the cash register, I noticed that Lee didn't have Lil's purse. He pulled some bills from his shirt pocket, saying, "Mr. Mason gave me some cash. I can pay."

Jean: "Please let this be my gift to you, Lee." He accepted and thanked me. On the drive home, Lee asked, "Why are you so nice to us? What do you want us to do for you?"

"I like all of you I have met, and I am sure I will like Esther too, whenever she's ready to talk to me. I have always liked Lillian. I just want you to be my friends and to let me be a friend to you."

Lee: "We don't have friends, except Lucy does."

Jean: "Will you be my friend, Lee?"

Lee: "I don't know how. I never had a friend before. What do I have to do?"

Jean as Narrator: It was an unusual question, but Lee was serious. I responded, "Just be you and talk to me. Know that I will never, never intentionally do or say anything to hurt any of you. Maybe you can help me with Amy and Esther."

Lee: "Doctor said you shouldn't ask for Esther yet. She's too angry and needs time. Amy is afraid a lot of the time. She had a lot of bad things happen to her, but she likes you."

Jean as Narrator: Lee was providing valuable information. "Is Amy left-handed?" I asked.

Lee: "Maybe, but she uses both hands a lot."

Jean: "How about you, Lee, are you left-handed?"

Lee: "Yes, and so is Julie. But Lucy is right-handed and proud of it! She could write the way that teacher wanted her to, and Lil couldn't. I will help you with Amy. Just ask for me anytime. You are doin' right with her."

Jean as Narrator: I had been teaching her the alphabet letters by mail. I didn't remember driving home because the conversation was so extraordinary. While getting out of the car, Lee said, "Thank you for takin' me, and thanks for the wood."

Lillian's Journal: "Today I really seemed to be coming and going. Here one minute and gone blank the next. Aunt Jean took Lee to get some teak wood. Aunt Jean said Amy was here. I knew it would happen, but I didn't want to think about it. I'm not a little girl! Or a boy either, but Lee is there, so I suppose Amy has as much right as any other one. Julie was here. I don't know about Lucy. Uncle Walter acts like I still am an okay person. Aunt Jean has been so nice. It's so peaceful here, even when the day seems so scattered. I woke up this morning and thought just for a moment that someone had left home, and here I was in a motel room again, but it was just a quick thought and a relief to remember Aunt Jean and Uncle Walter were where I was, and it's a good place to be."

Lee's Journal: "Mr. Walter talked with me okay. I was sure he would give me some lectures if I was around. He is an okay guy."

Julie's Journal: "I met a man today who takes organ lessons from Jean. I really was scared, but this man was nice and safe to be around. Jean calls him Colonel. He is an Air Force colonel. Jean's husband is nice too and funny. I don't think he hurts people. He said he liked to work without a lot of people around. Me too."

Jean as Narrator: Julie had told me that she and Lucy had a lot of questions about religion, and since I liked my pastor, Rev. Chris, so much, could they maybe ask him some questions.

We made an appointment. Julie was afraid but finally brought herself to ask him if it was all right for her to be inside his church. He responded with great compassion, and Julie liked him. Lucy appeared to say that she had a lot of mixed-up ideas and feelings about church and asked if she could discuss them with him sometime. We made an appointment for the following day. On the way home, Julie expressed her opinion of Rev. Chris. "He cares about people. Even I talked to him a little bit, and he didn't get mad at me. I wish I didn't get so afraid."

The next day, I was able to convince Lillian to talk to Rev. Chris. When we left the church, Lillian commented, "He was kind. I forgot about the time and maybe was there longer than we should have been. I lost time in front of him, and he seemed to accept it okay. He said a prayer for me after asking me if it was okay! In the prayer, he said, 'Thank you, God, for loving the parts of Lillian that she hates.' That was perceptive of him to know there are parts of me that I hate. He said something about asking or checking to see if there was a church of some kind that I could go to at home that would accept me as I am. I doubt if there is any church I could go where the others would go too, and it would still be all right."

Lillian's Journal: "Aunt Jean and I talked, and here it is 2 a.m.! I enjoy being here so much! It's so calm, and I don't ever need to worry about how I am, even with Uncle Walter."

Jean as Narrator: Tucked in the journal was a note from Lee. "Lil, you already have washed, taken your pills and drank orange juice today."

Lillian told me how ashamed she was that Dr. Robinson had seen Amy. We were standing near the dining room table. I wanted to see Amy again, but Lillian was reluctant. I reassured her that no one else was here, and it would be okay. Just then, Amy showed up to sit by the table with me. She prepared to get up on the chair by holding onto the back of the chair she was facing, then put one knee on the chair and hoisted herself up.

Amy: "Hi, Jean!"

Jean: "Amy?"

Amy: "Mmm hmm. Can we color?"

Jean: "Sure. What is your favorite color?"

Amy: "Black."

Jean: "Black? Why black? Most little girls I know like red or blue."

Amy: "Black be better. When Lil's mother take us out of coal cellar, our dress be dirty. Shoes too. She say, 'Naughty black dirty girl, spoiled her dress.' Face an' hands be black too. If dress an' shoes be black, can't see dirty. I like black."

Jean: "Oh, Amy! She put you in the coal cellar? Were you scared?"

Amy: "Mmm hmm. Dark down there an' rats an' spiders an' mouses. She locked door. Rats can jump far. You ev'r see rat jump way 'cross coal, Jean?"

Jean: "No, Amy, I never saw that, but it would scare me."

Amy: "One time, I's sleepin' an' somethin' on my face wake me up – a rat. It run down my arm an' run 'way. Don't sleep no more. Look see if 'nother and run see if 'nother rat come."

Jean as Narrator: Amy was totally unrestrained as she described her frightening experiences.

Jean: "Who goes in the coal cellar? Amy or Lillian?"

Amy: "Sometime somebody else, sometime Amy. That's 'cause we are bad. Lil bad seed. No good. Jean, what Dr. Robinson goin' do to us? I don't think he hits people. He goin' lock us in coal cellar?"

Jean: "No, no, Amy. Nobody will ever put you in a coal cellar again. I won't let them! Dr. Robinson won't hurt anybody. He likes you. You are not bad. Neither is Lillian. You both are good."

Jean as Narrator: It was apparent that she was not believing me. She was certain that she was bad, and Lillian too.

Jean: "That was wrong for Lillian's mother to lock anybody in the coal cellar."

Amy: "We are bad, that's why."

Jean: "No, Amy. You are not bad. You are a good girl. I love you, Amy. You are beautiful."

Amy: "No, Jean beau'ful."

Jean: "We are both beautiful. Amy is beautiful, and Jean is beautiful!"

***

Jean as Narrator: Julie spent a considerable amount of time with me. She was enjoying listening to classical music. I didn't see much of Lillian. Each time Lillian appeared, she began crying over the lost driver's license. Then, Lucy, Julie, Amy or Lee would take over.

Chapter 5
Amy's Halloween

Giving no indication of what is to come and bringing relief to the building tension associated with the reader's exposure to Lillian's abuse memories, Chapter 5 treats the reader to the personality of Amy.

Frozen in time as a 5-year-old child, Amy is irresistible – curious, spontaneous, good-natured and enthralled with Halloween.

FA

Jean as Narrator: When Lillian left the hospital, Evan drove her to our house in Virginia. They arrived just before Halloween. Amy had become so real to me, that everything within me wanted to write to Lillian and ask her to have Evan bring Amy along with them, but there were only two bodies – Lillian's and Evan's.

We bought a pumpkin for the front window. This was to be a very special Halloween for Amy; of that, I was aware. Little did I realize at the time what a unique memory that particular holiday would produce.

Evan, Amy and I gathered at one end of that familiar dining room table, now covered with newspapers. The pumpkin, a knife and a black marker were laid out.

"Amy, how about using the black marker to draw eyes, a nose and a mouth? Can you do that?" I suggested.

Nodding her head, she set to work. The first eye was a circle – a wobbly circle – but nevertheless a circle.

"Good girl," I exclaimed. "Now make the other eye."

It was a surprise to Evan and me when the second eye turned out to be an awkward square. "Okay?" Amy grinned.

"Sure, Amy! That's better than just okay. I like it! Nobody ever said a pumpkin's eyes had to match!"

I thought to myself, "Here is a perfect example of a small child's creativity before we adults begin to stifle it."

Amy was so intent on what she was doing that she stuck her tongue out as if this would make her marker work better.

The pumpkin's nose was a triangle, and the mouth curved down at the outer corners.

"O-ooh, Amy, he looks so scary! You drew a good face. Shall we give him a name?"

She giggled and looked him straight in the eyes, "Name is Jackalanum!" She was jubilant.

"Okay, Evan," I said, handing him the knife. "How about you cutting the top out so we can take the seeds out of the inside?"

"I think I can handle that."

And seeing Evan taking the knife in his hands, Amy cautioned him, "Be careful. Knifes is sharp. Might cut you."

She had been standing, but now, just as any small child would, she climbed up with both knees on the chair so she could see better. When the lid was lifted off the top of the pumpkin, she peered inside, and turning up her nose, said, "Yucky. Jean, look in there. That's yucky."

"Yeah, it sure is yucky. Evan, how about reaching in there and scooping out the inside with your hand?"

"No, not me!" Evan laughed.

"Okay, I'll do it," I said. I thought it was yucky too. I certainly did not enjoy pulling the seeds and stringy pulp out of the pumpkin.

"Don't you want to see what it feels like, Amy? See the seeds? Evan, don't you want to help?"

Evan replied, "No. You are doing such a good job; I'll just watch."

Amy agreed, "Yeah, let Jean do it. Jean does it good."

As I worked inside the pumpkin, Amy inquired, "Why you do that?"

"So we can put a candle inside and make a light inside."

"Can't make a candle. Fire is dangerous. No fire, Jean." Amy was teaching me what she knew.

My thoughts as I worked included trying to figure out if I could carve out the eyes, nose and mouth as Amy had drawn them. Suddenly, it came to me that if we had no fire, no candle, it would not be necessary to carve out the face.

Finishing the job at hand and wrapping the pulpy seeds in the newspaper, I handed Amy her marker. "Now, can you color in the eyes, nose and mouth all black, so they look like holes?"

"Yep." When Amy completed her handiwork, we put Jackalanum's top on him. We were ready for the night's festivities.

Amy did not want to go trick-or-treating. She knelt on her knees on the sofa, watching out the front window beside Jackalanum. We answered the door together, saying "Trick or treat!" I invited the children in so that Amy could see their costumes better. She handed out the goodies to the children and enjoyed their costumes.

Afterward, she said, "That was fun!" I had the most fun just watching Amy! But Lillian missed it all. She asked, "Did Amy get her candy given out?"

Lillian had Amy in her mind's eye as a little girl. When I told her what fun Amy had seeing all of the costumes, Lillian needed to know, "Was she all right? Was it okay for her to be there? Did Uncle Walter see her?" Lillian obviously perceived Amy as being a little girl in a little girl's body. By some miracle, she seemed to see, yet not see, Amy as a little girl. I saw no such change, but she did indeed act like a little girl.

"Yes, she was fine. She is very well-behaved, and no, Walter hasn't come home from work yet."

Evan had never seen Amy before. He was enchanted by her and made a special spot in his heart for his mother as Amy. New feelings of protectiveness welled up in him. "I wondered what you and Mom did when she came here so many times. I had no idea, Aunt Jean," Evan said.

I wondered how Evan dealt with his mother as Julie, Lucy, Lee and Esther. Was Esther angry with Evan?

It was an eye-opener for Evan. After they returned home, he remembered that his mother was afraid of lightning and thunderstorms, and that she was afraid to lock the door. He surprised her one stormy night by coming home early. "I know you are afraid when it storms like this," he told her.

Several weeks later, Evan and Lillian made arrangements to meet Keith, on leave from the Navy, and his girlfriend at a restaurant. Evan tried to explain to Keith what Amy was like. "Mom's just like a little girl when she is Amy," he said. But words were inadequate. Evan could see that his older brother did not believe him.

"Mom, could I show Amy to Keith?" Evan asked.

"If you want to see Amy, you have to ask for her, and if she wants to be there, she will," Lillian said.

With the blinking of an eye, a little voice said to Keith, "I know you. You are the Navy boy." The exchange was brief, and the bond between Lillian and Evan grew ever stronger. But Keith wasn't even sure he saw what he saw. He never commented on it.

Chapter 6
Sarah Ann and Celeste

Chapter 6 introduces Sarah Ann and Celeste.

Lillian finds herself overwhelmed by integration itself, not to mention the introduction of two previously unknown personalities.

Who are they? What trauma did they come from? What can be done about Esther?

Jimmy and James begin to show a growing comfort with each of the personalities, except for Esther. At the same time, Jean's relationship with Esther is growing.

In the face of these challenges, Chapter 6 signals a period of growth and stability. It seems as if all family members – Jimmy, Evan, Keith, James, Uncle Walter and Aunt Jean – take up helping roles where needed, but is this a step toward integration, or will it have the paradoxical effect of normalizing multiplicity?

FA

Jean as Narrator: Lillian was always pleased when I called her at the hospital. When she could, she would call me. Often, when she could not call, one of the others did. What Lillian could not tell me, another did. Lucy told me there were two more: Sarah Ann and Celeste. How would I ever have managed without Lucy's help?

Lillian saw a letter in her hospital room addressed to Dr. Robinson in an unfamiliar handwriting, so she opened and read it. It was from a new personality named Sarah Ann, introducing herself and telling of a Celeste.

Sarah Ann Wrote: "Jean, I am Sarah Ann. I usually say I'm 18 or 20. Celeste is 20. I don't have any twang. I have been practicing my diction, and my accent is not as noticeable as it used to be. Lil's stepfather would get very uptight when I was out and did any talking. So, we all tried to make our voices

80

as close to Lil's as possible so as to not cause attention. At school also, it was important.

"I hope we can be friends. I would surely enjoy hearing your son play guitar! I have been trying to memorize the song from *Deliverance,* where the banjo and guitar play together. I wish I had the sheet music instead of this trial-and-error way to figure out each note and write it down! I am not a good letter writer, so please do not ask me to start up any kind of correspondence. Sincerely, Sarah Ann."

Jean as Narrator: Reading Sarah Ann's letter to me seemed to be a show of strength and growth for Lillian.

Lillian Wrote: "Dr. Robinson, everyone wants time to do their thing, and it seems impossible to work out. Lucy wants painting time; also shopping, writing letters, sketching time. Lee wants more carving time and time to buy his cigarettes, magazines, cologne, etc. Julie wants a couple of hours at the library, letter writing and poem writing time, plus listening time for music. Julie says Amy takes drawing and coloring time. Esther might want to make clothes again. Sarah Ann probably will want to bone up on the guitar if it is found at home. Celeste paints portraits and will probably need some time too. I can't believe this! What about me? Will I have time for raising James, cooking, housework, laundry and Jimmy? Also, I want time for my painting, lousy as it may be, and my art class. With James seeing Dr. Alabiso on Tuesdays and me seeing Dr. Robinson on Fridays, it is no wonder some days I think I haven't done anything, and I am still tired! I don't have any answers for all of this."

Jean as Narrator: The next day, Esther made an escape attempt. She didn't want to talk to the doctor, and Lillian didn't want to know what Esther knew. Lillian got hold of a plastic bag, large enough to fit over her head. Julie begged her not to use it. Lillian wanted to decide for herself and asked via her journal that Lee, Lucy and Julie let her work it out for herself and sign their names if they would agree. They signed but added, "For one day only." The next day, Jimmy discovered the note about a plastic bag and reported it to Dr. Robinson. Thwarted again!

Julie Wrote: "We are home! I am glad to be back at my typewriter. Lil has an awful headache and is lying down, so I thought this would be a good time for me to write to you. Lil got a letter from her mother today. Her mother completely ignored what she had said to Lil over the telephone a few months ago. She invited Evan to come and stay with her and asked about James. She ended it with, 'Call me or write, and come for a visit.' Lil is feeling pretty bad. She says she just can't be around any of them right now or even write or call, and she thinks she shouldn't feel that way. Lil's mother always makes Lil feel guilty.

"Mr. Mason wrote on the back of the letter to Lillian's mother that he had opened the letter and was not going to show it to Lil. 'You said you never wanted to see or hear from Lillian again, so let's keep it that way.' He put it all in another envelope and mailed it back. Then he called the telephone company to have their phone number changed to an unlisted number. I think he is right.

"Mr. Mason cares about Lil, and I think he tries to be nice to us too. He even got Sarah Ann a guitar and then asked Lil if she wanted to buy a book and try to learn how to play again. Lil got the book but doesn't think that she'll have any time to fool with it.

"I heard Sarah Ann play 'Red River Valley' tonight when no one else was home. I was surprised how good she is. I like music. I don't care for Lucy's country music, but Sarah Ann's picking was soft and nice.

"I hope Lil stays away from her mother!

"The friend you introduced me to, the colonel, sent me a card while we were in the hospital. That was nice. I never thought a man would do things like that. Maybe some men are nice too. Lucy says I should try typing. I love you. Julie."

Jean as Narrator: For the first time, Lucy put her letter in the same envelope as Julie's. I detected bits of cooperation and positive changes. Lucy's typing improved. She loved the stationery she designed and that I had printed for her. It depicted a cat peering into the page from the upper right corner, some cattails and her signature "Lucy" on the lower left side. As I read Lucy's letter, I noted she referred to Jimmy as "Mr. Mason." I had never heard or seen Lucy call him that. Could it be Julie's influence?

Lucy Wrote: "Mr. Mason went out and bought a big calendar for us. We have to be sure if any of us wants to go to art shows or plays, we write it on the calendar ahead of time so Evan will know, because he has to drive us. Lil said she wished someone would show up who likes to do housework! Not me.

"Lil forgot to put Amy on the schedule. Amy wanted Tootsie Rolls like the ones James has. Lil didn't want to buy candy, but I will. That can't hurt anything.

"Lil was discouraged. She asked Evan if he wanted another mother, and he said, 'No, thanks. I have plenty of them now.' He must think we all are! We don't boss him. Now that I think of it, Lil doesn't either. Anyway, I sure don't want to be a parent to anyone. I like to play with her kid James sometimes.

"When I took the MMPI test, one of the questions was, 'Do you think someone is trying to rob you?' And I put 'true,' 'cause that Esther was taking my dimes and using them to catch buses to strand us out someplace! It asked if somebody was trying to control my mind, and I said yes to that 'cause Lil won't let us get out right away sometimes. Some wasn't fair questions, like, 'Do you go to church every week?' I had to put 'false,' but if I could get out, I would do that! Lee says he is going to take the MMPI test, but that Julie is scared to take it. Julie is scared of tests. I don't know why. She is smarter than me!

"Lil has a bad headache. She always blames them on us, but this one, I bet, is 'cause of that letter from you know who. That nurse in the hospital was a mean old witch. I was scared, well, just a little, while we were down there. Did you know, on that card you sent us at the hospital, even your mother signed 'Grandma Baker' just like we were one of the family? Grandma Baker is nice. Some others are. You were a mother once too, huh? I never thought of that before. I am tired. I better go to bed. Your friend, Lucy."

Lillian's Journal: "Lee fixed that chair Uncle Walter brought. Now three of us can sit down to eat at one time. Lee bought a desk. He and Evan put it together. All the others can put their things away now. The drawers have labels with their names on them. Thank you, Lee and Evan."

Jean as Narrator: Keith arrived for an emergency three-day leave from the Navy to help "take care of Mom." But while he was home, he spent most of his time with his friends, especially his girlfriend. When Lillian made out a grocery list for Evan and Keith, they found themselves in a quandary about one item on the list: drain cleaner. Evan insisted that they wouldn't dare buy it, because he knew that his mother wanted it for burning herself again. Keith was positive that drain cleaner had to be bought because, "She asked for it, and she is Mom!"

Evan would not give up, "No, Keith, we don't dare buy it." Keith went to the pay phone in the grocery store and called Dr. Robinson. Dr. Robinson confirmed Evan's decision, and no drain cleaner was purchased. When the boys returned without drain cleaner and apologized to Lillian, she thought they were making a big deal out of nothing. All they needed to do was not buy it.

***

Jean as Narrator: Two days later, my mailbox yielded another letter from Lucy.

Lucy Wrote: "Lil has had a bad headache all week. She is lying down right now. I decided, why waste the time, so I'm writing letters.

"We started that schedule this week, and it isn't going too hot, with her having that bad headache. Celeste missed her painting time today, but Esther went ahead and took some of the time for herself anyway. She should show up for her class all the time, and it was Lil who had the headache, not Esther anyhow. Evan just sort of shook his head when his mom said she was sick, and then right away, Esther asked him to take her to her class. Evan didn't argue.

"Lil, well, I'd better not say it. Never mind, she is jealous of me. I put a hickey on Jimmy just so Lil would see it, and she did. That will show her!

"Celeste saw a painting of a nude girl in a store today, got a paper out and sketched it, and then sketched it on new material and is embroidering it. It looks like tedious work to me."

Jean as Narrator: In the same mail was an envelope containing letters from Lee and Lillian. More cooperation?

Lee Wrote: "I don't write good, and I am a loner. I figured out I think I am neutral. No sex feelings for male or female. Is there such a kind of person? People are okay as long as no one gets too close. I don't want that. Maybe I don't belong nowhere. That's all. Lee Marvin. P.S. Are you against drinking too? No stamp. I will put this in someone else's envelope."

Lillian Wrote: "I hit the jackpot at the mailbox today! Besides another card from you, there was a letter to Lee from you, plus one of your community efforts to several of us at once, and a card from my Aunt Pearl. Tonight is my first painting class. I'm a little scared about going.

"Aunt Pearl wrote that my mother has moved close to her, and they take morning walks together every day. So, I think I will cut down writing to her, except for a birthday card. I just don't want to hear about my own mother from anyone, and I know that's not right. Oh, well, I'll have to work on it."

Jean as Narrator: Lillian's letter continued. She seemed not to know that it was Lucy who married Jimmy.

Lillian Wrote: "Aunt Jean, I'm going to say something you probably won't understand, but I resent Lucy asking you to tell me to give her more time with Jimmy. If she wants time with Jimmy, she takes it, and I don't have much choice. Just call me jealous, I guess. I know Jimmy thinks of her as me or part of me, but all I have is a blank time, where I'm aware after the fact that she and Jimmy have spent time together. I really don't appreciate becoming me right after it is over and feeling semen running down my leg!

"The doctor said when the time comes, I will be part of that, which may be true, but it doesn't help the way I feel now. Jimmy has put up with so much from me, I probably should be willing to recognize his needs and be glad he doesn't have a girl at some truck stop. Enough of this! Sometimes I say more to you than is really decent, don't I?

"Isn't this awful? Sarah Ann and I wrote so much, but thank you for all the listening you do for me. Take care. Much love. Lillian."

Jean as Narrator: Sarah Ann, in her introductory letter to me, claimed to be 18. She said she likes country bluegrass music, plays guitar, likes boys and is shy. She is afraid of Lillian's mother, has long brown hair and doesn't drive. Sarah Ann's writing had a strong back slant, and each line crawled upward. She dotted her "i's" with circles, wrote with a red pen and did not appreciate dirty jokes.

Lucy told me on the telephone that she was getting very angry about Celeste working on that nude. That was against Lucy's religion. "Jean, we don't have such things around this house! If even a magazine comes into this house showing a girl with bare legs, Jimmy takes a black marker and blacks them out. We don't believe in that stuff. No shorts for women either! If that Celeste don't quit, I am going to cut it up when she finishes it."

Celeste worked silently. She could not speak. It occurred to me that when the personalities first came out, they spent a lot of time doing something with their hands. The time spent with their hobbies could be devoted to considerable thinking.

I understood that. I had become aware of the relationship between nonverbal activity and solitary time in the body. Having done some embroidery and crocheting myself, I could relate to the satisfaction of producing a lovely piece of work, and I appreciated the serenity such work offered. I wondered,

"Is that when they seek out their personal preferences, beliefs and desires, and decide who they are?"

But there were other reasons for Celeste's not talking.

I began doing a bit of meditating on my own likes, hopes and goals, wondering whether I could state my "self" as precisely as Lillian's personalities did. My renewed interest in reading exercised my emotions and created a yearning to discover the "real me" too. At times, I could relate closely to certain characters and stories I read. Reading *The Thorn Birds* brought me closer to Julie. I saw it as a shared experience, even though she had read the book months before I did. She was linked to the characters in the book, and now, so was I.

The Taylor Caldwell books really hooked me. I wanted to read everything I could find by this author who was new to me. As I read, I wondered which of Lillian's personalities read the same books, so I asked Lucy, who said, "Sometimes when I want to read a book, it gets taken back to the library before I am finished. Julie reads slower 'cause she looks up all the words she don't know in the dictionary. Lillian reads fast. I read a lot slower. I never went to high school."

I was reading one quiet afternoon when I came to a new character named Esther Winslow!!! My pulse quickened, and I hastily read on. Esther Winslow lived in the South, and she had a mother and father who loved her! Bookmark! Telephone! "Lillian, guess what?! I found out where Esther got her name!"

Back to reading. I couldn't put the book down. I was awakened to the influence an author could have on a reader and was baffled by the implications. Another reader would have gone right on reading. Why did I read that book right now? Yes, I read it because I like to read. But I could have picked any of a dozen or more paperbacks on our bookshelves. Why that one?

I was experiencing nonverbal communication at its best. My mind refused to rest. Some nights, sleeping was impossible. I couldn't let it go. Perhaps Taylor Caldwell's books had more for me. Upon finishing one book, I forced myself to grocery shop, vacuum and do laundry before starting the next book. It was a good thing I had organ students to break what I began to think of as my selfish concentration on me. Teaching requires total involvement, and I was devoted to my students. I was excited to discover a new creativity and the ability emerging in my teaching. It was akin to a new dimension within my very being.

***

Jean as Narrator: Jimmy jokingly said that their health insurance should pay for medical expenses like canvasses for Lucy's, Lillian's and Celeste's paintings; Lee's carving tools, membership dues, wood, guns; Julie's typewriter; stamps by the hundreds; long-distance telephone calls to Jean; plane tickets to Jean's; tickets to plays and operas; art classes; Sarah Ann's guitar; desk; lawyers for Julie's wild drive; yarn and sewing supplies for Esther; and on and on. In just one year, the Masons' medical and hospital bills had come to over $11,000. They still owed $6,000, and it was only October. Jim and Lee had become friends. Jim was going with Lee to woodcarvers' club meetings, recognized that if someone was crying now, it was Lillian, not Julie, and began to see Julie as being calm and past her crisis. Jim initially called the doctor every time "she" changed personalities, but now only called when he sensed a crisis. He was good to all the personalities, buying them whatever they asked for. While he feared for his wife's life, he continued to love and support her in every way.

Jimmy got a new job driving 18-wheelers, or big rigs, long distances. He was often gone for several days. Evan strived to take care of his mother and James when his dad was at work. However, he experienced so much violence among his peers, both inside and outside of school, that he stopped attending high school. He relayed that those boys carry chains, knives and other weapons. Drugs seemed to be everywhere. Tempers flare, and fights erupt at the drop of a hat. Evan was taught not to fight. "It takes two to fight," his parents had said repeatedly. It was nice for him to be able to drive James and Lillian to Dr. Alabiso's and Dr. Robinson's offices for their weekly appointments, but he still had only a learner's permit. Evan was playing in a rock band and drinking, smoking and doing drugs, but not being rebellious at home. James continued to try to learn under difficult conditions, to say the least. James played cards and games happily with Lucy. He responded to Julie with cool respect and recognized that if classical music were being played, that was Julie listening. Lee carved a couple of animals for James and Amy to play with, and James went along to the woodcarver's club with his dad and Lee. Esther frightened James with her shrill voice and quick, punishing hands. James had been taught to call me on the telephone. Lillian encouraged him to call frequently and ask for Aunt Jean. She let him dial the phone and talk to me about anything. For James, this was a privilege. Sometimes, he called me to say, "I don't know who is here. Do you?" I would ask to speak to whomever was home and then report back to James. We were building trust.

Dr. Alabiso was establishing a strong relationship with James and was deeply concerned for his patient's safety. James and Amy began coming to James' therapy sessions together.

The child abuse reports that had been turned in on Lillian resulted in the doctor's search for alternate care for James.

Lillian's sisters continued to place guilt on Lillian. Each time she heard from them, Lillian hurt herself. I kept trying to get her to claim her freedom from the pain they inflicted, but she was determined to earn their love and acceptance.

Lillian had relieved Julie of Mr. Sampson's rape memories, had taken over the crying, and was no longer being cut and bled by Julie. So now Julie had time and energy to use for her own pleasure. She had to stick around, though, for the driver's license hearing. Each time they visited me, I saw Julie briefly, but the needs of the others were predominant, and Julie stepped into the background. Julie and the colonel were now friends. They wrote letters and sent cards to one another.

Jimmy decided to help Lee by letting his hair grow long so Lee could accept Lillian's longer hair. Lee had a better relationship with Jimmy, and James enjoyed watching Lee carve. Each time Lillian visited us, Lee craved male company and appeared when male students took their organ lessons, sitting at a card table in the studio, carving while I taught, his foot keeping time to the music.

I had been sending letters to Amy, teaching her how to communicate by mail. She learned to write the alphabet in lower case, then in upper case. I asked her to count by tens to 100. Next by fives to 100. Amy became 6 years old as soon as she learned to print. Hearing James talk about writing in cursive, she sent me a letter asking if "6 be big 'nuf to write like James." I found it necessary to remind myself that Amy was younger and smaller than James, not to my eyes but to Amy's eyes. Reality forced me to remember that Amy still, to me, looked exactly like Lillian. I also had to remember that she knew less than most 6-year-olds because she had had no social contact with children other than James. It must be nice for James to be older than someone. I saw myself as Amy's protector, James' too.

Lucy remained critical. Dr. Robinson found her to be angry. She put her fist through a window in their home every once in a while. I didn't see that side of Lucy. She was always peppy, happy and enjoying life when we were together. Lucy moved quickly and had a gleam in her eyes, unlike Lillian's sadness. Walter's friendship was crucial to Lucy, and she sent card after card to him, asking, coaxing, pleading and good-naturedly begging him to write her a letter. When he finally acknowledged Lucy by writing her a letter addressed to Lucy, she was so moved, she cried for the first time in her life. Walter's approach tended to be that they are all Lillian, and he refused to call them by any other name for months. Lucy and Walter loved to exchange jokes, trying to top one another's stories. She stated and restated to me that she was never going to be integrated. She referred to herself as "THE LUCY!" ("If anybody is going to leave, Lil can go, but I am staying! I will never leave!")

Lillian and I discussed her ability to write poetry like Julie, and I suggested that she could undoubtedly paint every bit as well as Lucy. So they began painting, and Lillian enrolled in an art class. I guessed that she could also learn to carve. We wondered together whether their talents would become hers when they were integrated.

I wondered how the others felt about my talking about integration because, after all, they were going to have to be integrated someday, and that meant they would no longer be!

Lillian questioned me repeatedly about the others. I am convinced that she couldn't see them, and she became convinced that I could and did see them. I was beginning to be more forward in my questions. A letter from the speeding-ticket lawyer called Lillian a split personality. Lillian was offended. She explained to me that split personality, or schizophrenia, means a person has two distinct sides. Schizophrenia is not curable, but it can be controlled with medication. Her mother, Jessica, was diagnosed as being a paranoid schizophrenic. Lillian couldn't remember her mother taking medication.

On the other hand, Lillian's diagnosis was multiple personality disorder. She had a split in the conscious process in which a group of mental activities broke away from the main stream of consciousness and functioned as a separate unit, as if belonging to another person.

Multiple personality disorder is curable!

One lawyer's letter addressed insanity or "impaired mental faculties," which had been corrected. Dr. Robinson objected. So did Lillian. Lillian had no insanity and no impaired mental faculties. Find another lawyer – No. 6.

Esther Wrote: "I opened the gift you left for me when you visited with Lillian and read the letters you sent. Thank you for your gift. Perhaps I was wrong in some of my thinking. Esther Winslow."

Jean as Narrator: Trying to be patient and not crowd her, I waited a week and sent Esther a simple card about friends. I added no writing, just signed my name.

Esther's anger worried me. I finally called Dr. Robinson to remind him that someone should be angry with me for telling Lillian, "You need to tell your mother" when she had visited us at age 16 and was being raped by Mr. Sampson. Could that anger cause Esther to be dangerous to me or Walter when she was in our home?

Lillian told me she gets afraid that some "personality" will show up who has done, or will do, something drastic.

Celeste finished her embroidered nude and wrote a note to Mr. Mason, asking for a frame for it. When her handiwork was all stretched and ready for framing, Lucy, just as she threatened, cut it to shreds. Celeste appealed to Mr. Mason in a note. "Lucy cut my work up. No one cares about how I feel about anything."

Lillian, having seen the notes and having viewed Celeste's work, feared that Jimmy would scold and that someone would get angry and leave, or hurt her. Sure enough, Lillian's blank time needs explanation.

Julie Wrote: "Lil, Mr. Zannoni would want me to tell you what happened. Lucy got mad at Mr. Mason and was already mad at me because of my religion class and Celeste because of her painting. She messed up Celeste's work, and Celeste felt bad, so she went for a ride. After she drove awhile, I got control and called Dr. Robinson. I told him what was going on, and that I would start home. Lucy got mad again. She took over and drove clear to Ohio and then changed her mind and let Lillian be there. Lillian was surprised but didn't let on."

Lillian's Journal: "Esther went to a class for crewel embroidery, and she let me back before she left the store. Someone was telling me 'I' didn't need to come back to this class, since I already knew how to do crewel. I don't. I had some items in my hand that they wanted me to buy. I had to make out a check. She seems to want her privacy, so I'll wait till she says she wants someone to see what she is doing. My fingernails have been bitten."

Lucy's Journal: "We saw our doctor tonight. He had the test back that me, Lillian and Esther took. It said I was impulsive, liked people, was friendly and felt alienated from my family. Also, that this type could become addicted to alcohol or drugs (and me a Christian!).

"The doctor said I could have caused serious trouble by driving the car when Lil didn't have her license, and we could have been put in jail or in some strange hospital if I had an accident, even if it wasn't my fault. Dr. Robinson says tearing up Celeste's painting was cruel, and I should let Celeste and Julie do what they want and not interfere in their lives, even if I don't agree with them. He even swore at me. He must have meant what he said. I was wrong. I never thought about how Celeste would feel. I used to break or ruin things of Lil's before, and she just looked at what was broken and never said anything or had any reactions. So, I didn't see that I was hurting anyone, but our doctor said I was. He said he would help me learn other ways to take care of my anger. Dr. Robinson said I could write it down and seal it in an envelope and mail it to him. Maybe I will try that. He is a cool doctor, but I don't like all that he says. Celeste, sorry I ripped up your painting. I will try not to do that anymore."

Julie Wrote: "Did Esther or Lucy or both of them do it? We are confused. The doctor suggested Lillian and Jimmy begin working on their sex life together. Lillian is aware that she is not being much of a 'wife' to Jimmy and knows that she has lots of hang-ups. Meanwhile, Lucy has been listening. She wrote to Dr. Robinson, 'Lil can't go to no sex instruction class. She don't allow any feelings for that.'"

Lucy Wrote: "Lil, Jimmy and I don't need you. Everything is fine now. Why try to change? You can't, you know!"

Esther's Journal: "That doctor of the others is trying to tell me he thinks I need therapy. He told me he has the results back from the questionnaire I filled out. He acted like the whole thing was bad. He had Dr. Alabiso there in the office, and they objected to me doing Lil's job with her kids for her. I never ever used any instrument of any kind to hurt her kids. I just hit them good. There isn't anything wrong with that. I don't care what they say. No one ever objected to me being hit with something, so what's the big deal now?"

Jean as Narrator: Dr. Robinson went over Esther's test with Lillian. He said that she was depressed, that she hides behind a facade, and that she daydreams and fantasizes a lot. He said her attitude puts people off, and it's a known fact that children who are beaten will beat their children.

Lucy's Journal: "There has been more of Esther hitting James. I decided to do something about it and called social services and made a child abuse complaint on Esther Winslow at Lillian's address."

Lillian's Journal: "Confusing? Yes, confusing. A child abuse report on myself? I must remember that Lucy and Esther see themselves as separate from me and separate from each other.

"The doctor told me that Lucy was worried about integration. He said no one is integrated until BOTH parties agree to it.

"Jimmy acts as if Esther has committed a crime by hitting James, when he, himself, has hit his own kids. What is he trying to prove? His church upbringing? He acts like I'm a criminal, and I haven't done anything wrong. I can't see Esther or control her."

Jean as Narrator: Without notice, Lee spoke out. "Mr. Mason asked me what was going on between Lil and Esther and Lucy. I said I didn't know. Man, no one is getting me into any fights!"

Dr. Robinson asked Esther what she got hit with. Esther said a baseball bat, razor strap, brush, horsewhip; whatever was handy. Jessica never hit Rosalind or Letty. The doctor asked Esther to go to a group for discussions of child abuse: Parents Anonymous.

Dr. Robinson asked Lillian about her mother. Lillian was surprised at how little she remembered between the time her stepfather died and age 16. That time was so vague. She felt terribly guilty talking about her mother. She called herself a "bad teenager." Later that night, Lillian again burned her arm with drain cleaner.

Amy used up her black crayon and asked me for "more black." I sent her a new one and some paper dolls. Amy and I exchanged letters and pictures every week or so.

Lillian noticed the letters ready to be mailed. There was one of them to me from Amy and one from Sarah Ann. Lucy wrote a letter, Lee did too, and so did Lillian. Asking Evan to mail the letters, Lillian watched him look at each one. She thought how hard it must be for the kids to put up with a mother like her.

Lillian's Journal: "James told me that he watched Lee do some carving, played paper dolls with Amy, and got hit by Esther for crying when she sent him to bed, and then I held him for a while. Seven years old, and he has to cope with this kind of mother. It just shouldn't be. I am down."

Jean as Narrator: Lillian called on Friday night. She talked of her jealousy of the others receiving so much attention from me. Dr. Robinson told her to talk to me about it. I thought that was a cop-out on his part. What made him think I could explain it and make Lillian feel better? I restated my love for Lillian and tried to make her understand that everything I did for the others was really being done for her. I attempted to hide my increasing interest in the others. It wasn't easy! Tuesday's mail included a new writing from Lillian.

Lillian Wrote: "Aunt Jean, your words were the right words and came just when needed. They were words of yours over the miles to me, fresh from your heart, and they brought the gift of love and gave me hope and strength. I learned over and over again the meaning of the word 'friend' this week. Until tonight, when I can't call again."

Jean as Narrator: What did Lillian's last sentence mean? Was Lillian again contemplating ending her life?

Chapter 7
Sarah Ann's Exorcism

The Devil

He comes out at night
an you gotta hide
But sometimes he gets you anyway.

I heard he gets in peoples
mouths
An he gets in peoples eyes
an even your ears
if you let hem near.

He comes out ~~mostly~~ at night
an you gotta crunch yourself up
real little in a tight ball.
But sometimes he ~~does~~ gets you anyway

by Ellen

Chapter 7 finds Lillian moving toward integration.

Finally, Lillian recognizes that she was the victim of abuse, not the cause of it.

Lillian is able to realize that her anger, driven by pain, is justified.

With this advance, Sarah Ann is finally able to give her trauma memories to Lillian.

FA

Jean as Narrator: Lillian wrote a letter to her mother dated December 19, 1979.

Lillian Wrote: "This is to let you know that I won't ever be seeing you or any of my 'family' I grew up with again. My choice. For 30 years, you managed to, among other things, make me cry every Christmas. Last year I didn't, and this year I won't, or ever again because of you.

"I am a multiple personality. That is caused by childhood trauma: something so bad I couldn't stand it, so 'someone else' did. Six of those personalities were there before I was 6. That's before any stepfather entered the picture. Mother, what happened in those first six years to cause those first dissociations? I remember some of it. Do you? Of course not. How convenient. It is known that all abusive parents develop amnesia when it is mentioned to them, so I don't expect you to concede to anything. And perhaps Rosalind would not think I had blown things 'a thousand times out of proportion' if it had happened to her also.

"I am not schizophrenic like you told everyone. I did not diagnose myself as a multiple personality. That was made by a qualified psychiatrist. It is curable.

"Made up? Maybe you can afford that kind of pretense, but we can't!

"Yes, I was Dad's pet. He trained me very well to serve him and other men. You had a very qualified 8-year-old prostitute as a daughter, with her stepfather as her pimp. And when you said, 'Herbert loves me, not you,' you were right. What happened to me didn't have anything to do with love. Your jealousy was for nothing. Oh, Mother, how could you leave me home alone with boys you knew didn't think of me as a 'sister'? HOW COULD YOU NOT LET ME QUIT WORKING FOR MR. SAMPSON AFTER HE RAPED ME? Because you raised your kids decently, and I wasn't going to spoil your record – I remember the words, and I'm sure you do too, somewhere back in your mind.

"Because of a caring doctor, a caring husband and some caring relatives who know the truth and accept me and love me as I am, the rest of my life will do a lot to make up for those early years that are still partly blank. You told me often enough how you didn't want me before I was born. Now it's true. You don't have me as a daughter anymore. You got your wish. My sons no longer consider you their grandmother. Merry Christmas. Lillian."

Jean as Narrator: The next time Lillian visited me in Virginia, Sarah Ann was "out." I wanted to try to understand. "Tell me more about giving Lillian your memories, Sarah Ann," I pleaded.

95

Lucy: "When Sarah Ann has a headache, lots of times it's because one of us wants to be 'out in the body,' and she doesn't want us to. We can give her a headache. Remember how bad she said her headaches were in the hospital? That was Celeste and me trying to get out. She sort of knew somebody was there, but she didn't want us to be. We can give her a memory too. And if it's too much for her, we can take it back. Sometimes they only give her a flash till we see how she takes it. Some of our memories are really bad. We don't want them. We want to get rid of them."

Jean as Narrator: "Aha, " I thought. When they give a memory to Lillian, they no longer have it. A theory was forming in my mind. Perhaps the only substance to the personalities was the particular memories each one owned. Could it be that when they gave all the memories back to Lillian, they would simply disappear? I was beginning to understand the fear of integration; the sense of loss of a part of oneself.

Sarah Ann's Journal: "A man comes to the house, and Dad and I are the only ones home. The man is partly bald on top. He asks almost immediately, 'Is this the child?' And Dad nods. His name is Rev. Kane. He is carrying a box. Dad offers him a drink, and he says, 'Let's get on with this. It can be extremely crucial to attack before they are aware.' Dad calls me and says he found a man who will make me be the good little girl I want to be. The man puts on a gown or a dress, and he puts some wide scarves on top of that. He puts some stuff out on the table and says it is important not to be interrupted, and Dad says, 'No worry there. There is no one else home.'

"It is dark outside and cold, and Dad says he will pull the air draft, but the man says, 'No, the coldness is good. Evil breeds fire.'

"This man said to undress the child for identifying marks. I don't know what he means. I am getting a sick feeling that something bad will happen. I just know it. 'Dad, I will be gooder.' He said to undress, but the man was there. Dad said, 'Don't give me that can't right now,' 'cause I had started to shake. I was scared. This was different. I looked from one to the other and started to run.

"Dad said, 'Stand still.' He had a grip on me. I stood still. The man pulled up my dress and my pants off. I didn't have no slip. My shoes were off. He just started feeling me all over. I was confused and close to crying. I thought of running, but Dad had a hard grip, and he started to feel all over me too and told this man that I had places I liked him to feel, but sometimes I talked back and wouldn't listen and even hit. A bad child forever breaking things, likes his hands where he puts them sometimes.

"Then he, the man, just put his tool out, and I started to fall, but he caught me, and he laid me on a table – the one we kept our Bible on. I said I was cold, and he put his hands where Dad's were and said definitely something about possibly wet with grease. (Here, another small child took over the writing.) It felt good, but he say move and hold sides sometime, and he sing then and put his tool like Dad's out. Make juice on stomick, and he shift 'er, and I scream. Cross pushed inside … cold … hurt. I pinned down. He scare me. He make ugly mess sticky stuff on me. I skreem a lot, Dad stop. I vomit. My stomach hurt. He pull out and away. He say child can be helped. I run to the cellar (Sarah Ann takes over the writing.) He brought my clothes, and he said to get dressed. Mother will be home. Lil's dad, stepfather, wash me, dress me. I crawl over the wall in cellar and whimper. Dad told mother I was sick, and he carried me to bed like I was a good girl now.

"Later, in the man's office, he did the same thing, feeling all over, and I was scared, but one place felt good, and that made me better for what was happening. I couldn't do like Esther and not feel nothing."

Chapter 8
Sarah Ann's Overdose:
It's Happening Now

In the course of healing, the recovery of memories is a necessary step in the process of integration, but it is not the final step.

*With each memory, the trauma is re-experienced not as something that happened in the past but as something that is happening **NOW**.*

Fear, terror, horror, body memories; all come flooding back as if the traumas of the past are happening in the present.

This period is one of high risk for self-destructive behavior.

In the aftermath of Sarah Ann's overdose, disconnected memory fragments come together, forming an integrated self – one body, one mind, one memory.

FA

Jean as Narrator: Jimmy called to tell me that Dr. Robinson wasn't making headway with Sarah Ann, and she was suicidal again.

Dr. Robinson was pondering over whether it was safe to release her from the hospital. He decided that she could be released only if she came to my house. My question once again to Jimmy was, "What if Sarah Ann or someone else takes their life while at my place?"

Jimmy answered that Dr. Robinson has a promise from all of them not to hurt themselves at my house. Thus reassured, I gave my consent.

As she (who?) approached me at the airport and greeted me with a hug, I noticed a small piece of paper in her hand. Taking the note, I recognized the handwriting. "Jean, this is Sarah Ann. I'm sorry. It just isn't working. Nothing will ever be right. Lil will never get her license back. Goodbye. Sarah Ann." My name and phone number were on the note.

Without her telling me, I instantly knew that Sarah Ann had broken the terms of her release from the hospital. In breaking her "contract for safety" with Dr. Robinson, Sarah Ann entered a new level of lethality. Her care for me and her gratitude for Dr. Robinson were not enough to protect her from a self-inflicted death.

I knew I had to get out of the airport quickly. Once in the car, I ordered, "Someone tell me what's going on!"

Someone said, "Sarah Ann took a handful of pills on the plane. She asked for orange juice and then swallowed them all."

I asked my standard question: "Who are you?" I had to know whether I was dealing with a child, a personality who didn't know me, one who was angry or Lillian herself.

Julie: "Oh, Jean, what are we going to do? If Sarah Ann feels that bad, shouldn't we just let her die?"

Jean as Narrator: "No, Julie, you should know by now that if Sarah Ann dies, I lose you, and I lose Amy, and most of all, I lose Lillian. Can you tell me how many and what kind of pills Sarah Ann took?" I asked. Talk about challenges!

"Maybe," Julie said, reaching into Lillian's purse for bottles.

Handing her a pen, I said, "Write it down: the kind and strength of the medication and the number of pills you think it was."

I didn't tell Julie, but I panicked at the thought of them, all of them, passing out and my having no information about what was taken. Only slightly relieved, I sped homeward.

Julie: "Are you mad at us, Jean?"

Jean: "No, Julie, but I want you to stay and help me with whatever I need to do to keep you alive. What we need to do is drive straight to the hospital and have your stomach pumped out."

Julie: "I don't think that can be done. It's awful. They always hold us down, and then we are so sick. Nobody wants to be seen vomiting, and the hospital attendants and nurses always watch."

Jean as Narrator: I raced toward home, knowing I had a student scheduled to arrive in less than an hour.

Arriving home and getting her seated in the big studio, I went directly to the telephone and called the hospital emergency room. The answering nurse confirmed the need to empty the stomach, but when I told her the patient refused to come to the hospital, she said to go to the drugstore and purchase ipecac. "Have her drink all of it. She should start expelling the poison from her system in a short time."

Thanking her, I returned to the studio. "Who is there?" I queried.

Julie: "Still Julie. Do you want someone else?"

Jean: "No, Julie, but help me. Somehow, we have to get some medication from the drugstore to empty your stomach. I am afraid to go and leave you here, and I am afraid to try to take you along in case you pass out."

Jean as Narrator: The door opened quietly. My student, the colonel, entered for his music lesson. One look, and he asked, "What's wrong? What can I do to help?"

Julie: "I am Julie, and Sarah Ann took an overdose on the plane on the way here."

Jean: "I hate to ask, but I can't figure out a way to get the ipecac from the drugstore. She won't go to the hospital. Do you think you could stay with her until I get back from the drugstore?"

Jean as Narrator: Without a second thought, the colonel suggested, "I'll go to the drugstore if you can tell me what to get."

With great relief, I thanked him, and he left.

Returning my attention to my hurting friends, I found that Julie had left and someone else was there. Lucy? "Who is going to take that nasty medicine? Not me."

Well, now I have a new challenge. Who indeed? Two or three others spoke up, "Don't ask me." "Not me. I didn't take no pills."

Julie said, "I don't think I could choke it down."

Someone else said, "I won't."

Finally, someone stated, "Let the one who took the pills take the medicine. It would serve her right." That must have been Lucy speaking.

My answer to that was, "No, Sarah Ann feels bad already. I can't ask her to do that."

Whenever nobody else wants to be in the body, Lillian is there. So, once again, they all deserted her. She had no recollection of how she suddenly found herself with me in our studio. The last she remembered, she was in the hospital in Niagara Falls. "Aunt Jean, what's going on?"

I brought her up to date. She expressed embarrassment that Sarah Ann burdened me with her overdose and said that she felt like Sarah Ann did; namely, "What's the use?"

The colonel returned with the medicine.

Lillian and I sat together for a short time, saying nothing. I realized that valuable time was slipping by, and I urged her, "Lillian, we have to get this done before Uncle Walter comes home. He would never understand. Besides, I'm not strong enough to get you up and into bed when you can no longer navigate, and you collapse on the floor. I'd have no choice then but to call an ambulance."

As Lillian stumbled into the bathroom, she said, "I feel I'm pretty woozy."

She reluctantly swallowed the medicine. In a short time, I heard her retching and thought to myself, "Thank God! One more time, her life is saved!"

Lillian relieved herself of the drugs, and I encouraged her to lie on the sofa in the living room, where I could be near her. She was quite moved by my wanting to be around her when she was sick. Nobody had ever shown her that kind of care before. I gently sponged her face with a washcloth.

Lillian slept while I prepared dinner.

Lucy was there when Walter arrived home for dinner.

Two days later, Lucy was her old jovial self, showing no signs of Sarah Ann's death wish.

Sarah Ann apologized for her trouble and asked if I was mad at her.

"No, Sarah Ann, I'm not mad at you now, but I was. Do you know that if you kill yourself, you also kill Lillian? If any one of you kills my Lillian, I will be very angry and terribly sad. I will cry for days. Don't you know how much I love her?"

Sarah Ann was completely taken aback by what I was saying.

"You mean you really like her? We are all bad. Don't you know that? Jean, how could you care about her?"

"Lillian is very, very special to me. She always was and always will be. I am her aunt, and she is my niece, and I want her kept alive. I need your help, Sarah Ann. Please promise me you won't ever hurt yourself again. When she hurts, I hurt. When you or one of the others hurts, I hurt. You may not be ready to know that today, but someday you will understand."

Sarah Ann disappeared, and Amy appeared.

Amy: "What're you goin' do to Sarah Ann? Burn her hands? Tie her up an' put her in a closet? Why didn't you hit her? I know, you goin' lock in the coal cellar."

Jean: "Amy, Amy, my dear sweet Amy, I'm not going to do anything to Sarah Ann but love her. She didn't think what she did was wrong, and I guess she didn't know how much I love Lillian."

Jean as Narrator: Amy curled up her nose. She was surprised and visibly disgusted.

"You mean you like Lil? She bad. She is dirty girl, and nobody likes Lil."

Aha, here's my chance.

"Of course I like Lil, just as I like you, and I like Sarah Ann, Lee, Lucy and all the others."

"But not Esther."

"Oh, but I do like Esther. She writes to me, and she talks to me now. I won't ever, ever hurt Sarah Ann or any of you," I assured her.

Shaking her head, Amy said, "Esther hit James." And she was gone.

Esther took over, standing erect with a refined demeanor and clipped manner of speaking. I was certainly aware that I was sending a very clear message to Esther that I cared about her. It was equally apparent to me that I had clearly and simply stated my love for Lillian.

Sarah Ann: "I'm sorry I caused all that trouble, Jean."

Jean: "And I'm sorry you had to feel so bad, Sarah Ann.

Lucy: "Jean, you shoulda' seen Fluffy last night! Lil was layin' on the sofa feelin' real bad, and Fluffy crawled up on her shoulder. Lil stayed real still, an' pretty soon, she started washing Lil's tears from her face. We like Fluffy."

Jean as Narrator: One month later, Lillian was back in the hospital – Sarah Ann was suicidal again.

Lillian Wrote: "Back in the hospital again. Dr. Robinson came in, and we just talked about me and therapy. He saw the letter I had written to be given to him after I killed myself, and he kept it. He said he would sure feel bad if I did that after all our hard work. He said I was making a commitment to keep on working with him in therapy. I asked if he ever got to feeling like he wanted to drop me as a patient and take someone else who wasn't so mixed up. I am glad he puts up with me when I get on the wrong track.

"A girl from the hospital told me she feels like I do. There are things that happened that cannot be forgiven. She was raped, and when she leaves here, she is going to kill that person. She can let her therapist believe she is ready to go home and get away with it. But if I lie, one of the 'others' will tattle. Yet she can go. She knows I can't forgive. She feels like getting even and plans to carry it out. I want to do that, but there isn't any way to keep it a secret for me. Does that make me a worse person than her?

"Dr. Robinson wants me to role-play. He wants me to play pretend games. They didn't 'pretend' with me. What's this role-play stuff? I'm not role-playing! I'm going to shoot my mother, my dear old mother, and use either the butcher knife I have or one of her own and cut her up into all the little pieces she has made of me. I hope she is still alive when I start to cut. You friends of Dad's and your sex games! I can't get away with cutting you up, but you can still be killed, and I can wait however long for all of you. I'm good at pretense. I don't understand why Dr. Robinson can't see the way I hurt. I thought he cared about me, and all he talks about is games."

Julie Wrote: "Some woman in here says we are evil possessions of the body, and she said she is psychic and reads cards and used to be a witch, and she can cast out demons. She thinks we are from Satan. I ask, even at 2 years old? And she said, 'Yes.' She scares me. I told the hospital therapist about her. The therapist says it's not true."

Sarah Ann Wrote: "I talked to Rev. Chris today about the exorcism stuff. It scares me."

Lucy Wrote: "I've been reading a lot of the Scriptures that were used at Lil's house growing up. Deuteronomy 22:23: 'If a damsel that is a virgin be betrothed unto a husband, and a man finds her in the city, and lie with her; Then ye shall bring them both out into the city, and ye shall stone them with stones that they both die.'"

Chapter 9
Amy's Broken Christmas Terri Beth:
Here and Gone

Lillian's reaction to a lengthy stay in the hospital at Christmas provides the reader with a better understanding of the potential for a setback.

In this chapter, the reader is also introduced to Terri Beth, a fragmented/splintered ego state having a single function.

Giving such ego states a history and personal characteristics such as a name and a fluid relationship with the other personalities may act to "create" more of a personality than is necessary or needed.

Terri Beth is one of those personalities: no name, no interaction with the others, no knowledge of the past 20 years, no future, only a past.

Such personalities are best noted and left alone.

FA

Jean as Narrator: Lillian, Jimmy, Evan and James spent Thanksgiving with us.

The men and Lee watched football in the afternoon. Lee joined in with kibitzing about the game and the referees' calls.

Celeste was present long enough to make delicious dinner rolls.

It was hard to remember that only one body was available for Amy, Lee, Julie, Lucy, Esther, Sarah Ann, Celeste and of course, Lillian herself. It had to be a fragmenting experience for Lillian.

We planned for Lillian to return again, two days after Christmas. Upon her return to New York, we received a Christmas card made by Lucy and signed by Lucy and Celeste. Lucy noted that Celeste had offered to do the printing on the card for her if Celeste could sign her name too. I guess they got over being mad at each other!

Lucy told me that Amy had experienced sadness and disappointment at Christmas. The first Christmas after their mother married that man, there was a lot of excitement around the house. There was much merriment and many, many gifts. Amy was the youngest of all the children, and on Christmas morning, when she saw all the gifts under the tree, she wondered which one was hers. But when all the gifts were distributed, there was none for her. The older kids each received several presents, but Amy was left out.

"That's 'cause bad kids don't deserve presents," the other children taunted.

Amy was certain that Santa Claus just forgot, and that he would come back after he delivered all of his other gifts and found Amy's present still in his sleigh. The other children left and played with their new toys, occasionally taking time off from their gifts to tease Amy and remind her that Santa Claus doesn't bring anything to bad kids.

All day long, Amy stood with her little nose flattened against the window, watching for Santa. But when bedtime came, and Santa still had not reappeared, Amy finally gave up and went to bed, convinced that she was indeed bad, and that Santa would never, never bring gifts to her.

My heart ached for little Amy (or little Lillian, as you choose). No wonder she didn't like Christmas.

But Lucy's story didn't end there. The day after Christmas, "Mother found" Amy's presents in the closet! But the damage was done. Amy never looked forward to Christmas again.

So, of course, Ms. Fix-It Jean took up the challenge. Lillian and I went shopping. Next to talking, shopping was our favorite pastime. Walking in the department store parking lot, I said to Lillian, "I would like to have Amy in the store for a while."

Lillian sighed and asked, "What for?"

"I would like to let her see all the toys. All children like to look at the toys in stores."

"Aunt Jean, what if someone sees her. I don't want you or me to be embarrassed." Lillian obviously experienced Amy as looking like a little girl.

"Amy will be right beside me. She is very good. Other shoppers will be intent on their own shopping and won't pay any attention to us," I pleaded.

"I worry about my purse if Amy might be there. Little girls aren't used to taking care of purses, and she would probably put it down somewhere and lose it."

"I will be glad to take care of your purse, Lillian," I said. Her purse was immediately handed to me, and Amy took my hand, just as any small child would.

"We are goin' in the toy store, Jean?" she asked, all smiles.

"Yes, Amy. Won't that be fun?"

"Mmm hmm."

Going directly to the toy department, we began talking about the different toys. I was trying to discover what appealed to Amy so I could buy her a Christmas present of her own choosing.

"What do you like best, Amy?" I asked, showing her the dolls. "A doll?"

"No. No baby." She was adamant and walked right past them.

I noticed that Amy looked at things arranged on the lower shelves. Did she think she was little? My attention somehow focused on the higher arrangements, and I reached up and held some items down low for Amy to see. She looked and smiled at each one, and then in her sweet little-girl voice, she admonished me. "Not s'pose t' touch things in stores."

"Right on," I thought! "Now, how do I explain this?"

"That's right, Amy." Children shouldn't touch things in stores, but grown-ups sometimes have to get things down from the high shelf to show the children." I hoped she would buy my story.

"Oh," was all she said.

We looked at various toys, and Amy was enjoying every minute of it. Finally, my eyes lit on a stuffed figure that I was sure Amy could identify. It was a Sesame Street Big Bird. He was wearing a red fireman's hat and jacket fastened with Velcro. We both stooped down and studied Big Bird. Amy was fascinated with the jacket that could be removed.

"Would you like Santa to bring you Big Bird, Amy?"

Shaking her head, all she said was, "No, no presents." Then she was gone, but my mental choice was made.

Lillian asked, "Did you do what you wanted to do with Amy?"

"Yes, we looked at all the toys, and she told me I wasn't supposed to touch things in the store," I related, handing her purse back to her.

"And she is right!" Lillian replied. "I'm glad she knows that."

***

Jean as Narrator: Word spread among Lillian's family members that Lillian is "talking to a doctor and telling lies." Several family members wrote to either Lillian or the doctor. Each time Lillian answered and tried to explain, they piled on more guilt and disbelief. Her mother had written to Dr. Robinson again and sent snapshots of Lillian as a smiling child. When Lillian asked if she could read the letter, Dr. Robinson asked why she would want to read it when her mother obviously upsets her so much.

Lillian's Journal: "I feel like I'm 15 instead of 40! Doctor said he knew, and I needed to learn that no one has the power I think Mother has over me. He says he believes me, and I trust him completely. He asked if I ever wondered that maybe the concern Rosalind and Mother are showing is because they don't want the truth to come out. If I am lying, what I say couldn't make any difference in their lives when they live so far away. Doctor gave me an example of why they know me as a liar. The vase broken in the basement that I said I know I didn't break was actually broken by Lucy. To me, I was telling the truth, and to them, I was a liar because no one knew of Lucy. Okay, but I still don't understand why I don't remember some of the things the others talk about. If it happened in my life, why don't I remember what Esther talks about happening to her? What anyone writes to Dr. Robinson about me when I was young has to be bad. I was considered a liar as a teenager. To use my mother's own words, I was 'incorrigible.' I ran away time and time again. Anything bad anyone wants to say could be said about me.

"Jimmy, Aunt Jean and Uncle Walter, please believe I am me and real, and I count as a person. Listen to dumb me. I'm pretty bad off when I beg for friends! I have this awful feeling of dread that I have found people who believe in me, and now dear Mother will work her magic, and Lillian will disappear again. There will never be anything I can do to make things right with Rosalind or Mother or Letty. I said that to Dr. Robinson, and he agreed with me. Why should they matter to me? I never mattered to any of them – not really. I am in the pits.

"I am so down. Nothing is right. I will never get better. Doctor said once that he thought he could help me, but it hasn't worked. I will never be any different. I'd just rather not be. Doctor suggested to me once to let someone else take over if I was down, so I hope someone else does now. They can just live the rest of my life for me as far as I am concerned. They won't fail nearly as bad as I do at everything."

Lee's Journal: "Mr. Mason gave Amy a doll. He said she could have it, but she is scared that she has to love Herbert to earn it."

Jean as Narrator: In the past, Lillian or one of her personalities had to do sex to earn a gift.

When Lillian and I talked that Friday night, Lee interrupted and told me about Lillian's reaction to Jimmy's gift to her. I told Amy Big Jimmy wasn't like Herbert. I told her that Big Jimmy would not hurt her. She had remembered something that had happened when age 8 rolled around and wanted to know if it would be okay to stay 6 years old. She was worried that I would be mad because she regressed in age. Frankly, I had been unaware that Amy was getting older. She insisted that she did not want the doll. It was pretty, she said, but scared her. Amy asked me what to do with it. I told her to give it back to Big Jimmy to put away so she could have it later if she changed her mind.

"Not change mind! Amy not want doll!"

"I will tell Jimmy that Amy does not want the doll and to take it back to the store. Okay? I love Amy!"

"Okay. I love Jean. Bye."

Amy was gone. Lillian was now on the phone. She had burned herself again, was suicidal, and was talking about pills and ending it all. My words somehow never seemed to be quite enough. I reminded her that we had already set a date for her to come to Virginia right after Christmas.

Lillian's Journal: "In the hospital again. Why can't I just get shock treatment so I won't remember anything of my life or anyone else's? I am getting all the feelings and the memory of a whole year of rape. Mother wouldn't let me quit working for Sampson. She said I couldn't tell the police and spoil her reputation. She said since I didn't scream like the Bible says, I should be stoned. I even let him drive me home! She said she talked to him, and I believed she did. Only, it kept happening. Mother said I lied because I wasn't hysterical. I told Rosalind, and she hit me for lying, and I said I didn't know what rape meant. I told Aunt Pearl. She believed me, I think, but I was too mixed up. I told the preacher at youth group, and he called Mother, and she said I had always lied.

"After a long time of weekly sex rape to me, I started crying at school and couldn't stop. Mother got mad because I interrupted her at work when the school called her to take me home. She asked our family doctor to talk to me. He told me what a problem I was being. He said how hard it was for a mother to raise kids. I ran away several times. I 'lost' a whole year. I know now why Julie was 'there,' but what bothers me is I don't know why Lee was there, or Amy or Celeste. I can't go through this again! I don't want to know about their memories! I don't need these people. EVER!"

***

Lillian's Journal: "In the hospital for a voluntary admission. Doctor says he doesn't think I'm letting anyone down by being here over Christmas. It's okay.

"Saw Dr. Robinson today. He asked about an incident last night. I didn't remember any 'incident.' He asked to talk to someone who did, and I asked to be released. I know, and doctor knows I can't be released yet. Later, I figured someone must have tried to leave, but Dr. Robinson said he talked to 'Pat,' who said something about tying sheets or someone coming into my room (Pat?). I guess it wasn't anything to worry about. I forgot to ask if Pat is he or she and what the age is. I don't really care. I tried to walk out – me. No other personality. Started crying and couldn't stop. Everyone is so kind and patient with me, who seems to be trying to make some kind of record of doing wrong things in here. I fell, and my tray went all over. I smell like essence of coffee! They had to change the wrist bandage where I burned myself with drain cleaner. I hurt my finger when I fell. I called Aunt Jean. She is always so optimistic.

"Can or will someone tell me about Pat? Or will you, Pat?"

Lee's Journal: "Leave Pat alone."

Lucy's Journal: "You don't need to bother about any Pat. He don't matter. Be happy."

Julie's Journal: "Don't worry about Pat. Things are taken care of. Will be seeing Jean soon."

Sarah Ann's Journal: "Don't go looking for no trouble. Pat is okay. Let him be. Have a good Christmas."

Lillian's Journal: "Today I cried over such a trivial thing. Felt so ashamed. Rosalind sent me a Christmas card. No words or photos. Just a signature. I didn't send to her or Letty or Mother. I can't. Me wrong again?

"Dr. Robinson just left. I had sent a note to James' doctor, and Esther wrote in it too and said Celeste loved him. Dr. Robinson knew Celeste gave me that memory. Thanks a lot, Esther; I don't need your so-called help. Love is one of those things not to be thought about. Dr. Robinson talked to Esther. I wanted to leave. He said Pat is 20. He? I don't want to know anything else about any Pat or anyone else. I fell a couple of times. Maybe medication.

"Lost some time. The calendar says Christmas is in three days. One of the staff told me Lucy went down to the coffee shop with the group and tried to leave, just when I felt this time in here was better with 'the others' than before. Please be patient.

"Doctor just left again. I shared the letter Rev. Hobgood sent me. He asked me if I understand what the Rev. Chris is saying. 'If I own the anger, the need for outward signs such as burns, etc., is no longer there.' No, I don't understand.

"Blank times this afternoon. Don't know who was here. Maybe Lee. My mouth has an awful taste, but don't see any cigarettes around. I hope he didn't bum any."

Lucy's Journal: "Lee was here. He just smoked three or four cigarettes. I called Jean. She says if your broken finger hurts, put it higher than your heart. She says she'll still call on Christmas Day. Jean says the muscle relaxer for the charley horse might make me off balance a little, so watch it. Since it was the left finger, I could still write with my right hand."

Lillian's Journal: "Tomorrow is Christmas. Looks like I'll still be in the hospital. I talked to Jean. She called here! She says she bought something for Amy for Christmas, and it should be brought in. Jimmy brought a skateboard and slipped it to me to give to James tomorrow. I lost some time."

Lucy's Journal: "Lee was here and talked to two staff members in the lounge. Amy sucked her thumb night before last. She is afraid Santa will think she is bad this year. I told her there wasn't no Santa, but she says, 'James says yes, and he knows.' I got a letter from Rev. Chris, and so did Julie. Julie must have sure asked a lot of questions about God and hell and everything else! Lil got a letter from Jean about home and where it is, and she saved it and cried. Jean said home can be wherever you feel loved. Lillian cries easy lately."

***

Jean as Narrator: Christmas Day, afternoon. At our house in Virginia. With gifts exchanging and Christmas dinner over, I was working in the kitchen when the phone rang. Answering with "Merry Christmas!" I was pleased to hear Jimmy's voice. He responded in kind. He was calling from the hospital. He told me Amy wanted to talk to me.

"Just a minute, Amy." I heard him say to her, then to me, "She's taking the telephone away from me!" He was laughing.

"Jean, Jean, I got presents! Do you know you sent me presents? Mine! For me, Jean! How long can I keep them?" Amy was so excited.

"Hi, Amy, Merry Christmas!" Amy couldn't contain her surprise and delight.

"Merry Christmas! You should see!"

"Tell me about your presents, Amy. What did you get?"

"I got Big Bird an' he got a red hat an' a jacket I can put off and on! He is yellow."

Her excitement thrilled me, and I felt really happy that Jimmy was near her and could share her joy.

"Do you like Big Bird, Amy?" I asked.

"Oh, yes, my Jean. How long can I keep him?"

"Amy, sweetheart, you can keep Big Bird forever," I responded. An ache came over me as I remembered her disappointment on past Christmases when gifts were given, with price tags still attached so that Mother could return them to the stores and get the money back.

I continued, "You can keep Big Bird with you always and always. You can keep him with you there in the hospital, and when you go home, take Big Bird with you. He belongs to Amy, and nobody can ever take him away. He is yours!"

"I can keep him all day?"

111

"Yes, yes, Amy, all day and all night and tomorrow and tomorrow and next week and next year. What else was in your package, Amy? Did you get anything else?"

"Yes, I got a candy cane an' I broke it an' gave James half. We like it." She didn't mention the little tube of hand lotion that I had sent or the gift I sent for James.

"Well, I am glad you got presents and that you like Big Bird. Merry Christmas, Amy."

"Merry Christmas!" She hung up the phone. I had to call back to talk with Lillian.

***

Jean as Narrator: Lillian was still in the hospital. Jimmy called to say that Lillian had dissociated again. "When I walked in, she was asleep. I called, 'Lillian,' but as soon as she heard me, she cringed and asked me who I was. She was confused and frightened and didn't know who she was either. She wouldn't talk to me. I got two nurses, and the three of us spent an hour with her. She asked for a dictionary, and it said one of the causes of blank time was alcoholism. She asked if she could be an alcoholic without drinking alcohol," Jimmy said.

"Jean, she is really mixed up and scared. But she knows you somehow. I told her to call you. Will you talk to her?"

Poor Jimmy. What next?

Whoever it was called me from a pay phone in the hospital. I could hear the operator ask her name, and while she was trying to explain that she didn't know her name, I recognized the voice and accepted her call. She thought she was in Mercy Hospital in Ohio, and it was 1957.

"This isn't Lillian. I don't know who I am. Do you?"

I responded, "I know you are not Lillian. I am glad you called. I don't know who you are either. Maybe we can find out together."

A lengthy conversation ensued. She wanted me to get Lillian back. I told her it was okay for her to be there, and that Dr. Robinson would be in to see her, and he would be able to get Lillian back. I was sure Dr. Robinson would want to talk to her.

This new girl didn't know anything about Lucy, Julie, Amy or the others, but she had seen their names in Lillian's hospital room. She said she didn't have any clothes. I told her she should wear Lillian's clothes; that Lillian would want her to. I asked her to write in Lillian's journal, and I asked her to write me a letter. I assured her that the doctor was nice and would keep her safe, that she could trust Jimmy, and that I would call her again the next day. She was relieved when I told her that we would take care of her and that she would never have to go back to Lillian's mother's house.

Who was the mysterious person?

Three days later, I received a letter. The letter was addressed to Aunt Jean and Uncle Walter.

The only personality who referred to me as Aunt Jean was Lillian. Yet, the letter read as follows: "Dear Aunt Jean and Uncle Walter, Mr. Mason said I should have asked what the charges were on the telephone, and I didn't remember. I will try and send the money when they let me out and I get some.

"There is a building right across the street from my room, and it's only for cars and nothing else. You can drive up inside it – no offices or anything, just to park cars.

"Did you know a newspaper costs 20 cents? For one paper to read! And 15 cents for a postage stamp, and there isn't a 2 cents deposit no more on pop. No one ever heard of pedal pushers here. Women wear boots inside and dresses real long or real short or no dresses but pants like guys, only different colors.

"Some guy with long hair says his cigarettes cost 70 cents and not a quarter. Boy! I'm glad I don't smoke! There are male nurses. Female doctors. No one wears white uniforms. No one's camera opens at the top to look down through no more.

"The Christmas tree here isn't real. I don't know what it's made of, but it comes apart, and you can use it again. It looks real. I have glasses. I never had glasses to wear for eyes before. The telephone number on the address ends still don't make sense. There is a gas station that says 'self-serve.' Does that mean they are giving it away if you take it yourself?

"I could wash my clothes, and they don't need no ironing and no wrinkles either. They have pop with no sugar and gum with no sugar, but I'm still fat. I still can't think of my name. There are supposed to be charts at the end of the bed, but it's not there to read what my name is. Doctor says he don't know either. Then says I am Lillian and Amy and Julie and Lee and Lucy. Did you

113

ever hear of such a thing? Maybe I shouldn't be where people have so many names. No wonder I can't remember one of them. How many names do you have? Do you think I am crazy? I hope they let me out sometime. That Dr. Robinson is a nice man. I hope I can believe him. I always bit my fingernails. I don't, no more! They have been filed smooth. No one wears bobby socks or little scarfs around their collars or no bright lipstick either. The television man don't say no rain or no snow. He says percentages. That's cheating. I'd better stop. I am trying hard not to be crazy.

"From your Aunt Jean's and Lillian's friend – me."

Jean as Narrator: The next day, I called the hospital to talk to whomever was there. Again I talked with her on the phone. She pleaded with me to get Lillian back. Since I thought that doctor might want to work more with her, I really made only a halfhearted try and failed.

Lillian: "Dr. Robinson told me to pick a name. I don't know how to do that. I have more names than I need."

"You may have part of my name if you want it."

"What is it?" she said eagerly.

"My middle name is Beth, and I never used that part of my name."

Jean as Narrator: That evening, Jimmy called to report, "Here's the name for you: Terri Beth."

During my next conversation with Terri Beth, she told me Terri was the name of one of the nurse's daughters, and Beth comes from me. "Do you like it?"

"I do. Yes, Terri Beth, that is a pretty name. I do like it, and I am honored that you chose part of my name for yourself." I used it a lot in that conversation. I also sent her another letter using her name, now that she had a name. I talked with Terri Beth three or four times that weekend, but she wasn't around long enough for me to see her at Lillian's next visit to my house.

Jimmy took Terri Beth home on pass from the hospital to see if she would remember him or the mobile home they lived in. She went into the trailer reluctantly, obediently following him from room to room, then said with disdain, "Take me back right now. This is trailer trash. Nobody I know lives here."

The next morning, Lillian was the one who awakened in the hospital. At last, Christmas was over! She had lost three days. When she called me, she had already seen Dr. Robinson.

Dr. Robinson informed her that Terri Beth had taken over. She had been the one who took over when Lillian was pinned under the porch as a little girl, and again when Lillian was hospitalized and given shock treatments a year after leaving my house at age 16. She only appeared after long confinements, the doctor told Lillian. Lillian had been confined to Memorial Hospital for two weeks. Terri Beth seemed to have gone away after shock treatments and lost 20 years!

Dr. Robinson sent word to me that he did not want Terri Beth developed. So I never saw or heard from her again.

Chapter 10
Identity Obsession

It is difficult for others to understand why Lillian is so fixated on the return of her driver's license. Time and again, she is fretful, often near panic at the thought of losing her license.

Lillian's driver's license represents more than her driving privileges. It is tangible proof that she has an identity.

Lillian's license is the only piece of paper she owns that confirms her existence, and she clings to it.

It represents the part of herself that ties all the other parts together, and following Julie's "wild ride," it is gone.

There is no provision under the law that does not hold the host personality responsible for the acts of the other personalities.

Imagine the challenge for an attorney in trying to convince a judge that it was Julie, not Lillian, who sped down the highway at 100 mph.

Imagine the judge's dilemma: It was Julie who exceeded the speed limit, but the suspension was on Lillian's license. Furthermore, while Lillian had a license, Julie did not. Should Julie (Lillian?) be charged with driving without a license and without insurance? Should Lillian be held accountable for what Julie did?

Do the acts of the other personalities fall under the mental illness exception in the law (i.e., not capable of understanding the criminality of one's acts)?

What about qualifying for Social Security disability when one personality is capable of working and the others are not?

Indeed, the suspension of Lillian's driver's license strikes at the very heart of her identity.

FA

Jean as Narrator: Everyone was worrying about the hearing for Lillian to get her driver's license back. For the past many months, either Jimmy or Evan arranged their lives to be able to take Lillian to her doctor appointments. It was really hard for Lillian to have to count on someone else to do all the driving. When she came to visit in Virginia, either Jimmy or Evan took her to the airport. It had been Julie who was driving so fast, crying while doing more than 100 miles an hour, hoping for help after leaving Dr. Robinson's office. The state trooper who took her license said he regretted writing the ticket after Julie explained, in her own way, about multiple personalities. But the ticket could not be undone. She (Julie? Lillian?) would have to appear in court if there was any hope of getting her (Lillian's) license back. Jimmy had a hard time finding a lawyer who would represent her. It was a heavy burden for all concerned. After all, it was Julie who was driving but Lillian's license that was taken away. Could she get it back?

Julie made another apology to Lillian about the driver's license. She offered to take a bottle of pills if Lillian wanted her to.

Julie talked to me too. She was still extremely suicidal. I reminded her that if she killed herself, she would also kill Lillian and all the others. I insisted that normal people would consider that murder. Rethinking that, it seems pretty crazy that Julie could kill Lillian (same body), and that I would accuse her of murder. I realize that I was thinking like "they" did.

When Julie talked to the doctor, he told her that the way to leave was by integration, and she was not ready for that yet. She was so frightened about the motor vehicle hearing; I found that I couldn't even speak about the hearing to Lillian. Never have I seen anyone so totally consumed by the desire for a driver's license. It got so ridiculous, I wished I had never heard of it. How could it be that important? Lillian clung to it.

The lawyer told her that most people don't believe in multiple personalities. They don't believe she is really unaware of the various handwritings or what is written until she reads it later; that time is really blank for her. That lawyer's opinion confirmed that the personalities were not real.

Lee Wrote: "That damn driver's license weighs on her. She should forget it!"

Sarah Ann Wrote: "Jean came last night on the 10 p.m. flight. The lawyer called and canceled the meeting for yesterday and made it for this morning. I wish this was over. It is all so unfair. I am glad Jean is here for Julie and Lil!"

Lillian Wrote: "Today was our hearing at traffic court. Dr. Robinson was sick all week but was there anyway and saved the day. I will get my license as soon as they hear back from Albany. I am very fortunate to have this doctor. Aunt Jean and Jimmy were there too. The judge called the role of personalities to get each one's promise not to drive, and Amy piped up, saying she was 'too little to reach the pedals.' The judge and lawyer pretended not to hear her.

"I found a thank you card for the state trooper who saved my life. Now I need to find where to send it. I have to send thank you cards to Dr. Robinson, the lawyer and Aunt Jean. I feel very alone. James says Celeste played the organ. I know Esther and Julie were here. Jim is at work. I am lonesome. Are my neighbors afraid of me because of all the police or because of rumors?"

Julie Wrote: "We got a note from that nice lawyer, saying he was going to frame the thank you note from us! Can you imagine that?! He was really nice. He is president of family and children services in this area. He is enthused about the possibility of doing a program with us."

Lillian Wrote: "We got a refund from one attorney and a bill for $1,300 from another. It was worth it. I just hate to have it cost Jimmy so much money for me all the time. I wonder what Dr. Robinson's charge is going to be for this. I won't worry about it. Dr. Robinson is good about it, and Jimmy never blames me for all the bills that I cause. There really are some beautiful people in this world!"

Julie Wrote: "I just realized that when we are integrated, Jean will be my Aunt Jean!

"Now I can rest easy. Now that I got my license back, I have proof that I am."

Chapter 11
Lizabeth and Pat

Jean as Narrator: Two letters from Lillian in the next week reflected her feelings. The first was addressed to her Uncle Walter. "I know you probably know a lot more than you care to know about me and my illness. I think of you being my father's brother and wonder if my father would be ashamed or embarrassed to have someone like me around if he was alive or, like you, be related to me. I don't want to lose any tolerance you might have had for me by me visiting your home simply because Aunt Jean can tolerate me (or us). I very much don't like what I am. If you prefer not to see me again until I am a whole person, I will understand. I don't want to be a nuisance."

The second letter told of how nice Jessica is and that the whole problem is Lillian herself. "Aunt Jean, thank you for talking with me so long Friday night. I am sorry I get so down. Bothering someone else when I'm like that isn't right. You are a very kind person. Someone else would have said, 'Call me back when you are more rational.' Every day, I thank whoever is in charge of things for your special friendship and also Uncle Walter's patience with me."

Lillian Wrote: "I just wrote Dr. Robinson a letter and told him I just can't see any way out of this. I must have a lot of resentment inside. Sometimes I think I hate Dr. Robinson for the way I am. I have feelings now. I don't know how to handle them right. As time goes on, more and more of the wrong things I do are going to show up.

"It bothers me that somehow you and Uncle Walter might not think as highly of my mother as you did before we became friends. My mother is a very nice and kind person to everyone she comes in contact with. What happened to the way Mother and I get along is completely separate from any feeling she has for other people. I have had different people tell me how Mother listens to their problems and is a big help in their lives. Anyone being around her would like her manner.

"I know that things were always wrong between Mother and me. I don't know why. I think I am going to hate myself more than I do now when whatever despicable thing I did to cause her hate comes to the surface, and I see myself as she sees me. I don't want my actions or feelings to have any negative effects on your opinion of Mother. It isn't right for me to influence anyone in the way they feel about her. I know the kindness and love she has in her for other people, and what she feels about me I have caused. She has had a hard life, and I must have made it harder. Am I saying too much? Or do you understand what I am trying to say?

"Aunt Jean, I feel so awfully guilty, and I don't know why. Mother has to know. And so do Rosalind and Letty. It's really a good point for Mother to not have told everyone how awful a daughter she had to raise. And now I'm repaying her by not being able to be around her and having awful dreams about her. Oh, Aunt Jean, do I sound confused? I really feel that way. This is probably one of those letters I shouldn't mail.

"I hurt very much. How do I change inside? There just doesn't seem to be an end to any of this. My head is splitting. Aunt Jean, don't let me impose on you more than you can put up with. You have given so much to me, and I don't seem to be able to give back. I'm sorry for that failing on my part. With much love from Lillian."

Jean as Narrator: Lillian's relationship with her neighbor Liz became a concern. Liz insisted that Lillian have an exorcism. I kept telling Lillian it wasn't an exorcism that she needed. Lillian turned to Rev. Chris, and he told her the same thing. Liz gave Lillian a box of books to read, and after Lillian finished them, she brought them to me to read. Every single book was about evil spirits, possession, Satanism and the ways to deal with "being bad." Lillian was shocked when I reacted negatively about all those books and the effect they were having on her mind. She said, "I thought everything written in a book or printed in a newspaper was true."

It was a big issue between us, but she was, as always, eager to hear my thoughts and just as eager to embrace my beliefs. She showed me another item that she had written:

Evil in me has taken hold,

See an exorcist. I was told,

I don't know what the future holds for me or how long it will take to feel free,

I do know my doctor is the right way out,

I resent people who don't know what they are talking about.

***

Jean as Narrator: I received a letter from Sarah Ann. Evidently, I had written a letter to Julie, referencing additional personalities and addressed the envelope to Lillian in error. Sarah Ann admonished me for letting Lillian know of others.

During her next visit to our house, Lillian complained that her hand and arm had been getting numb off and on during the past week. She was puzzled about it. She also wondered why "… Someone has been biting my fingernails. I stopped that over a year ago."

She (they) had been at our house for a short time when Sarah Ann appeared and introduced herself. "Jean," she said, "Look at my fingernails. Tell Lil nobody is biting any fingernails. I'm filing them. Can you guess why?"

"Your guitar! You can't play guitar with long fingernails. Right?"

"Right! And, Jean, my hands get numb sometimes, like Lil's. I'm worried. Do you think we are demons, and that's why Lil's and my hands or sometimes my foot gets numb?"

"No, Sarah Ann, you are not demons. Do you think I would invite demons into my house? You are part of Lillian. I don't know much about you yet, Sarah Ann, but I want to be your friend."

Later, Sarah Ann told me about Lil's mother tying her hands and feet and putting her in a closet. When Lil's stepfather was ready to leave work, he called to say that he was on his way home, and that's when the tying took place.

Lillian's mother would put Sarah Ann into a closet in Mother and Dad's bedroom so she could watch them having sex. Lillian's mother, while putting Sarah Ann into the closet, would keep saying, "Dad loves me, not you! You just watch, and you will see!"

The child's hands were often tied so tightly that her circulation was cut off, making a hand or foot numb. Sarah Ann was giving Lillian that memory, and that's why Lillian was getting a numb hand or foot.

Sarah Ann told me she first appeared when Lillian's mother took her to visit family down in West Virginia. "They believed Lillian had demons, and they knew how to get rid of demons. There was to be a tent meeting, and she was taken there. They were said to know how to 'cast out demons.'

"Lillian was forced out behind the tent, where there was a bucket of water. They shoved her head under the water and held her there. She couldn't breathe. So I took over, and when I couldn't breathe either, Rachel Ann took over. We finally got loose and ran away."

Perhaps that's where and how Sarah Ann got her speech pattern; her West Virginia twang. Not showing much emotion, she nonchalantly changed subjects.

"Doctor wants us to make friends. I'd like some friends my own age. I am 16 now. Know any teenagers? Nice ones that are like me?"

"I have several teenage organ students. They are nice. I will introduce you to some of them," I said.

"There's somebody new named Pat, Jean. That Pat's all mixed up now," Sarah Ann offered.

Dr. Robinson told me not to ask for Pat.

"Celeste can't talk, but Pat can. Pat is doing things that are wrong and will have to be dealt with," she added.

I had my hands full with the original five, especially considering that Esther was angry, and I didn't know why. But now come Sarah Ann, Rachel Ann, Celeste and Pat. I need more notebooks!

Sarah Ann had my attention, but I was satisfied to leave Pat alone. I later learned that a handful of pills was dissolved in some Kool-Aid (Esther? Lillian?), but when it was handed to James, Pat knocked it out of James' hand.

I tried to picture it. James had to be confused. All the same hand, but who gave James the pills?

That evening after I finished teaching, Lillian talked about her hand being numb, and I told her that Sarah Ann said her hands had been tied and she was put in a closet. Lillian had been receiving that memory from Sarah Ann. Her version of Sarah Ann's memory was essentially the same.

Lillian: "I wonder why she did that. It happened more than once. At first, I was little, and she had to lift me up into the closet. It was a different kind of closet from most. It had two or three drawers at the bottom, and then two doors that opened, and clothes could be hung in the top part. I remember that when I got big enough, she would tie my hands together tightly and tie my feet together and say, 'Don't dare make a sound.' I could sit in the closet and pull my feet up. Why would she do that, Aunt Jean?"

Jean: "I have no idea, Lillian. What do you think?"

Lillian: "To teach me sex? They always went right to bed. She made sure the closet door was open a little, so I watched sometimes, but I could never understand. After he went to sleep, she came and got me out. I had to be quiet. Sometimes I was there all night. She would forget where I was, and I had to keep quiet. She said so."

Jean: "Oh, Lillian, no wonder your hand was numb. Is it still numb?" I was curious.

Lillian: "No, it isn't. I don't understand, but it feels fine now."

Jean as Narrator: The next day, Lillian described hearing glass shattering in her head.

Lillian: "Most glass breaks, shatters, falls and gets quiet. This sounds like it is in an echo chamber. It keeps going on and on. Did you ever hear anything like that, Aunt Jean?"

Jean: "No, I never did. What do you think it might be coming from?"

Lillian: "I don't know, but I do know that I am never able to help you in the kitchen. I feel bad about that, but it frightens me to even think of picking up a dish or a glass. It seems ridiculous, but there is something there."

Jean as Narrator: Thinking while I cleared the dishes, washed, dried and put them away, I came up with a suggestion that we intentionally break some glasses I no longer wanted. "Maybe if you break them and you see that nothing happens, you will get past the shattering in your head," I suggested.

She resisted but allowed me to talk her into trying. We took the glasses to the studio, which had a concrete floor. I knew the glasses would break the instant they hit the floor, and I was prepared to do an extensive sweeping afterward.

As Lillian and I stood by the card table holding the glasses, she began to shake.

Lillian: "Aunt Jean, I am scared. Do we have to do this?"

Jean: "No, we don't have to, but maybe it will help."

Jean as Narrator: Even though I seemed to be coaxing her, I admit to some concern over what reaction the crash would cause.

Sarah Ann: "I can tell you why Lil is afraid. It happened one day when I was late getting home from school. I played with the other kids down by that old fallen tree. I ran home and into the house. I hoped Rosalind wasn't there yet, but she was, and she was mad. I didn't dare take time to change my clothes. I remember what I was wearing: my new skirt and a white blouse with saddle shoes and bobby socks. Dinner was a casserole that night, and Rosalind already had it in the oven. I rushed, setting the table.

"When Lil's stepdad got home and everybody was at the table, I opened the oven and reached in for the dinner. I started to turn around to go to the table, and I DROPPED IT! It smashed! Everybody's dinner was in that dish. I started to run. I ran and hid! They found me and cut me!"

Jean as Narrator: I thought I had my explanation about the shattering glass, but I hadn't quite caught on. Sarah Ann had told me her memory. Then she began giving the memory to Lillian. We changed the subject.

The next day, without my realizing who was speaking, Lillian picked up the memory and said, "Aunt Jean, I can see it all like it's happening right now! Everybody was sitting at the table, waiting. That's all we had for that meal, and I broke it!" She put both arms over her head, as if to protect herself. She was shaking all over.

"It's okay, Lillian! It's okay. We don't need to break the glasses! Take your arms down. Nobody is going to hurt you!" I put my arms around her.

Lillian: "I can see that little girl. She was wearing a red pleated skirt and a white peasant blouse. And her shoes, I can see them!" (She changed from "she" to "I.") "I ran and hid. But someone came and pulled me out. I can't see who pulled me out!"

Jean as Narrator: We sat down and tried to relax awhile. When I asked who pulled her out from her hiding place, she didn't know.

Lillian: "I can't see who it is! Isn't that funny! I could see the whole episode, but I don't know what happened next. It had to be Herbert or Mother. I don't remember Mother ever hurting me."

Jean as Narrator: Lillian was drenched with sweat. Didn't she say earlier that her mother had hit her on the head?

Jean: "Lillian, I think Dr. Robinson would want to know what happened here today. Somebody should write to him."

Jean as Narrator: I needed him to close the incident, and if necessary, to tell me to refrain from such things in the future if I had, as I suspected, gone out of bounds.

During the next few days, Lillian and I talked a lot about her mother. Julie and Lucy gave me enough information to know that Jessica had mistreated Lillian. I wracked my mind over ways to get her to stop wasting time on getting love from those who hurt her. It was so frustrating to me that they had a hold on her that my care and attention could not break. Could she accept our home and love as a replacement for the guilt and pain they constantly inflicted on her?

We tried to time Lillian's visits to coincide with monthly recitals by my organ students. As they learned more about her and the personalities, several more students became friends with certain personalities, especially Sarah Ann.

Since Dr. Robinson's therapy was only one hour weekly, except when Lillian was hospitalized, and my time with her stretched into days at a time, the personalities often told me their memories before giving them to Lillian. It became more and more apparent that I had become an important link between these memories and each personality. They looked to me for my reaction to the horrors they had endured. I understand in retrospect how much they trusted me.

As the personalities recounted their compartmentalized memories, my role was changing. More than just a friend, I was looked to for solutions to make it okay. I often said, "Lillian was not wrong. She is not guilty. She could not have stopped it. I could not have stopped it if it had happened to me. I would have felt the same way if that had been done to me."

Sarah Ann was afraid an exorcism would be forced on her or Lillian. She talked to Rev. Chris. She talked to Jimmy. She talked to me. We kept assuring her that we would keep her safe. Lillian also questioned whether the personalities were demons.

Jean as Narrator: Sarah Ann wrote that she had been locked in a coal cellar all night. At the cellar door, Dad asked her to show him some love if she wanted to get out before the other kids in the family find out how and where she spent the night. As he unties Sarah Ann, he asks her to "Give Daddy a good feel" before he lets her go, so he will know that she understands why she must be treated like this. Sarah Ann obliges to get away quicker, but first she has to tell "Daddy" she is sorry and won't tell Mommy. To make sure Sarah Ann will obey, Daddy says, "You pee in here, and then I will put this bottle inside. If you tell anyone, they'll be damn shocked our little daughter did things like that to herself!" Daddy goes on saying what Sarah Ann has heard many times before. "If you take it out, shit ass (one of his favorite nicknames), you will spend more time in here. Remember, no one will believe you. I'll tell your mother, and she will see what kind of kid she's got!"

It is now 8 a.m., and Sarah Ann has left for school, afraid and tired and wanting to cry, but it never helps. At school, there aren't any friends. It's hard to sit. Daddy will be waiting when she gets home. But no, not yet. One of her foster brothers – the oldest – teases her in front of the other kids. "Third grade and pees in bed." Sarah Ann hides in the lavatory until recess is over. She wishes she were dead sometimes. At least school is better – a place to try not to be noticed. Her teacher asks, "Why can't you be more careful – skinning your arms and knees like that! And honey, have you thought about washing more often?"

Eleven-thirty. Lunchtime. Maybe Daddy won't be home. But he is home, and he likes what he calls French kissing. Sarah Ann lets him.

Three p.m. – school is out. Sarah Ann has 15 minutes to walk the mile home. It would have been fun to stop and play on that old dead tree, but she can't take the chance after what happened with the casserole dish. Good, just her sister is at home. They start supper. After supper it was Sarah Ann's turn to wash the dishes. She let Lucy do them, but sure enough, Lucy broke one, and because of that, her hand was put in the hot water on the stove. Her clumsy hands that hurt already, and the dishes still needed to be done.

Sarah Ann cries inside and wishes she could tell someone to please love her, and she'd be good from now on. Dishes are scary, and her foster brothers laugh when they see her cry over "a little burn." Sarah Ann thinks, "Someday *we* will be strong, and we can burn them and make fun and laugh and lock them up in the coal cellar and never go back. Just let the rats eat them!"

Then, feeling better after having those thoughts, Sarah Ann stops crying and worries about what will happen to Esther when Daddy takes her for a ride. She crawls behind the couch, but Daddy finds her, and she is resigned to being Daddy's money source for a couple of hours. It was only later when Sarah Ann's memory was given over to Lillian that she understood what Sarah Ann meant.

Sarah Ann: "It would be nice to die, God. Why won't you let us die? Don't you care even? No! No one does. This story is true. I know because I was 8 years old; now I am 16. At 8 no one cared. Does anyone care now? Will anyone ever care? There is no way out."

Jean as Narrator: Dr. Robinson asked Lillian, "What did Sarah Ann's story stir up?"

Exhausted and overwhelmed by what she had written, Sarah Ann was no longer able to bear the pain of these horrific memories. Sarah Ann gave the body back to Lillian.

Lillian Wrote: "Now that I remember Sarah Ann's story, will I ever stop associating sex and love with the hurting punishment they were then? I don't want to lose Jimmy. I want to please him, but his pleasure would be in giving me pleasure. That puts it all on me. If I don't act right, the whole thing is wrong. Always it's my fault."

Jean as Narrator: A few days later, I telephoned Lillian, but it was Amy's voice on the other end of the phone.

"Hello, Amy, do you know who this is?" I asked.

Amy: "Yes, but I can't see you!"

Jean: "That's right. I can't see you either, but I can hear you. That's funny isn't it, Amy. Is this the first time you dialed the telephone all by yourself?"

Amy: "Yes."

Jean: "Amy, I like all the nice writing you are doing. You are doing lots of practicing. Your writing is very good."

Amy: "I know."

Jean: "Keep on writing and drawing."

Amy: "Okay."

Jean: "Amy, is there anything you would like to tell me?"

Amy: "I like letters."

Jean: "Oh, yes, I do too. I will send you some more letters. I like to get your letters. I sent you some books. Did you get them?"

Amy: "No."

Jean: "Well, you will get them next week. One is a storybook. Do you have any storybooks?"

Amy: "James does. James has books."

Jean: "Can you read James' books?"

Amy: "Sometimes."

Jean: "Do you have any books of your own?"

Amy: "No."

Jean: "Well, I sent you a book about a little engine that tried and tried and thought he could. It is your book. It has your name in it. If you find any hard words, copy them down and send them to me so I can help you with them. Do you have anything else to say to Jean?"

Amy: "Thank you."

Jean: "You are welcome, sweetie. Anything else?"

Amy: "I got stars."

Jean: "Good. What will you do with them?"

Amy: "Me and James put on our school papers."

Jean: "Do you go to school?" (I was puzzled). "Now Amy, I am going to talk to Lillian in a minute. I will talk to you again sometime. I want to talk to Lillian, but first I want to tell you goodbye. Goodbye, Amy."

Amy: "Bye."

Jean: "Now, let me talk to Lillian. Lillian?"

Jean as Narrator: Seeming to have no memory for what Sarah Ann had revealed, Lillian came to the phone.

Jean: "Thanks for letting me talk to Amy."

Lillian: "Is she all right?"

Jean: "Yes, she is fine."

Jean as Narrator: I never thought about it before, but what if James and Amy were there alone and needed help? What would they do? He's only 9, and she's even younger.

The next day, my phone rang. It was James telling me that his mom was teaching him to call me on the telephone if he ever got scared or just needed someone to talk to.

Jean as Narrator: I wrote to Lee and asked a lot of questions.

Lee: "I was here first to help Julie. I thought I told you that. I was 14. I am 26 now. Julie is 29 years old. Julie is older but not as mature. Maybe she is now. She has grown a lot in the last year, you know. Lucy and Lizabeth were the first, as far as I can figure."

Jean as Narrator: Lizabeth? Another one? I just found out about Sarah Ann, Rachel Ann, Celeste and Pat; now Lizabeth?!

My next letter flew off my pen. Does Lizabeth know me? Would she like to have me for a friend? What does she look like? Are there more?

Julie: "Yes, there are more. We have to respect their privacy until they are ready to let us see them."

Jean as Narrator: On Friday night, Lillian told me that Dr. Robinson talked to Sarah Ann. The person who had pulled her out from behind the piano after she dropped the dish was her mother. Mother grabbed up a piece of broken glass and ran after her. "You broke it! How did you think that dish felt when you broke it? Here, let me break you so you can see how it felt!" And she slashed (Sarah Ann's) arm with the broken glass!

It was terrible information for Lillian to learn that her mother had intentionally cut her.

Lillian Wrote:

"This year the awful tactless remarks you make won't be heard.

This year your anger and my jealousy won't clash.

This year no one will remind me of my failures.

This year I'm not supplying tears caused by your criticisms.

This year the silence will be nice.

This year I have grown."

Jean as Narrator: My friend Rev. Chris began receiving more letters from Lucy and Julie. Lillian also wrote to him. Chris' interest was growing, and he took on more responsibility for Lillian and the others. At first there were five personalities. Now in just one month's time, the number increased to nine, plus Lillian. And Julie said there were more!

Lillian's self-torture and suicide attempts were uppermost in the minds of those of us trying to keep her alive. Rev. Chris saw Lillian each time she came to Virginia. He and Lillian entered into a covenant together. She would not take pills or try to commit suicide without first asking for help.

At night, Lillian's dreams persisted and got worse.

Lillian sensed that the worst was yet to come.

Chapter 12
Celeste, Rachel Ann, Buddy, Lil, Jackie, Nancy

Fortunately for Lillian, Jean was never trained in psychotherapy.

Likely, if she had been, Lillian may never have been integrated!

It was Jean's qualities as a person that Lillian (and the "others") found irresistible – always curious, always welcoming, always genuinely interested and always authentic.

When Jean was asked how she developed her method, she replied – "I didn't know any different."

In Chapter 12, we meet Celeste, so damaged by her abusive past, she is literally unable to speak.

Celeste's recall of the abuse that left her mute liberates Lillian's intense fear. However, Celeste does not integrate, suggesting the possibility of more memories.

Not every personality responds to trauma in the same way, even when the trauma itself is identical for each one.

Up to this point, with the exceptions of Esther and Lucy, most of Lillian's personality states have been docile and self-effacing.

Even 16-year-old Sarah Ann is timid. Then comes 15-year-old Rachel Ann.

Having been exposed to identical trauma as Sarah Ann, Rachel Ann went a different way. Rebellious, oppositional and occasionally defiant, Rachel Ann's external behavior conceals crushing pain.

As with the "others," her memories have to be turned over to Lillian before she can integrate.

Unexpectedly, Buddy, a never-before-heard-from personality, shows up, followed by the first "split within a split."

FA

Jean as Narrator: Celeste was a challenge for me. I began writing short notes to her as soon as I learned her name. She sent short letters back. Here is the way I coaxed her to become friends:

"Dear Celeste, how are you doing? Okay, I hope. I hope you can come to my house when next Lillian and the others visit. I especially want to meet you. I would like very much to talk to you, even if you just listen, but I won't know you unless you tell me when it's you. You may even hand me a note if you like.

"One of the special things to me is to help those who are shy and uncertain of themselves to overcome whatever difficulties they have so that they can begin to blossom.

"You are important, Celeste, and I want to thank you for helping Lillian when she needed you. She still needs you, my dear, and I need you to help me to help her."

Celeste: "Dear Jean, you are nice to write. I don't have any definite likes or dislikes. It is safer not to have any preferences about anything. That way, you never have to worry about being disappointed.

"I never visited people. Just home and school.

"Does anyone ever care? No. Thanks."

Jean as Narrator: Celeste didn't write. She printed all in capital letters and with lots of curves and curlicues.

At the same time, Sarah Ann seemed anxious to spend time with me. Lucy had been my facilitator, but now Sarah Ann became my new informant. She told me one day that Celeste was afraid. I asked if I could see Celeste. Sarah Ann replied, "If you want to see her, you will have to ask for her. But you know she can't talk."

"She won't have to talk. Sarah Ann. May I please see Celeste?"

Sarah Ann's cheerfulness was gone, and before me sat a tense and frightened adult. She wrung her hands. Her eyes stared at her lap. She shook all over. She removed the gold wedding band and laid it on the table.

"Celeste?"

She nodded her head affirmatively.

"Celeste, I am pleased to meet you. You are a very brave lady. I don't know what you are afraid of, but Celeste, I will do my best to help you feel safe. Are you afraid of me?"

Eyes now on me, Celeste shook her head no.

We were at the dining room table. "Will you pull your chair closer to the table so I can talk to you better?"

As she arose from the chair to move it, she quivered so much, I was afraid she would have a heart attack. I wanted to ask her so much, but she was terribly frightened.

"Celeste, may I hold your hand?"

Question marks were all over her face. I quickly explained, "I just want you to know I care about you. I won't hurt you. You are safe here."

She gave me her hand. "Thank you, Celeste, for being here when I asked for you. I won't keep you long, because I don't want to worry you. You are welcome here. Will you let me see you again sometime?"

Affirmative, and she was gone. Lillian was in her place, saying, "Who was here? I feel shaky."

"Celeste was here. She put your wedding ring on the table."

Lillian slipped the ring back on her finger, saying only, "Oh."

The next day, I again asked for Celeste. We were sitting, this time, at the card table in the studio. I purposely got pens and paper before requesting Celeste's presence. Again, she was shaky and frightened but apparently wanted to be there. I asked questions, and Celeste wrote her answers. Celeste also wrote questions. "Would Walter ever get mad and hurt Fluffy? Would your sons get bored and hurt Fluffy?"

At first, I wrote my answers but soon realized that she was not deaf, just mute, and I laughed to myself about it. "No, they would never hurt Fluffy. Watch them talk to Fluffy, or hold and pet him. You can tell how much they like him. They wouldn't let anybody else hurt Fluffy either," I said.

Celeste Wrote: "Was your daughter bad like we are? What things did your two sons do to her?"

Jean: "No, Celeste. My daughter is good, and you are good. So is Lillian. My sons never did anything to hurt their sister," I assured Celeste.

Celeste Wrote: "How do you know what you didn't see all the time?"

Jean: Well, that one caught me off guard. I was stunned by the realization that something might have happened that I never knew about. "You are right, Celeste! I will call her and ask her. I will tell you what she says." (My daughter's answer was that our home had been safe.)

Jean as Narrator: Amy had asked me to teach her to play the organ like my other young students, and now Celeste wanted me to try to teach her. Of course, I would.

Later that day, I asked for Celeste to go with me to the organ, and she did. We took long paper for written notes, not musical notes! I kept wanting to answer her questions in writing! We made a good start on the lesson, and when I got up the next morning, I could hear the organ being softly played. I went to her, and when I spoke her name, she jumped right off the organ bench and disappeared. Sarah Ann was there for a second, until I said, "Celeste, please come back. It's okay. I am glad you are practicing."

Celeste reappeared, and I gave her a hug and left her again to practice while I dressed and prepared breakfast.

But upon their return to Niagara Falls, Celeste gave some of her fear and her memories to Lillian, and everybody became frightened. Lillian reported that a letter had arrived from one of the foster brothers. He wrote, in effect, "Jessica says you are telling lies about us. Why are you trying to ruin Herbert's good reputation? If you don't stop it, I will tell your old man how we boys could all have sex with you any old time we wanted to."

I know that the wording was stronger and more vulgar because Lillian wouldn't read it to me over the telephone. She was terribly upset.

Lillian: "That's blackmail, isn't it? Why are they making me out to be the bad guy?"

Jean: "I would consider that blackmail, Lillian. It appears to me that they are all trying to stick together and hide what they know. You are supposed to be the weak one, but in reality, you are the only strong one. Did you tell Jimmy or the doctor about the letter?"

Lillian: "No, I could never do that! Jimmy thought he married a virgin. Matter of fact, so did I!"

Jean: "I understand that, Lillian, and so does Jimmy. Once you tell Jimmy what is in the letter, that boy won't have anything to hold over you. Jimmy loves you very much. You have had that letter four days now, and I am sure Jimmy wonders why you are so upset. He probably thinks he did something wrong and can't figure out what it might have been. He will understand. Tell him."

Lillian: "No, Aunt Jean, I just can't."

Jean: "Well, then, since Dr. Robinson is out of town, call Mr. Zannoni and take the letter to him."

Lillian: "No, oh, no! He and Dr. Robinson already know too much about me. What if this turned out to be true like some of the other things I didn't know about?"

Jean: "But you know you can tell Dr. Robinson anything. You can trust him. He trusts you, and he can help you."

Lillian: "But what if it turns out to be true?"

Jean: "Lillian, the letter only told one side of the story. We don't know the other side yet. One of the other personalities might know something you don't know yet."

Jean: I knew I was skating on thin ice. "I am saying you must either tell the doctor about the letter or one of the personalities should tell him. He needs to know."

"Lillian, when you first called me tonight, you thought you couldn't tell me about the letter, but you did tell me. You shouldn't destroy the letter. You may want it sometime in the future for proof. If you can't show it to Jimmy, tell him you received a letter. It is important for you to tell him."

Lillian: "Maybe, I thought maybe I could tell you because you are a woman, and just maybe you might not put me down."

Jean: "And did I?"

Lillian: "No."

Jean: "And neither will Jimmy or Dr. Robinson. I will call you again tomorrow, Lillian. I love you."

Lillian: "Still?"

Jean: "Yes, still and always."

Jean as Narrator: When I called the next day, my first question was, "Did you tell Jimmy about the letter?"

Lillian: "Yes."

Jean: "What did he say?"

Lillian: "He said to talk to the doctor about it."

Jean as Narrator: We talked a little more, then Lillian told me that the letter was now torn into little pieces.

A couple of nights later, Lillian called unexpectedly, not on a Friday.

Lillian: "Aunt Jean, I have drain cleaner, and I don't want to use it, but I feel so down. I hate Jimmy, and I hate you, but mostly I hate myself. I think I need to talk to Rev. Chris, but he is not at the church. Do you think it's too late to call him at home?"

Jean: "No, it's not too late. I am sure he would want you to call." I hunted for Rev. Chris' home phone number and gave it to her.

Jean: "If you don't reach him, will you call me right back?"

I knew she was in crisis again. Desperation was coming through loudly and clearly, but at least she was trying, for the first time, to get help.

Lillian: "Yes, I will call you."

Jean: "Promise?"

Lillian: "Yes, I promise."

Jean as Narrator: She did call Rev. Chris and also called me back about a half-hour later.

Jean: "Did Rev. Chris help?"

Lillian: "Yes, he helped me. He told me what I needed to hear. He said I was not guilty, that I could not have stopped those big boys from doing what they did."

Jean as Narrator: I hung up the phone, feeling relieved.

I was eager to make my next regular Friday night phone call. Lillian answered on the first ring. She had seen the doctor that afternoon.

Lillian: "Well, I don't like to say it, but you and Rev. Chris were right again. What was said in that letter did happen. Dr. Robinson talked to Esther today, and part of what she told him also helps explain why Celeste can't talk. Dr. Robinson said Esther told them that those boys were so mean to animals; really cruel. They caught a cat and cut its tongue out. They told Celeste if she ever said one word to anybody about things that they did to her, they would find her and cut her tongue out! So that's what Celeste is afraid of!"

Jean as Narrator: It became clear to me that this was the reason why Celeste needed my reassurance that my sons would never hurt Fluffy or their sister.

It made me shudder just to hear the words.

Celeste gave the memory to Lillian, and now Celeste, though still mute, was enjoying playing the organ, embroidering and painting with watercolors.

Celeste, Lucy and Lillian had painted a deer in a forest setting. Lucy painted the animals. Celeste and Lillian did the forestry. It was beautiful. Jimmy asked me to keep it at my house so none of the personalities could destroy it. I hung it in the studio, never dreaming of its future.

Meanwhile, Jimmy and Lillian began the arduous task of finding a new location for their house trailer. That letter from one of the foster boys produced great fear that she would be hurt for talking to the doctor. Since the letter was correctly addressed, she could be found, and the threat carried out. There was desperation in their search. So much fear! Celeste and Sarah Ann, as well as Lucy and Julie, were afraid. Esther was giving her anger to Lillian, but Lillian still couldn't allow herself to be angry. She had successfully locked away her ability to accept and express anger.

Lillian and Jimmy considered the threat to be serious. In reaction to Celeste's fear, they changed residences several times, moving their trailer each time.

A childhood friend of Lillian saw her recently and was encouraged by his wife to send a letter to Dr. Robinson.

Remembering Lillian at about the age of 11 or 12, he recalled that she was not only generally quiet, at times she had no voice (Celeste?). Her family always seemed odd, but he could never put his finger on specifics. He remembered Lillian as always being cut. He used to wonder if she did it to herself, but that explanation made no sense to him, since she never wanted anyone to see the lacerations and never complained. At times, she seemed helpless, only to be in total command minutes later.

He described seeing her tied to the back porch. She smelled sour.

Lillian Wrote: "Summertime, 10 years old, noon, and I already wish this day had never begun. Sour milk all over my head and hair and dress, and the wasps and hornets won't leave me alone. This morning was going to be the start of a good day. I was going to be a big help with washing jars for Mother while she got tomatoes ready for canning, and then I did it again. Spilled some milk while pouring us a glass for breakfast, and Dad was there so quick and poured the whole gallon all over me and in my hair and was yelling. Why do I make all my days turn out so badly when I never mean it to happen?! It's being a bad seed again, but why can't it be someone else just this once?

"Dad uses his belt and ties my hands onto the railing at the side of the back porch, not close enough to the step, so I can't sit down, and the sun is so hot, and I'm tired of having to stand. My arms hurt, and I got to go to the bathroom, and I hate to be. Wish I could just be outside of me and watch someone else be here instead of me! (Celeste?)

"Oh, no, here comes that Charles. I never wanted my one friend to see me looking this messy and smelly. Now everyone will know how bad I am.

"The afternoon is about gone, and I've been stung again by another one of those wasps. At least it isn't as hard as it was earlier, and the other kids will be coming home soon for supper. I wish Mother wouldn't call me 'naughty ungrateful child' so much. I would never have wet my clothes if I could have used the bathroom.

"I wonder if this means I am going to get cut and bled again to take some more of the evil out. I just got to stop thinking. I dare them kids to say anything. I just can't stop crying sometimes, and I know how mad it makes everyone. It's hard to not ever do anything right or even know what I should do to be good. It always seems like no matter what I do, it's always wrong.

"Now I itch everywhere. My shoulders hurt and my arms too, from being tied. I hope nobody tells on me. I can't cry anymore today.

"Supper is ready. Now Dad will come in from the garden and let me loose. Please, I hope he doesn't need to feel me all over to make sure I'm not hurt. I know he is going to check me over after I wash up for supper, and everyone is waiting at the table – no time to heat water. I will have to wash my hair and all of me in cold water. I have to eat, and everybody has to wait for me cause Dad always says, 'None of my kids ever went without supper.'

"I don't like him to see me naked, but he will just call everyone in to watch unless I keep quiet and just let him feel me. I got sunburnt, he says, and he went and got some stuff for it so everyone can see how he takes extra good care of me. I HATE HIM and myself too."

Rachel Ann

Jean as Narrator: Rachel Ann was out during Lil's next visit to our house. When I first met Rachel Ann, she said she had brown eyes and long brown hair, and she liked to wear braids. She often asked me to French braid her hair. She had a lot of "how comes?"

When I asked her about numerous recent events involving interactions between the other personalities and me, she did not know what I was talking about. I said, "Rachel Ann, you should watch and listen."

Rachel Ann shuddered. "I don't want to see bad stuff."

I responded, "You should pay attention. Bad stuff isn't happening now."

Rachel Ann was 15 years old, and she and Sarah Ann, who was 16, pretended they were twins. Rachel Ann had first come to spell off Sarah Ann when she was being tied up in the closet. As if waiting to say goodbye before Sarah Ann left, Rachel Ann didn't make her presence known until Sarah Ann was ready to integrate. Rachel Ann clearly did not want to be involved in "what was going on."

After "they" returned to New York, Rachel Ann sent me a letter.

Rachel Ann Wrote: "Jean, here is a letter you asked for. My name is Rachel Ann. I am right-handed. Sarah Ann and I are friends. I will miss her a lot. I got my name from Sarah Ann's mother, Rachel Ann Nusiyrua, who was born in 1940 and married George Sixt. They had lots of kids with Ann as the middle name: Elizabeth, Martha, Ruth.

"Me and Sarah Ann liked to pretend we were twins, but she is – was – really a year older. I don't play guitar or nothing. I like reading. I don't go to churches for nothing, ever no programs, not even to see Sarah Ann. Mostly adults go, and they just pretend to be nice to kids. I like kids till they start bugging me. I don't trust nobody. I don't get sick as much as Sarah Ann does. That's all. Yours truly, Rachel Ann."

Jean as Narrator: Rachel Ann's letter mystified me. Was it just babble or the fantasy of a 15-year-old?

In March, Jimmy and Lillian came to visit us again. While they were here, Rachel Ann decided to run away. One of the other personalities talked to me about it. I suggested that Rachel Ann walk on our street or in the 10 acres of woods adjoining the house, which also belonged to us. I thought she would be safe there. I offered to walk with her. It was very cold.

Rachel Ann, like any other 15-year-old, had to do it her way. I saw her leave at about 4:30 p.m. I gave her about five minutes, and then took her gloves and her hat, got in my car, and searched for her. When I found her, I stopped the car and rolled the window down.

Rachel Ann: "I don't need any help to walk. I can do it myself," she said angrily.

Jean: "All right, Rachel Ann, you walk. But when you have walked enough, you walk back home. Don't leave Lillian out in the cold someplace to try and find her way home. That's not fair."

Jean as Narrator: Yes, I was angry. Rachel Ann's coat was hanging open. She didn't take her gloves or hat when I offered them. All my maternal instincts came leaping to the surface. Why did she have to be so stubborn?

I returned home and waited. I knew Rachel Ann needed time. In about 10 minutes, Jimmy drove around to try and find her, with no luck. Waiting around 30 minutes, I took my car and looked again. No sign of her, but I did find two Fairfax County police cruisers, so I reported Rachel Ann as a runaway (a 40-year-old runaway?).

The police officers asked all the appropriate questions. They asked about her parents.

I was pleasantly surprised by their acceptance of my description of a multiple personality.

The officers asked if she might become combative. I explained that she would likely be very frightened and become apologetic and appreciative of being brought back to my house. I further explained that she likely would respond to the name Lillian.

Off the officers went, one in each direction. Once again, I returned home after promising to call police headquarters if Rachel Ann came back.

Jimmy and I paced and worried, and at about 1 a.m., we retired for the night. About two hours later, Jimmy got up and looked out the front door. There, sitting on the front steps, was Rachel Ann. No! It was Lillian, teeth chattering, sitting on cold cement steps, freezing. When she saw Jimmy, she said, "Why did you let me sit out here so long? I am freezing!"

Jimmy brought her into the house, called the police to report that she was home, and put her to bed, rubbing her arms and legs to warm her up.

"At least now Rachel Ann got that out of her system," I thought.

I tried to figure out why so many of the personalities ran away or attempted suicide.

Rachel Ann had been headed for the interstate. She intended to walk in front of a truck. She was not walking along the road but taking shortcuts through backyards, so we couldn't find her. She came upon a dog that barked and growled. She froze instantly, as if being paralyzed by fear. Every time she moved, the dog, actually small in size, growled. She finally sat down, too frightened to move. After a considerable passage of time, probably two hours, she got so cold, she jumped up and ran.

In that instant, she saw that the dog was chained and could not have reached her anyway.

Tired and cold as she was, Rachel Ann did what I told her to do. She came back home. She didn't let Lillian take over until she was sitting safely on our front steps. Lillian, of course, had no idea what had occurred.

Lucy's Journal: "We are at Jean and Walter's, and Jim came too. We saw Rev. Chris. Jim told Rachel Ann he wanted her to promise him she wouldn't take pills when she got mad. Walter got mad because Rachel Ann and Jim argued in front of him (but Walter wouldn't admit that he was mad). Walter was in bed. He just got home from the hospital from an operation on his neck. Rachel Ann left and went for a walk and wasn't going to come back, but she did at 3 a.m. Things are heavy around here."

Rachel Ann's Journal: "Everyone wants to tell me how I feel. Jean's husband don't like any of us, but he don't like Jean either. He says leave what's happened in the past behind. He told Jimmy today that when Jean talks to him about us, she makes a big deal out of nothin' and says, 'That was a major breakthrough,' when it is something everyone is born knowing. I don't want to be here in this house this time at all. Everyone is against each other. I want to run away. I want to be dead. I am scared of Jean and Jimmy. I wish Dr. Robinson was around. He don't judge or yell or get mad, and he hears the words I say. Jean don't or Jim. Jean ought to put herself in our place and think what she'd feel like in a body like Lil's when she saw her friends and looked in the mirror! Maybe she thinks she cares, but she don't understand."

Jean as Narrator: Choir rehearsal was the following night at the church. I sang in the choir, and Jimmy liked to sing with the choir whenever he was here. Rachel Ann wanted to spend some time with Rev. Chris' daughter, so they arranged to get together and visit in the social hall on the ground level while Jimmy and I attended choir rehearsal.

When we returned to the social hall at about 9:15 p.m., Rachel Ann was nowhere in sight. We called. We searched. We called Rev. Chris' daughter at home. Rachel Ann was gone! Rev. Chris came back to the church with keys to all the Sunday school rooms. Jimmy, Bill Gunter (the choirmaster) and choir members hunted and hunted. Rev. Chris and I opened every door, turned on every light and looked into every room. We found her purse but no Rachel Ann.

I said disgustingly, "Doggone her! I don't know why she is running again!"

The longer we looked, the more certain I became that she had, in fact, run away for a second time in two days. Jimmy and Bill continued to search the church while Rev. Chris and I got in his car and drove toward the interstate.

Rev. Chris drove, and I went into stores along the way, checking out the ladies' restrooms and asking cashiers if they had seen her. Our emotions swung wildly from anger to worry. I expressed my anger to Rev. Chris, and he replied, "Yes, sometimes I have to make myself remember that Rachel Ann is not your everyday, run-of-the-mill teenager."

Meanwhile, back at the church, Bill took his flashlight and went upstairs to look all around the balcony, also in the pantry and storerooms on the ground level. Finally satisfied that Rachel Ann was not in the church, he left for home. He had to go to work the next morning. Jimmy remained and continued the search.

Later, when Rev. Chris and I decided to check in at the church, Jimmy said, "I found her. She's upstairs, hiding in the balcony. Only it isn't Rachel Ann. It's someone real young and really scared. She doesn't know me, and I don't know who she is. I just waited 'cause I know you two would know what to do. She is afraid of me."

Rev. Chris went up to the balcony. There, huddled on the floor behind the huge floor-to-ceiling beam, quaking with fright, he found her. I wanted so much to go up and hold her and tell her everything would be all right, but I didn't want to overwhelm whoever that frightened child was.

I could hear Rev. Chris speaking softly to her but could not quite hear what he was saying. After what seemed like an eternity, they emerged from the darkness, and I, now standing at the bottom of the stairs, could see them at the top. It was pathetic to see how terrified she was.

I asked, "Who is it?"

Rev. Chris answered, "It's Rachel Ann. I know she is 15 years old, but right now, she thinks she is 8. She is afraid of you, Jean. She thinks you don't like her because she ran away last night, and now you'll think she ran away again. I told her that you love her and that you were worried, not angry."

Rachel Ann glanced at me and looked down at the steps in front of her. "Come on, Rachel Ann," Rev. Chris said softly. "One more step."

Rev. Chris was in front of Rachel Ann, backing down the steps one by one, keeping between Rachel Ann and me so that she would feel safer and also to catch her if she fell or jumped. I don't know if I have ever seen greater fear, and it was me, Jean, whom she was afraid of.

Rev. Chris spoke. "Rachel Ann is afraid of what you will do to her. I told her you would just be glad that she is safe."

What tremendous love and patience Rev. Chris possessed. I will never forget the moment or the intensity of it. Jimmy and I stood at the bottom of the stairs, helplessly. There, before me, was a grown-up woman's body dressed in the familiar green winter coat that I had hugged so often, but this "being" was a frightened 8-year-old child.

As Rev. Chris backed down the steps, he reached to hold Rachel Ann's hand. At that moment, I felt a great surge of love for this caring man. His faith and loving kindness were unequaled in my experience. It has been said that "Fear and faith cannot coexist."

When they finally reached the bottom of the stairs, I eased forward, speaking softly to Rachel Ann and reaching out with open arms. She pulled back. Rev. Chris said, "Let Jean hug you. It's all right." And she did.

That hug broke the tension. I could feel Rachel Ann relax.

"Me too!" I thought. Whew, safe again! How many crises must there be? How much more can she (they) go through?

Jean: "Are you ready to go home, Rachel Ann?" I asked.

Rachel Ann: "You still want me t' go t' your house?" she said.

Jean: "Of course I do, Rachel Ann. I love you."

Jean as Narrator: I was relieved, to say the least. Jimmy and I thanked Rev. Chris again, and with Rachel Ann safely with us, we headed for the parking lot where my car was parked. I was thinking, "How grossly inadequate the words 'thank you' are." How many times had Jimmy and I said thank you to Rev. Chris? We had no idea how many scary times were yet to come!

Recognizing that Rachel Ann thought of herself as having no friends, Jimmy suggested that he ride in the back seat of the car, hoping that by sitting next to me, she would begin to feel safe.

I wondered if anyone ever really appreciated or understood how patient and supportive Jimmy was to all of her personalities.

Rachel Ann: "When Rev. Chris' daughter left the church to go home, I went into the ladies' room. Coming out, I saw a mouse. I thought it was a rat. I took off runnin' as fast as I could. I seen them steps an' everythin' changed. I was back in the old house. They were after me, an' I had t' get away. I ran. I had t' hide. I looked at the tower. I thought I could hide there. I thought I was someplace else. I held my breath. I used to hide in a corner cupboard. They never found me there. I heard people talkin' and callin' me. Then they came in with a flashlight. They walked right to where I was hidin'; I scrunched myself up so little. I couldn't breathe. I waited for 'em to hit me on the head with that flashlight. I di'n't know where I was.

"When the flashlight went away, somebody big in a red jacket came, and I know'd he is after me, but I di'n't know who he was.

Jimmy: "That was me – Jimmy. Bill looked for you with the flashlight."

Rachel Ann: "When Rev. Chris come, I di'n't know him. I di'n't even know who I was. All I could say was 'I…I…I…I…I.' He told me I was in the church balcony. I couldn't believe that. I thought you'd be mad at me for runnin' away again. Are you?"

Jean: "No, Rachel Ann. I was angry when I thought you had just run away again, but I was so happy to see you okay, I forgot all about being angry."

Rachel Ann: "Tomorrow you will think about it. Then you will be mad."

Jean: "No, I understand now that you did not just run away. I am sorry you were so frightened."

Rachel Ann: "You are not mad?" She had a hard time believing it.

Jean: "No, Rachel Ann, I am not mad, and I am not going to be mad tomorrow."

Rachel Ann: "I'm hungry. You got anythin' at home t' eat?"

Jean as Narrator: Rachel Ann heaved a great sigh of relief, as did I.

Lillian's Journal: "Rev. Chris was here and talked with Rachel Ann, me and Aunt Jean. Rev. Chris said Rachel Ann told him she wouldn't kill herself till I said it was okay.

"Boy, that sure lays it on me.

"Rev. Chris was very kind and didn't put me down because of how Rachel Ann acted yesterday. He said she was scared to death. We talked, and Rachel Ann remembered, 'Our garage had an open pit under where the car would be. I hid in there. I was afraid of rats in there.'"

Jean as Narrator: Rachel Ann asked why we went looking for her. She said that she had run away often and was gone sometimes for two days, but nobody ever searched for her. She saw no police cars or anybody looking for her. She could sleep at night in the vestibule of a church or in someone's screened-in back porch. It was easy for her to hide during the day. When she finally went back home, nothing was ever said. She was baffled that we had searched so many hours for her.

Afraid of a threatening letter Lillian received from one of her foster brothers, Lillian and Jimmy decided to move. Jimmy called to ask if Lillian could stay with us until he could relocate their trailer.

The second day she was with us, Jimmy called to say that he was having trouble getting the trailer moved. Could she stay four more days so he could get the water, electricity and telephone turned on? But I had planned to paint our master bedroom at that time. I didn't tell him that, thinking I would just put it off.

When they arrived, they asked what I was going to do, and I told them that I planned to paint the master bedroom, but I knew Lillian was highly allergic to paint. They told me to go ahead and paint, and they would take over for the four days, and they did, showing no signs of allergies.

That evening, Rachel Ann visited me.

She explained, "Mother usually beat me over the head, but 'Dad' preferred hitting bare legs. His favorite weapon was a razor strap, but a garden hose, rake handle or riding crop would do if the razor strap was not convenient."

Lillian Wrote: "James is at Gateway Home for Children. He said right at the last minute, 'Mommy, I am scared!' It tears me up inside just thinking of what he has gone through because of me. I do love him so. I wish so much he was in his own bed right now. Jim's at work. Will there be days without tears? James had some today. I hope not like me tonight. My son James, when you cry, I cry too, and the ache in your throat, it's mine too. One day, James, this will be over, and we'll be a real family, where every minute will belong to us.

"I miss James. It is so lonely here at this trailer. No one around.

"A new personality named Buddy, along with Lucy and Amy, wrote letters to James, but he can't read them. Nine years old and still can't read. He is keeping it a secret that his mother is a multiple."

Rachel Ann's Journal: "Lil, can I take your pills, or can you get some pills for me to take them all? I promised I won't unless you say it's fine with you. No one wants freaks like me around. Please."

Lillian: "Rachel Ann, wait awhile yet. Okay? I know how you feel."

Jean as Narrator: I got a phone call from Rev. Chris' daughter. Rachel Ann had just called her to say goodbye because she was going to take pills.

Thanking her, I hung up the phone and quickly called Dr. Robinson. Damn all the miles between upper New York and Virginia!

Lucy: "Lil, what's going to happen? Can you speak up better 'n that to Rachel Ann? Wait a few days? For what? To see if you feel bad enough by then too?

"There is no way Rachel Ann is going to take my life! Cripes, Lil, can't you do more positive than saying, 'Wait awhile'?!"

Lillian's Journal: "Gateway called today about James. I am to see their school psychiatrist on Wednesday.

"Rachel Ann, I know you are struggling with some ideas. Being 15 is very hard. Rachel Ann, please think of this: I, Lillian, do not mind dying. I'm not afraid of it, but I want to be the one there when it happens. Let it be me, and let it be my choice, not yours."

Jean as Narrator: When Rachel Ann realized that she was only occupying Lillian's body, and that she really did not look like she thought she did, she said, "It's a bummer."

***

Buddy

Jean as Narrator: "Someone" could hardly wait to tell me, "There's somebody else. There is Buddy, but don't let Lillian find out. She couldn't handle it right now. Buddy is a girl. Do you think Buddy could be a girl's name? She is 11."

Jean: "Sure. A buddy is a pal, and girls have pals just like boys do. Tell me more about Buddy."

Someone: "Well, she likes horses a lot, and she is really shy."

Jean as Narrator: I said I was shy when I was 11, and so is my 10-year-old granddaughter when she is around strangers. I liked horses a lot when I was 11, and so did my daughter and now my granddaughter.

That made it very easy for me to enjoy Buddy and to know what she might be like.

Someone: "Don't ask for her. Dr. Robinson doesn't know yet."

Jean as Narrator: Later, Rev. Chris told me that since I suggested, "Wouldn't it be fun if a new personality showed up at my house?" Buddy decided to be the one. I was afraid I had encouraged her to create a personality and was relieved later to learn that Buddy was from her past. That's a little scary to be able to make a suggestion and have it carried out. Rev. Chris agreed.

"It's difficult to find yourself in your position," he said.

Buddy told me her stomach hurt. She didn't think she was supposed to be here. I told her she could leave if she wanted to, and she did.

Buddy thought uniforms gave people the authority to kill "bad people" and wanted to grow up and get a uniform and go "kill some people."

On another visit, the colonel invited us to his home. Although only two bodies went, several were there, including Lillian, Julie, Rachel Ann, Amy and Buddy.

I asked for Buddy and asked the colonel to show his Air Force uniforms. He talked to her about his work, stating firmly that his uniform had nothing to do with the killing. Buddy said, "I was going to kill somebody once, but I decided not to."

I asked, "What made you decide not to?"

She wrinkled up her nose. "Too messy … all that blood."

Colonel said, "Yes. I think you are right."

Buddy still thought a uniform automatically gave the wearer the right to kill people.

Lillian believed that too. She and I had a near argument on that subject when I told her about Buddy's conversation with me.

I treated Buddy to lunch at McDonald's one day. We had an easy conversation. Part of the conversation went like this:

Buddy: "Dr. Rob asked Lil to draw the rooms like they were in her house growing up. So she drew the upstairs and the downstairs and even the basement."

Jean: "I guess he wanted the drawing so he could understand better."

Buddy: "Those foster boys could do anything they wanted to Lillian, and anybody could watch. They tied her hands together over her head. She never knew who was watching. She asked for a door, and everybody laughed at her. She thought if she had a door, she would find some way to lock it and block it so they couldn't get in. Being watched just made Lillian feel more badder."

Jean: "Well, Buddy, little friend, I will tell you how that makes me feel. It makes me mad, and the more I think about it, the madder I get. Lillian was not bad! Those boys were bad, really bad, and so was everybody who laughed at her."

Buddy: "Well, it didn't matter if she had a door or not 'cause they just made holes in the wall. Those walls were just made of cardboard. Anybody could punch a hole easy. Then they could watch her. They had holes to watch her everywhere."

Jean: "So that's why she dressed and undressed under the covers?"

Buddy: "Doesn't everybody?" Buddy asked.

Jean: "No. When I was a kid at home, I could go in my (and my sister's) bedroom, shut the door and do anything I wanted to. Nobody could see me unless I stood in front of the window."

Buddy: "Oh."

Jean as Narrator: I got a cold and a sore throat and consulted my doctor. Lillian and the others were in the hospital, and they wished that they had a nice card to send to me. I said, "I would like the one you make yourselves. That kind is better than any you can buy."

Sure enough, three days later, a collective card arrived. It was made of paper I had bought for Buddy. Each personality wrote something different. Buddy was last, and she drew a horse carrying a container of flowers on its back. I loved it! I cried when I read it. I have reread it many times, and I cherish it. I thought, how many ways could I say, "I love you"?

Lucy told me Buddy has decided to be a boy, and Buddy plans to get older. Buddy wants to get some uniforms and ammunition for a vigilante group with other kids and go kill some bad people.

One of my neighbors was a policeman. I explained multiple personality to him the best I could and asked him if he would have any interest in meeting with Buddy. He was greatly interested, and the meeting time was set.

I remained at the table when Buddy and Officer Tom met. Buddy had lots of questions. "Do you have a gun? Do you have a uniform? Do you have bullets? Do you like shooting people?"

Buddy was quite surprised when Officer Tom did not like even the idea of shooting at people, and he said that he had been shot at himself. The conversation did more to enlighten Buddy to a policeman's role and the potential dangers that policemen encounter. The meeting with Officer Tom did more for Buddy than I could have ever done. Buddy had a lot to think about.

***

Lil

Lillian's Journal: "When I was at Dr. Robinson's office, the secretary wrote 'Lil' on my bill. That seemed like a good name for 'her.' Lil got separate from me. Did I consciously create another me?"

Jean as Narrator: I wasn't prepared for what came next.

Lil: "I am Lil. I know you. I have been to your house. I am the other Lil."

Jean as Narrator: Now there was Lil (different from Lil) – a split within a split? I asked if Lil would talk to me. I didn't know what I was asking for! The same voice said, "This is Lil."

Jean: "Which one are you?"

Lil: "I'm the other Lil."

Jean: But the names Lil and Lil sounded exactly alike to me.

Lil: "I am me, and she is her."

Jean: "Unreal!" I thought. "How old are you, and what do you look like?" I was groping.

Lil: "Same as her," someone answered.

Jean: "Which one are you?"

Lil: "The other one."

Jean: "Never mind! Let me talk to Lucy!"

Lucy: "This is Lucy. Jean, you should have seen Dr. Robinson today! He was talking to Lillian and writing like he always does while we are in the office, and when Lil and Lil started up with their names that sound alike, he just gave up and set his pen down and said, 'I don't know what's going on. This is a good place to stop for today.' He was shaking his head when we left."

Jean as Narrator: I decided to hang up the phone while it was still Lucy.

Lil Wrote: "Lil, I wrote your Dr. Robinson today and told him just cause you decided you don't need me anymore doesn't mean I'm not going to be. His secretary acknowledged me. I can do things you can't."

Jean as Narrator: Two days later, I received a phone call.

Lil: "Jean, this is the other Lil. Did we confuse you Friday?"

Jean: "That's the understatement of the year! You are the other Lil?"

Lil: "Yes, and I called to ask you what you think about my taking a ceramics class."

Jean: "I think that would be fun. If I ever had the time, I'd like to try that too."

Jean as Narrator: Lil did, in fact, take a ceramics class. She made a pair of horse-head bookends for James and a large pumpkin with an electrical outlet for a light for Lillian. She gave me a lovely pineapple-design spoon rest, which I keep on my stovetop. On the back is written, "Jean Lil, '81."

Lillian Wrote: "Aunt Jean called. It's Friday night. She has written some for the doctor. He had asked for an overview from her. She is writing of her family history. Sometimes it's like the doctor asks for someone, and they are there, and so am I. And so is Amy and Celeste. I can see them."

***

Jackie

Lillian: "Aunt Jean told me Jackie says she wants to have a baby – a boy. That's scary. Jackie, you may be 19, but I am 40! I don't think I could do justice to a baby, let alone how would you accomplish the fact? I couldn't handle that! Jackie, I don't think I could handle an abortion either. Wow! Jackie, please don't!"

Jean as Narrator: I received a panic call from Lillian. She had become "herself" in a motel room, and there was a man singing in the shower. She had a robe on. She knew it wasn't Jim in the shower. Her little suitcase was nearby. She quickly dressed, grabbed her purse and suitcase, and tore outside.

Lillian: "Thank God my car was there, and I had keys. I thought Jackie had already done something. I went to a drive-up phone, sat in the car and called our old number. No answer. So I called you. Have you heard from Jimmy?"

Jean: "No."

Jean as Narrator: What a predicament! She drove home to their old address. She just couldn't think.

Lillian's Journal: "I am so glad nothing happened! Jackie, I will go crazy if I ever get in that situation again. I know that you know it too. No second time. Ever."

***

150

Nancy

Jean as Narrator: Seemingly out of nowhere during one of Lillian's hospitalizations, Nancy appeared. Nancy had no last name or established identity. Yet, after writing two brief letters to Lillian within 24 hours, in an attempt to establish an identity, she "disappeared," not to be heard from again, but not before helping to keep Lillian alive.

Nancy Wrote: "Jean, you said to write you a letter. I don't know very much. I know today is Sunday. Some lady came in and asked about you. I told her you knew Lillian and some of the others. I told her Jackie said there was someone she knew who couldn't have kids. Lillian needed someone who could stay alive for her. I can stay alive, and I don't need any kids around. I can stay composed. Lillian was bad, but I'm not bad. I'm good. I don't want to be Lillian. I want to be me. I told the nurse. She called me Nancy. I sound just like a person when she let me be called that. I'm not a child. I'm an adult. I'm not sure how old. I don't have a last name."

Chapter 13
Esther

By the time the reader starts Chapter 13, the personalities are distinct enough that the reader is able to recognize them by personality, attitude and trauma history.

Indeed, the reader has mentally become part of the story, such that some readers may even find themselves silently talking to themselves or to the personalities!

Chapter 13 provides a fuller view of Esther's identity and her rage toward multiplicity itself, a rage that Dr. Robinson considers to be dangerous.

FA

Jean as Narrator: I received a letter from Esther finally. The handwriting was small. It was so straight, I decided she must have held a ruler or some other straightedge along the bottom of each line. The handwriting was completely different from that of Julie or Lillian and much neater than Lucy's, Lee's or any of the others'. The descriptive word that comes to mind is "stilted."

Esther Wrote: "I noted recently in one of your letters to one of the others that you asked if I knew you. Naturally, I am aware of things that enter into the life of the one and the use of the body at a particular time. I presume you have at least figured out that I am Esther. I am not one of the 'sickies,' who, unfortunately, you control.

"Julie I consider a sissy who plays at poetry. Why she is encouraged in this is beyond me. Lillian and Lucy obviously cannot paint worth a damn. No one has taken it upon themselves to enlighten these people, which causes me to wonder at the mentality of their Dr. Robinson. Lee, it took him six weeks to carve one animal! You call that talent?

"I have no need for therapy or communication with anyone in this world. No one can be trusted or counted upon in any circumstance. I need no one. All men are cruel and dangerous. All women are liars who use their children to get things for themselves. There is no such thing as a friend. I am simply biding my time until I have the necessary means to leave. I will then join my own family, who live in the South. Their name is Winslow. Perhaps you have heard of them? Unlike Lillian, I have both a mother and a father who love me dearly.

"I have not expressed my views of the others to the doctor. Obviously, he has his hands full. Perhaps you might suggest to the doctor that Lillian should be encouraged to go away in her head more often. She is losing her ability to do so at will. Further communication is not necessary, as there is no such thing as a friend, and I have nothing you want. Esther Winslow."

Jean as Narrator: I called Lillian and told her about the letter from Esther. She asked so many questions, I finally just read it to her.

Lillian: "Are you mad, Aunt Jean? That was not a nice letter. She sounds so sarcastic and critical."

Jean: "No, of course I am not mad. I was worried that Esther might be angry at me. Her letter is intriguing."

Jean as Narrator: I answered Esther's letter very cautiously. I told her I appreciated her letter and all the information she offered, and that I had called the doctor, as she suggested. I replied that I had not heard of the Winslows but expressed an interest in meeting them someday. Then, agreeing that the doctor, indeed, has his hands full, I told Esther about my family: my parents, brothers, sisters and children. I closed my letter by inviting Esther to make herself known to me when next Lillian and the others came to visit and by stating that I cared about her.

What did Esther mean about Lillian losing her ability to go away in her head more often? Did she mean create blank time so the personalities could be out more, or did she think Lillian should dig deeper in her mind for her childhood memories?

I called Dr. Robinson's office to report Esther's letter. When I told him what Esther had written about men not being trustworthy, he said, "Yes, I am aware of that." I also advised him that someone should be angry at me for saying to her, "You need to tell your mother" when she had visited me at age 16. I needed the doctor's advice as to my safety. Walter was afraid she might hurt me. Dr. Robinson thanked me for calling him but probably already knew everything I knew and much more.

The journals, which Lillian gave me for writing this book, began telling the story better than I can.

Lillian's Journal: In 1978, Lillian wrote in her journal: "Nothing is right. Nothing will ever be right again. If Esther comes from a family down South, I wish she'd go back. I don't need her or anyone. None of us is of any use. I miss the letters from my sisters and miss writing to them. I have no one to just chat with. I hate the world. I hate God. I hate responsibility for me or anyone else. How can I hate? I'm not allowed feelings. It isn't working anymore."

Jean as Narrator: It was Julie who answered the phone when I called Friday night.

Julie: "Lil's throat hurts so bad and closes up when she tries to talk. She plays a game of charades with James with signals for turning the television off, getting ready for bed, brushing his teeth and everything. He laughs, but do you think he wonders why Lee, Lucy and I can talk and she can't?"

Jean: "Yes, I suppose James does, but maybe he thinks she is just playing a game. What happened in the doctor's office today, Julie?"

Julie: "Esther talked to him some, and Lil told him about her dream. It was about a cellar house. But Lil's throat hurts so bad she said she couldn't swallow. She drove around for a long time after she left Dr. Robinson's office. After we got back to Lil's, Esther took off walking."

Jean as Narrator: I noticed that Julie was more at ease on the telephone than she had been a few weeks ago, but what was that "dream" about? I would just have to wait to see.

I wrote to Julie and made an attempt to respond to a poem she wrote for me about friends.

Lucy wrote a letter that Esther and Dr. Robinson didn't like each other.

Lucy Wrote: "We are going to take an art class. Esther crocheted a couple of bibs this week. I wonder who is going to have a baby? I don't think she has any friends. One of the other personalities is vengeful. I guess I have done some things when I got mad a few times, but not deliberately to hurt someone. I hope Dr. Robinson don't make her mad, and she gets even by hurting Lil. She has hit James a couple of times. Don't tell Lil or Jimmy, because he'd just get mad at Lil, and Lil already feels bad about how she sometimes feels about James. Did you ever see an explosion that just happens, and it's too late to do anything to stop it? I think Esther is like that, and all she wants to do is hurt people. I don't like her. Maybe I'm just afraid of her. Now I sound like that Julie. Maybe next time Esther is out, I will trip her or something." (How could Lucy trip Esther? Same body!)

"Esther sounded just like Lil's mom a couple of weeks ago. She even said 'Judas Priest' like that woman does. What's that mean? It must be swear words, 'cause Lil's mom always used it when she was yelling. Does Dr. Robinson think she is bad? I don't like anyone to fight or yell or raise their voice or get upset. Lil is changing, and she says more things now, and maybe things will be bad here if she yells about something. I don't like to worry or stir things up.

"Can Dr. Robinson stop the way it's changing? Can you tell him so he won't get mad and make everything seem like it's nice again? I mean, everyone is supposed to be happy and not ever fight. I don't want anyone to fight. Esther yelled at Dr. Robinson, and I just hate for that to be. Does he have to ask to talk to her? She won't back down from a challenge.

"I better stop. Well, you can sure write a lot more faster on a typewriter and maybe say more than you mean to. That must be what's bad about typing and thinking the thoughts at the same time. Writing is slower, and you can stop the wrong words before they are out for anyone to see. I don't think I will type any more letters after this. You could just talk and talk, and what you want to say could be lost in the words, and maybe something important would be said, and you wouldn't even see it because of all the other words.

"Can you ask Dr. Robinson? Oh, Jean, things aren't smooth anymore. What if Lil gets mad? I thought I wanted her to take up for herself, but now I've changed my mind. I want things like they used to be. I mean, I used to see when Lil couldn't take it anymore, and I could just take over, and now, I mean, did you see that letter Esther wrote? Lil don't do or talk like that. Why can't things stay like they were before? I usually can say exactly what I want to, but maybe this once, as a friend, you could ask Dr. Robinson what's happening and to change it all back? Okay?

"I'm not typing any more letters. They say too many words and get what I am saying mixed up. Well, see you soon. I hope I said something with all this typing. If I don't make sense, or maybe the doctor would get mad, don't tell him, okay? Friends??? Lucy."

Jean as Narrator: The next Friday night, there was no phone call from Lillian. When I called at our agreed-upon 11 o'clock time, there was no answer. As the story unfolded, following Lillian's appointment with Dr. Robinson, Esther drove 400 miles, and Lillian found herself sitting in the car in front of her cousin's house in Ohio at 3 o'clock in the morning. She thought about driving back home immediately but decided to ask to sleep on the couch in her cousin's house. She slept in the car until her cousin was up. Then she asked to come in.

Later that morning, Lillian said goodbye to her cousin. She intended to drive back home, but Esther took over and headed for her parents' home in the South. She was driving in the fast lane of a divided highway at a pretty high speed, when suddenly a wheel went rolling down the road ahead of her. It narrowly missed the car she was preparing to pass, rolled across the road ahead of her, across the median strip, across the oncoming lane of traffic and wobbled into the ditch.

Esther fought for control as the car came down on the axle. She brought the automobile to a halt in the median strip and left the body to Lillian!

Looking around, Lillian saw other cars slowing down, and a van pulled up onto the grass behind her car. The driver got out and came running to her. All four doors were locked, and the van driver knocked on her window, yelling to her to get out of the car. Lillian unlocked the door, grabbed her purse and exited the car. She was shaking. The van driver put his arms around her and told her he would help her, then rushed her to his van, where his wife and two other adults were waiting.

Offering to take Lillian to a telephone so she could call Jimmy, the occupants of the van complimented Lillian on her excellent driving. "You should have seen what we saw! When your wheel came off, the sparks flew higher than your car! You went careening across the median strip and just missed two oncoming cars on the opposite side of the highway. You went clear across that other lane and wheeled it back across that lane onto the median strip! I never saw such good driving!"

Lillian collected herself and realized that Jimmy would be at work, so she called Jimmy's father, Pap. Pap and a friend of his came to get her. They put the spare wheel on the car, and Pap's friend drove the car back to Pap and Grandma's.

When Lillian got into Pap's car, she finally gave tears, but looking in his rearview mirror, Pap said, "We'll have none of that!" So she dried her tears.

His "don't feel" message was explicit reinforcement of all that the doctor was attempting to rid her off.

Apparently Esther was not wanting to hear the doctor when he explained that she was part of Lillian and not a separate entity. Not understanding integration, Esther thought she could just go home to her parents in the South.

But they no sooner got back to Pap's house than Esther took off driving once more. When she had worked off some of her anger, she let Lillian back. Lillian was so tired and uptight that she pulled off the highway and passed out. A state trooper stopped and said she couldn't drive until a doctor checked her out. She followed him to the hospital in Erie, Pennsylvania, and into the emergency room, but Julie walked out and drove on home to New York.

Lillian was so tired, but she didn't want to be home. She started out from home again, walking. Jimmy stopped her. Lillian decided to take every pill in the house. She went into the bathroom and locked the door. She took a bottle of aspirin and all the Vivactil she had – 25 in all. She had taken that many before and knew it wasn't enough. She opened a bottle of pyridoxine.

Jimmy broke the bathroom door down and stopped her. Evan restrained her while Jimmy called Dr. Robinson. She was admitted to the hospital as an involuntary patient, signed in by Dr. Robinson. After spending three days in the PIC room, Lillian just wanted to die.

Lillian Wrote: "It's all me ... Lillian. When I do remember something, Mr. Zannoni and Dr. Robinson say it was still me doing everything bad. I don't want to believe that it is me. I really was and am an evil person. When the things Aunt Jean bought were destroyed, I did it. The car – 100 miles an hour, I did it. The guns, the grass, the sex things – I did it. Everything was and will always be me doing it, even if I think otherwise. Those blank times that I can't see, I can't live with that kind of me. I don't want to. Why do Dr. Robinson and Mr. Zannoni allow them to have names when it's me who does these things? I am the bad person in the things I remember. I don't want to remember anymore. I don't want to live anymore.

"Four days since I last wrote, and I'm still here in this awful room with the door that can be locked anytime. All I feel is dread when I look at it – some phobia to have. Jimmy and the kids all knew I was afraid of locked doors, but I never dreamed it would be as bad as this!"

***

157

Chapter 14
Rocky Chair

Chapter 14 gives the reader insight into Jessica's cruelty.

The chapter also captures the curiosity of Amy as a 6-year-old child.

For the first time, two of the personalities appear to have a conversation with one another as Amy and Celeste set out to buy a gift for Jean.

This section is particularly fascinating as Celeste and Amy switch back and forth in rapid succession, almost as if two people are physically present to each other at the same time. Although physically impossible, the rapidity with which the switching occurs even leaves Lillian believing that Celeste and Amy can talk with one another.

FA

Jean as Narrator: Amy and I talked about our cellar. She was afraid for me to even open the door to the pantry shelves Walter had made between the rafters inside the basement door. She wanted to know whom I was going to put in the coal cellar. When I finally convinced her that I had no such intention, she asked if that was where I put my kids when they were bad.

Insisting that she stay and watch, I opened the basement door and showed Amy that there was no lock on either side of the door. Finally I coaxed her down two or three steps to look downstairs and see that there was no coal cellar, no rats and no spiders. When back upstairs, Amy spied and wanted me to pull down the attic door from the ceiling near the basement door. "What's that?" she queried.

"That's the attic door. Let me show you," I said, reaching for the cord and pulling the hidden stairs down.

"No, No, No! No attic." Amy was frightened of the attic too. Again, pressing my luck, I started up the steps and asked her to follow and see what was there.

"That where you put your kids when they are bad?" she asked.

After much explaining and cajoling, Amy came up just enough steps to peer into the attic. She was shaking with fear but trying so hard to please me. Her confusion mingled with absolute terror kept me from expecting any more of her. I was satisfied that I convinced, if not Amy, then one of the other personalities, that I had not, in fact, ever locked my children in the attic, coal cellar or basement. My conversation was full of statements like "Children are not bad" and "Nobody has the right to lock any child up, no matter what the child has done."

I wondered what impact this experience would have on Amy. A few days later, I reported to Dr. Robinson that there must be more about the attic because there is still so much fear.

Amy seemed unable to believe that she was not dirty. She was afraid to sit on any chair but the folding chair by the table in the studio. I wanted her to be with me in the living room, and she thought she had to sit on the floor so she wouldn't spoil the furniture. Very firmly, I invited her again to sit on all my furniture and all of the beds in the house. "While I am out teaching, Amy, I want you to go all around the house and sit on every chair, sofa and bed in the house." I had told her this once before.

Between students, I went into the house to see what Amy was doing. At first, I couldn't find her. Then, walking into a bedroom, I spied her crouched down on all fours, hiding and shaking. Going to her, I said, "You don't belong on the floor. You don't have anything or anyone to be afraid of here. No one will hurt you. Please come with me to the studio. I want you to be near me. I like for you to be with me."

She got up and obediently followed me to the studio. I did not know who it was. I never asked.

After teaching was finished, I was greeted by Amy.

Amy: "Can I sit in your rocky chair, Jean?"

Jean: "Sure, Amy. Do you like to rock?"

Amy: "Mmm hmm. I had a little white 'rocky chair' once. It was my real daddy's. I like to rock. Sometimes I scare myself; I rock so high I almost tip over."

Jean: "And did you ever tip over, Amy?"

Amy: "No. I didn't, but one day I's rocky, way up high an' I's singin' 'Daddy, Daddy, Daddy, Daddy, rocky chair, rocky chair,' an' Sister say,

'Mother, she doin' it 'gain makin' noise in that chair'. You-know-who yell at me an' say, 'You like that chair so much, you can just stay in it!' And she tie me in it.

"I cry. I say, 'No, no, too tight, hurts my tummy!' She just tie tighter. She tie hands on sides of chair – too tight, too tight. 'Mommy my hand cold.' I cried. She be mad. Then Rosalind push my rocky chair hard. I tip over my back and I cry harder. I scared. I cry more. Rosalind call me a bad word and put a scarf in my mouth." Amy leaned closer to say softly to me, "She call me shit ass."

Jean: "Oh, Amy, you poor little thing, what happened next?"

Amy: "Lil's mother an' sister get their coats and say, 'Let's go for a walk and get away from that brat.' I hear front door slam. They gone long time. I 'fraid they never come back. Aunt Pearl came by. Untie me an' take me away."

Jean as Narrator: I do remember my horror at Amy being tied and left alone while the mother and sister went out of the house. Now writing these words, I ache for this little girl as I see her lying on her back, tied to the beloved "rocky chair" and with a scarf stuffed in her mouth. Were they trying to kill her?

That afternoon, Amy and I went for a walk outside. We played shadow tag, laughing and stepping on our shadows. I recited a nursery rhyme to Amy. She loved it.

Amy wanted to learn to play the organ. On prior visits, I had encouraged her to try pressing the organ keys, and she sometimes watched while I taught a child's lesson. I chose a quiet time one morning to invite her to the organ. Placing her hands on a sheet of paper, I traced around them, then drew a fingernail on each thumb and finger and numbered them. We talked about the number assigned to each finger, and I placed her right hand on the keyboard and instructed her to press one finger at a time. We counted finger numbers as she played. The look of sheer joy that stole over her face revealed her excitement. Printing her name on a music book, I gave it to her to take home with her. Each time she visited after that, I taught her another lesson. One day when Amy was having trouble keeping her left hand high enough on the keyboard, she said, "Lil's tummy too big. My hand can't reach 'round it."

It was recital time. I had been teaching both Celeste and Amy to play the organ. Celeste wrote notes to me, asking questions about the music. Amy played it like any other 6-year-old would.

They decided to buy a present for me since I was now their music teacher. Off they went. Celeste, of course, was driving. Lucy described the trip to me.

Lucy: "Jean, you should have seen them! They were so cute! Here's Celeste who can't talk and little Amy who can't see the top of the counter or count money."

Jean: "That must have been a sight to see, Lucy," I said. I was trying to imagine that clerk's reaction. "Which one made the choice?"

Lucy: "Well, they didn't know what to get. Celeste looked at scarves and gloves, then Amy spied a little table. All that was on it were these red roses. Amy remembered hearing Jimmy tell Lil that red roses mean love. So she asked Celeste, "Do we got 'nuff money for this?" Celeste nodded her head. "Do you like it for Jean?" Another nod.

So they agreed on the red rose. Celeste counted out the money, and they took it to the clerk. Amy had to do the talking 'cause Celeste couldn't. In her best little-girl voice, Amy said, "We want this."

The clerk asked, "Would you like it gift-wrapped?' Amy looked at Celeste. "Can we?" Celeste nodded her head. Amy spoke for her. "Yes, please."

"They were really pleased, and they both thought you'd like it," Lucy concluded.

"The poor clerk," I thought. When her customer was Celeste, her hands trembled, and she looked frightened. A blink of the eye, and her customer was speaking in a small, excited child's voice, and the hands were calm.

Suddenly, Lucy was gone, and Amy was there. "It's pretty, isn't it? It's a red hankie all folded into a rose, but you can't blow your nose on it!"

Jean as Narrator: Long afterward, Lillian related the rose purchase through her mind's eye. "I see three people," she said. "Lucy is standing back watching. I see a big person who looks and acts just like you described Celeste, and I see a little girl beside her."

***

Jean as Narrator: The following day, the two of us were in the car. I say "two" because I didn't always know which personality was there. "Who is being so quiet and looking out the window?" I asked.

"It's me, Amy," and she flashed me a big smile.

"Hi, Amy. Do you watch out the window when Big Jimmy or Evan is driving?"

"Sometimes."

"Oh, look, Amy, there are some people making a sidewalk," I explained.

When my own children were small, riding in the car offered a wonderful learning experience, as together we explored the scenery and activities we viewed. Riding with my children offered many opportunities to teach my little ones. They learned to recognize their first letters from highway signs, differentiated horses from cows, sheep from pigs, red lights from green. We often recited nursery rhymes or sang. I couldn't resist the opportunity to teach Amy something she might not have known before. I drove around the block and stopped the car across the street from the sidewalk being laid.

"How they do that?" Amy was all eyes and ears.

"Do you see that big bucket with its mouth open, turning 'round and round?'"

"Yes."

"The workers shovel some sand in it and some dry concrete and pour some water in it. Now do you see the box that they made at the sidewalk?"

She nodded her head.

"Well, Amy, after they mix up sand and the concrete and the water real good and runny, they pour the cement into the box and smooth it down. Then overnight, it stops being runny and sets up."

"Sets up!" Amy interrupted. "I never seed a sidewalk set up! You sure, Jean?"

As I realized Amy's "sets up" means "sits up," we erupted into laughter. We giggled and laughed for a long time before I could settle myself down enough to explain "set up."

Then I said, "No, no, Amy, it doesn't 'sit up.' It 'sets up' like Jell-O."

Another interruption: "Jell-O can 'sit up'? I never seed it do that!"

Another outburst of laughter from me. Amy joined right in, though I am sure she didn't know what I was laughing about.

"No, Amy, you know how runny Jell-O is when we are making it. Then we put it in the refrigerator and it 'sets up' so we can eat it with a spoon. That's what the cement does."

We laughed again, and I will never know if Amy understood what happens to cement and Jell-O, but we had a grand and memorable time.

Did Amy's being able to tell me about her "rocky chair" enable her to laugh and joke with me? Yes, I am sure of it. Each time one of the personalities shared a bad memory, that personality was relieved of the suppressed pain. The memory and the pain were then returned to Lillian, and she was a step closer to integration.

After her return to New York, Lillian, upon reliving Amy's memory and its accompanying pain and fear, again became very angry at her mother and sister. Lillian felt Amy's fear and pain as her own.

Chapter 15
Compliance

In Chapter 15, Esther speaks of abuse factually and without emotion.

The effect of abuse on a child's thinking is one of the last and most difficult symptoms to change. Many abused children believe that they deserved to be abused. Indeed, some abused children believe that they wanted the abuse to occur. The untangling of these confabulatory beliefs is a long and arduous process.

In 1983, Roland Summit, M.D., wrote about abuse accommodation syndrome – a psychological bond that develops between perpetrator and victim in which the victim's sense of safety becomes tied to pleasing the abuser.

Ultimately, the victim comes to feel proud of their compliance as if it changes the victim in the eyes of the abuser from a hated child to one who is valued.

Children trapped in these situations confuse cause with effect.

Dr. Summit wrote, "The child cannot safely conceptualize that a parent might be ruthless and self-serving .... The only acceptable alternative for the child is to believe that she has provoked the painful encounters and hopes that by learning to be good, she can earn love and acceptance. The desperate assumption of responsibility set(s) the foundation for self-hate."

FA

Esther: "Five years old, and a new stepdad joined Mother and Sister. My new dad said, 'Let's play a game – a trick on Mother." He had her lipstick, and we would hide it so that she couldn't find it. It sounded like fun. When he showed me where he would hide the lipstick, I wasn't sure. It didn't seem wrong, but Mother always said to keep your hands away from that place. But Dad liked to do that. This was one game when Dad would pay attention to me. It was my and Dad's secret. It left Mother out instead of me. Only sometimes, he put something in me and made me keep it in. I felt confused and afraid someone would tell I had something inside. Sometimes it was uncomfortable. Sometimes it felt good. No one else talked about this. It must be what all dads do. I looked at other girls and wondered what they had inside them. Then Dad put something up my ass. That hurt, and I didn't like Dad's game anymore, but he said it was time to learn the facts of life. It was time to be a help to the family. So 1 learned the facts of life. There were other men who didn't have little girls to take care of them, so Dad showed me how to touch them and make their sticks get big. He told me these other men would teach me other ways to help, and I was to let them do whatever they wanted.

"I started to keep more to myself. I was scared and didn't want to be Dad's pet anymore. I was 8 when he first took me to someone's house. They lived in a cellar house, down a lot of stairs, and it was scary. I didn't want Lillian's dad to leave me there alone. He promised he'd be back, but only if I did everything these daddies wanted and remembered that Mother was counting on the money. And I was helping, doing something right, and I could sleep in my own bed that night and not be in the coal cellar.

"I was afraid Dad wouldn't come back. I tried to use my mouth fast so it would get over and Dad would come back quicker, but I couldn't swallow that bad stuff, and I got hit. Dad said it wasn't pee or snot, but I didn't want to swallow that sticky stuff. I learned I could stick my finger down my throat and throw up after I got home. So I figured I had outsmarted them.

"The men gave me money. The first time the man offered me a quarter or a paper bill, I took the quarter. I was no dummy. I knew Dad would take the paper money from me, and I wouldn't have anything. So I got a quarter, sometimes two or three in one trip. It didn't take too long, and I would just let myself not think of what had to be done. I knew Dad would come back. He never let me down that way. He watched out for me. He never let anyone go clear inside unless it was the back, and he got extra money for that, and nobody was allowed to hurt me.

"I told Dad once that it hurt, and he put a piece of broomstick inside back there. He got in a rage. So I didn't let it hurt me after that. I stopped feeling or thinking with my body. I was helping the family when Dad and I went for rides, and the other kids at home thought I was Dad's pet. Dad said I was good, and he said he was proud of me. I wanted him to like me.

"I was glad there were 'others,' not just Lillian and me, but I had to keep myself separate. Besides, the others had their own various problems. Lucy would get mad and break things, then leave. Lillian would deny that she broke anything, and so she got the reputation of being a liar."

Chapter 16
Robin Jean

There are therapists who hold the belief that the more one inquires about the existence of a personality state, the more one encourages the personality to take on an identity of its own, thereby creating more, not less dissociation.

Faced with this possibility, Jean ventures forth in an exploration of a personality with no name and discovers, to her surprise, that sexual abuse before the age of 5 sometimes can have an unexpected outcome.

Robin Jean's appearance raises many unanswered questions. Was Lillian sexually fondled before she was old enough to walk, and by whom? Can a person at such a young age develop a personality alter before the child's personality itself is actually formed? Every answer seems to raise another question.

However, in meeting Robin Jean, an unexpected discovery is made – Lillian, as Robin Jean, has a sexuality!

FA

Jean as Narrator: I often wondered during those early months how a personality decides to "come out." Jimmy didn't know either, but he had learned to recognize the signs. Jimmy called one day to say, half in desperation, half in warning, "There is somebody new, Jean. Don't ask me how I know. I can't tell you." Something in his voice made me wonder.

My first hint of that new personality's emergence came one day when Sarah Ann asked me, "What name would you pick if you could have any name you wanted, Jean? How do you pick a name?"

I said, "If I didn't have a favorite name, I would try to find a suitable variation of the name of someone I especially liked or a combination of two names." I gave her these possibilities from Rev. Chris: Christy or Christine, and from Dr. Robinson: Robin, and from Jean: Jeanna or Jeannie.

I accompanied Lillian (Lucy) to Rev. Chris' office the next day. Lucy reported right out of the blue, "Robin Jean said she could take over for a year." Rev. Chris and I looked at each other questioningly. We didn't know there was such a personality.

"Lillian doesn't need a Robin Jean or anyone else to take over for her," Rev. Chris declared.

That comment led Robin Jean, whoever she was, to believe that Rev. Chris didn't like her.

Later, talking to Julie, I asked about Robin Jean. "Do you think that it would be all right if I talked to her?"

"I don't know if she will talk to you," Julie replied. "She hasn't talked to anybody who knows who she is yet. She spends time with Jimmy, but he does not know her name."

I had become confident in my ability to deal with just about anything that the personalities threw at me, but I never really knew what or who would come next. I confess I had some concern about my safety as I met each new personality for the first time.

"Well, let's find out. May I please see Robin Jean?"

The figure sitting before me changed abruptly. She threw back her shoulders, raised her head, crossed her right knee over her left knee and hiked her dress up well above her knee. Slipping her right shoe off at the heel, she began bouncing her foot. I couldn't keep my eyes off that dangling shoe, wondering at what instant it would fall to the floor.

"Hi, Jean! How do you like my name? Named after the two sexiest people I know: you and Dr. Robinson."

There was a seductive quality to this one for sure; the voice, the twinkle in her eyes, and the way she cocked her head to one side and smiled.

We were soon chatting like old friends. "Could we go shopping together sometime, Jean?" she asked.

"Sure. We can go this morning if you like."

"I am sick of wearing those tired old rags Lucy buys. I want something snazzy. Jimmy gave me some money and said maybe you'd have time for us to shop."

So, this is the one Jimmy couldn't tell me about!

She went quickly to "their bedroom," applied bright lipstick, and put on gaudy, dangling earrings and high heels. She unbuttoned the top two buttons on her blouse. I could see that she had either shortened her bra straps or hooked the bra one notch tighter. She was overweight, but she saw herself as being beautiful and trim, well, maybe voluptuous, as Lillian had been at the age of 18.

"What's your favorite color, Robin Jean?" I inquired.

"Green to go with my green eyes," she replied.

"When did you first appear, Robin Jean, and how old are you now?" My curiosity could not be contained.

"Jean! You don't ask a lady her age! Anyway, I never thought about that. I guess I would just say I am the age of consent. I was around from the time Lillian was real small, not even walking yet. I came to take over the good feelings involved in sexual things – nothing else. I became what I call 'aware' or maybe 'more separate' as soon as Lillian left home and moved into that little apartment."

It wasn't until a long time later that I remembered her saying that she had sexual feelings before she was old enough to walk.

"Before she was old enough to walk?" I thought.

Robin Jean continued. "Lillian worked in an insurance office. She worked late one night, and one of the agents offered to drive her home. But when he stopped at his place and invited Lillian in to 'see something.' Well, he put the make on her. She started to run, but I decided to stay and find out what the sex talk was all about. And I discovered that I enjoyed sex!"

As we talked and shopped at the Springfield Mall, we were looking for something green. We bought a pretty print blouse that was predominantly green. I bought her a green pen with green ink. Then Robin Jean wanted to look around. She hadn't been in a shopping mall for some 20 years, and never with me.

"Window shopping doesn't count," she said. "It's no fun when someone else is in the body, and you are just watching. You got to go in and touch things."

When we came to the display window at Frederick's of Hollywood, Robin Jean's eyes lit up. "Let's go in here!"

So we did. And we found all kinds of frilly lace lingerie. She pointed out a tiny bikini. "How would I look in this, Jean?"

"Sexy! But do you think it would be safe to put it on? Jim would flip!"

"Hey, look, Jean, here's a slinky black teddy, just your size! Shall we buy it?"

"I'm afraid Walter would have a heart attack, and if he didn't, I might be the one suffering an attack!" I giggled, trying to keep up with her frivolity, but she was a master of innuendo. She soon had me in stitches, and I began acting like a giddy schoolgirl.

"Look at this, Robin Jean! Did you ever see a pair of panties with a hole in the crotch? Imagine buying undies with holes in them before you even wear them!"

"Here is a bra to go with that! Two holes, you know where!" she laughed.

When we came upon a display of strawberry body gel, we just had to smell it. I was laughing so hard I had tears in my eyes. About that time, I realized the clerks were not sharing in our hilarity.

"We better get out of here while the getting is good, Robin Jean," I whispered. "I think we have become personae non gratae. Besides, I have to find a bathroom!"

We left but soon returned. Robin Jean had spied a basket of aphrodisiac soap and wanted to buy some to try out on Jimmy.

After about two hours of shopping, lunch and gabbing, we were ready to go back to my house. "Did you get everything you wanted, Robin Jean?" I asked.

"Yes, I did. I had fun."

"I had fun too. Does anybody else want to do any shopping?" I asked.

"I don't know why anybody would ever wear heels for shopping," a voice said. "Can we go home?"

"Who are you?" I asked.

"Sarah Ann and my feet hurt," she said, stopping to remove the shoes. Sarah Ann carried her shoes, limping back to the car in her stocking feet.

Sarah Ann rode home with me. Saying she was tired, she yawned and left. Lucy appeared to inform me that Sarah Ann had always been the sickly one; she was anemic. I thought about Julie bleeding herself. She had allergies, so she couldn't play with Fluffy, and she tended to go to bed earlier when she had control of the body.

Now in Sarah Ann's place came Lillian. "Did Robin Jean get her shopping done?" Lillian queried. "Did she buy anything?"

"Yes, it's in the bag there. See if you like it." I knew she hadn't seen the blouse before. She did like it and went to put it on as soon as we got in the house.

"I never thought of wearing green before. Do you like it?"

Robin Jean's Journal: "I met Jean today, and she acted like she accepted me. I don't see any reason to have a name, but all the others kept arguing with me, saying I had to name myself or they would!"

Jean as Narrator: Robin Jean was flirtatious, but only when she felt safe. She enjoyed the company of men more than women and had never had a woman friend before me. We enjoyed one another's company. She dressed in style and with good taste. She cherished the green pen I gave her and always wrote in green ink. She was artistic and designed her own stationery with a tiny drawing of a bird (a robin, of course) on the edge of a nest containing three eggs. She did some scratchboard art, but her real hobby, she confided, was men.

Robin Jean had an intimate relationship with Jimmy, which I thought Lucy resented.

"That's not so," Lucy countered. "Lil is envious."

Jimmy bought a red lace negligee for Robin Jean, but "the others" cut it up before she had a chance to wear it. Someone later told me she cut it up because Jimmy was not being fair, buying Robin Jean a special present. If Jimmy had bought it for Lillian, they all could have worn it. Rational thinking or irrational? Who is to judge?

Robin Jean accepted her sexuality and her beauty. When Lillian saw a videotape of her, she said, "Robin Jean is prettier than I am."

Lillian, in trying to accept Robin Jean, said, "Doctor says my mother called me a prostitute. So maybe I, as Robin Jean, became one. I wonder what all I'm going to find out about myself from this Robin Jean. Aunt Jean, it really worries me!"

"I don't consider that Robin Jean is or ever was a prostitute," I assured her. "Enjoying sex with Jimmy isn't prostitution, even if he is your husband and not hers. Robin Jean is not a loose woman. She was not promiscuous, nor was she ever paid."

Robin Jean's presence seemed to awaken a desire in Lillian to become closer to Jimmy. "I wish I could have spent more time with Jimmy," Lillian said. "We cashed his check, and got a prescription, a couple of cards and stamps, and a few groceries. The next thing I knew, two hours were gone, and he was called to work."

At Dr. Robinson's office the next day, Robin Jean introduced herself and repeated what she had told me.

Lillian was hospitalized once more after receiving Robin Jean's memory of having been sexually abused.

Lillian felt compelled to set the record straight on her morality. "Robin, I ran away that night from the guy who worked in the insurance office! Please say I did! I got away! It was only insinuations he was saying. If you were there, you had to run too. Please tell me we both were able to not have anything happen. Robin, I am not like that! No part of me! No way!"

Robin Jean Wrote: "Sorry, but you left, so I was there and figured I might as well enjoy it. We wouldn't have gotten away anyhow, Lil, so why not? It was (is) fun."

Jean as Narrator: Following her release from the hospital, Lillian and Jimmy went shopping for a second dresser. Lillian had accepted Robin Jean's memory of the insurance man but not the good feelings Robin Jean talked about. After all, Lillian herself had not yet experienced sex, except for the very beginning of the rape by Mr. Sampson. Julie and Lee had taken that over for her.

Chapter 17
Will I Ever Be Clean?

Statistics today state that one in every five girls will be abused before she becomes an adult. The statistics for women are equally high.

Some remember, others don't. Those who don't, often don't want to be touched.

Plagued by the thought that she is soiled, Esther recalls her murderous rage toward her stepfather when she was 12 years old.

Like many young girls who have been sexually abused, Esther thinks of herself as "dirty." These children, even as adults, wash themselves compulsively, taking long showers as they symbolically cleanse their bodies of the shame they feel inside.

Indeed, such behavior is one of the primary symptoms of sexual abuse.

Chapter 17 depicts a dangerous period in Lillian's recovery from abuse as several personalities, with either suicidal or homicidal impulses, surface at the same time.

The risk of acting out is highest during these periods and accounts for the majority of suicide attempts made by individuals with multiple personality disorder.

FA

Jean as Narrator: Esther made her appearance in my living room.

"Dad got the paper money, and I got the quarters," she said.

"Esther!" I shrieked, "You said he got paper money, and you got the quarters?! Think about that! He was getting 10, 20 or 50 dollars, and you thought he was doing you a favor by giving you the quarters?! What are you saying!! He was selling the services of his little girl!"

My outburst surprised Esther. My anger was matched by her disbelief.

"Jean, I never saw you mad before!"

173

"Well, I never heard anything in my life that made me so mad before!"

Esther stared at me in amazement. Slowly she allowed herself to become angry, but she kept in tight control. Not until I expressed my revulsion could she stop thinking as she did as a child and permit herself to reason out the implications of the money exchange.

Esther: "One day when I was 12 years old, Lillian's stepfather came in the house from mowing the lawn. It was a hot July day. Mother had gone to the store, and Letty was taking a nap. Rosalind was upstairs.

"I had just finished scrubbing the kitchen floor on my hands and knees. He saw a place where I had splashed some dirty water on the baseboard, and he ordered me to scrub the whole floor again, and 'This time, do it right!' He ordered me to take all my clothes off.

"Then he went and got a light bulb, an elongated one, like the one in your curio cabinet; he was going to put it up me. I ran from him, but he caught me. I fought, trying to get a knife to protect myself! He held onto me, and we struggled. I raised my arm with the knife in my hand. He clutched his chest and fell to the floor, gasping, 'Get your mother!'"

Jean: "You must have been really scared, Esther!"

Esther: "I was. I ran and put my clothes back on. Just then, Mother came home from the store. She called the doctor and sent me and Rosalind and Letty to the next-door neighbor.

"The doctor went into the house but soon came back out onto the front porch and looked across at us on the neighbor's porch. 'He's dead,' I told Rosalind.

"I was right. I watched them take him away. I waited for the police to come and take me to jail. What I didn't know was that even though I thought I had killed him, there was not a scratch on him; no stab wound or mark of any kind.

"Herbert had a heart attack once before and was hospitalized for it. However, his job would have been in jeopardy if it was known that he had heart trouble, so he told them at work that he had suffered stomach cramps."

Jean: "Esther, all these years, you have carried that burden. Now you will be relieved of the memory, but Lillian must get all of those feelings back. Is she strong enough?" My head was reeling. Did I understand Esther correctly?

Esther: "It is very hard for Lillian. I have to give it to her a little at a time. It helps her to be able to talk to you. A lot of things she thinks she could never tell anybody, but then you make it okay for her to tell you."

Jean as Narrator: The next day, Lillian told me about Herbert's death. I was as shocked with the second telling as with the first.

That night, Lillian awakened from a dream. As she recounted the dream, she began to sob. In the dream, she, as Lillian, plunged a knife into Herbert's throat.

I held and comforted her for a long time, reassuring her of my care for her and my compassion for the personality, Esther, who had kept these hideous memories for so long in order to keep Lillian alive.

Strangely, all this brought back a memory of my own "lost time." I was about 10 or 11. We had neighbors who sometimes bought a dozen eggs from my mother. Our cat, Snuggles, had gone over to their barn. So my brother and I were sent off to deliver the eggs and get Snuggles. Since I considered the cat mine, we decided I would go to the barn and get her, and my brother would deliver the eggs.

When I got in the barn, the man who lived there asked me if I would like to be up on the horse. That sounded like a nice treat. I had seen him working his horses in the field just behind our house, and I sometimes stood and watched.

So, he lifted me up high. It was a very big horse, too high for me to get down by myself. I remember that it was a cold winter day, and I was wearing my snow pants. Old George tried to get his hand up under the leg of the snow pants, but it wouldn't fit. Then he reached down from the waist inside of my snow pants. Now, even these many years later, I cannot recall the next passage of time. My brother came back to the barn to get me. Years later, when I asked my brother about it, he said, "You bawled all the way home."

It's a memory that I can't get even today. What words could I have used to tell Mom? How did she find out? All I know is that Dad drove me to the doctor's office. Dad took me to the juvenile probation office. I answered the officer's questions but was totally shocked when he held up my bloody underwear and asked if it was mine.

Old George was arrested that same night.

I continued going to school on the school bus that stopped at our mailbox. Who knows? Do the kids at school know? I was ashamed.

Long story short, Old George spent a year in prison. As his year came to an end, Dad moved us several miles away. Every time I thought about meeting new people, I wondered if they knew. My dad did everything right. Nobody talked about my experience, not my mother, not me, nobody. I was taking piano lessons at the time and loved it. I think I lost myself in my music.

What happened was not my fault. I was a little girl. Now I know that what I needed were WORDS, WORDS, WORDS.

As we held each other and cried together, Esther knew that I understood more than she thought anyone could. We were bound together by our painful memories.

Esther's/Lillian's memories started coming out more rapidly than Lillian could process them.

Lillian: "I never before mentioned a personality named Rose. She dissolved pills in Kool-Aid and handed the glass to James. One of the personalities (Pat) knocked the glass out of James' hand. Rose thought a kid would be better off dead than having to endure what she experienced. She suggested a poster: STOP CHILD ABUSE! KILL A KID TODAY! She said if enough parents had to get involved in kids' funerals, child abuse might get the attention polio did. Kill enough kids, and someone will come up with a cure."

Jean as Narrator: Rose had murderous tendencies, and Dr. Alabiso said that James had to be removed from the home for his safety. Meanwhile, Lillian wanted James home with her.

When next "they" visited me, Rose had a knife, and she slashed the painting of the deer, the one Jimmy asked me to keep safe for him.

***

Jean as Narrator: Lillian struggled to shut her mother's voice out of her mind. What she was hearing was being yelled at for being sick and bad and wrong. She stopped referring to her mother as "Mother" and spoke only of "Jessica."

She told me, "Rosalind says she will still love me, and things will be just like before if I am willing to forget this farce."

The following Friday night, Lillian reported that the doctor probably thought she had a good session because it took so much out of her.

Julie talked to me too. Julie was extremely suicidal. I reminded her that if she killed herself, she would also kill Lillian and all the others. I insisted that normal people would consider that murder. Rethinking that, it seems pretty crazy that Julie could kill Lillian (same body!), and that I would accuse her of murder. I realized that I was thinking like "they" did.

Julie was very worried. She told me that Lillian wants to put acid on her face so the world can see the ugliness of "them." Julie went on to write, "What if the whole world thinks we are evil and shouldn't be allowed to be here? The everyday world does not want to even believe I am me or that anyone else is there. We represent filth."

Lillian Wrote: "Made a complete idiot of myself by crying at church tonight. They were there singing of being clean. Sure leaves me way out in the left field! We don't belong there. We can't ever be clean. We are the dirt people don't want to be reminded of. I don't care. God has his people, and then there is us."

Julie Wrote: "It is true. I feel dirty and wrong, and that man who thinks we are evil is probably right."

Esther Wrote: "I wish I was clean."

Chapter 18
Hatred

In his treatise on entrenched hatred, noted psychoanalyst Stephen Demby, Ph.D., describes the parent-child relationship that results in a personality marred by a hateful parent as follows: "These children are subject to relational trauma .... This is the trauma of children growing up with a parent or parents who are chronically and significantly misattuned and unresponsive to the child's emotional and other needs, who cannot tolerate the child's expressions of distress, who are intrusive and controlling of the child and/or who use the child to meet their own emotional needs. As a result, the child experiences excessive fear, helplessness, humiliation, shame, and abandonment .... The experience of childhood trauma can leave an individual with chronic personality vulnerabilities ... that the world is not a safe place and that there is no dependable source of security to turn to."

Parents presenting with this pattern are insensitive to their children. They lack tender emotions. They show no kindness, no warmth. Yet, they claim to love the child.

FA

Esther Wrote: "Dr. Robinson asked to talk to me today. I told him about the gun Lee got and how I tried to talk Lee into killing someone. I wish they were all dead."

Jean as Narrator: Esther called me in the middle of the day. "Jean, this is Esther. I have written something for Dr. Robinson, and I wonder if I could read it to you. Do you have time? You can tell me if you think it's okay to send it to him."

Jean: "Esther, yes, I would like to hear it."

Esther: "How do I make these feelings of hate go away? Dr. Robinson said to write it down. He said people today are more aware of child abuse.

More aware? That's a laugh! Not on my street. But don't worry. It doesn't matter. No one wants to be involved. The law protects the abuser. By fighting back, I will be getting even! It is easy for you to say that I can't. You weren't tied up for days. You weren't locked in a closet. There are no mental scars in you. No burns from cigarettes or scalding water. No rope burns. No electric shocks to watch you jump. No sex abuse. Nothing put inside to hurt you or to hide it from Mommy. No night terrors from being locked in the dark. No ridicule from other kids who don't let you forget that they know you are filth. You can't kill the one who tried to kill you. You tell yourself, 'Someday it will be their turn.' So, I survived because I was Lucky. Lucky?!! The past lives within me. It haunts my dreams, and you, all of you, tell me I can't get even. You make me sick! And now a therapist says I can't hit back. I can't hurt anyone. Why live in the past? It's over. Forget it. All of you who can't dial a telephone to report abuse or don't want to be involved make me sick, and now you tell me I can't even get even! I feel rage. I read the paper, and I want to scream. I listen to neighbors and fight to keep from letting the anger and frustration show. Is everyone asleep? Doesn't anybody care about what's happening on the street? Next door? I cry inside. I can now, but there was a time when I couldn't. I want to tell someone how it was, how it is. And make them wake up and care. I remember being scared all the time. Bedtime was a release before Lillian's new dad came to live there. Lillian had wet the bed – a sign that everything said about her was true. She was a bad seed. She didn't deserve to live. Guilt for being alive. Guilt for not liking to sleep in a wet bed. Bad, bad, bad. We learned fast that love means we are hurt because Mother has to teach us not to be so bad. Her new dad taught us too, for our own sake, so we could get along in the world. Dad had to teach us, punish us, so we wouldn't forget, because he loved Lillian. The coal cellar, the burns, the arms shoved in the scalding water because he loved us. I wondered about other families. How did they know which one of their kids was the bad one – the bad seed? We played a guessing game and tried to pick out which kid in other families was like us, the one who didn't do anything right, the one who spent dark nights in the coal cellar. We wondered if they were afraid of the dark. Of rats? We wondered how they stayed so clean. I remember the shame. I remember being afraid someone would notice me. What would I say if they asked how I got hurt so often? Why was I so clumsy? I would rather let them think I fell. It was an accident. If they knew how I got cut, then they would know I had been punished. During the years away from the house, we were in a home visiting and watched a father put a cigarette out on his daughter's arm in front of us and the whole family. No one said a word. A couple of years later, another daughter from that home got married, and Lillian was in the home when this young wife's husband hit their baby. We sat there and didn't say a word. We believed that this was the way it was in most, if not all, families. Lillian felt the wrongness, but hadn't we been subject to the same things? Lillian talked to the girl from the house about why her man did that, and she said his father had held a gun to his head when he was little. Wasn't getting hit better? And besides, it was just a kid, and that's how it is. You learn to live with it. I read in the paper about a child's death, and the neighbors knew there was no heat in the house in zero weather. The neighbors knew the kids were fed warm tea or water to live on, and the authorities are considering prosecuting the parents. What about the neighbors who did nothing? The girl or boy in school who is so cold and distant, the one the teacher just can't like. Usually, teachers find something to like about every kid. But no one tries to find out why that child is the way she is. Does anyone care? Yes, I hate!"

Jean as Narrator: Dr. Robinson was at a conference to learn more about multiple personality disorder, so Lillian drove down to spend the weekend with me. I was always glad to see her no matter who she was. We chatted all evening and went to bed late. But the next morning, she was gone. No note. No clue. She was gone all day Saturday, Saturday night and Sunday. I called Dr. Robinson's office and was told we would just have to wait.

Sure enough, late Monday afternoon Lillian phoned me. She lost a couple of days, but now she was back in control of the body. She was somewhere in Ohio. Was she on her way to Jessica's house? There was a gun on the seat of the car beside her, and she didn't know what to do. I did some fast thinking and asked her, "Is there a receipt for the gun?"

"Yes."

"Look at it. Do you know how to get to where the gun was bought?"

My heart was beating fast. I said, "Take that gun back and return it. Tell them you changed your mind and don't need any money back. Then head for home."

Chapter 19
Co-consciousness

Haven't we all, at one time or another, thought of ourselves as having opposing parts?

Don't we frequently say to ourselves, "Part of me wishes I could just do what I want to do, but another part of me knows better"?

Unlike those who suffer from MPD, most of us have never endured trauma severe enough to fragment our consciousness.

We, the fortunate ones, think of ourselves as one person.

Having been invited to speak publicly about her experience in assisting in Lillian's recovery, Jean seemed to intuitively know that MPD healing requires bringing out the personalities in service of bringing them together.

Chapter 19 – Co-consciousness – captures an extraordinary moment in the process of becoming "one person."

In this chapter, we witness cooperation among the personalities for the common good of speaking out against child abuse.

Rather than experiencing her personalities as fragmented and unwanted parts, Lillian begins to view them as the parts that make up a unified self.

This process is referred to as co-consciousness.

The achievement of co-consciousness in and of itself is thought to be a critical milestone in the healing process.

The debut of the personalities captures the public's fascination with MPD itself.

FA

Jean as Narrator: A student of mine was in charge of organizing public information programs at a center in Washington, D.C. He asked whether I would be willing to provide a program on child abuse, with each part speaking for her/himself. At the time of the request, Lillian was hospitalized after yet another suicide attempt. She was trying to find a reason to live. This program, I thought, could be at least the start to an answer.

We planned a two-part program. The first part, given by me, would overview Lillian's journey. The second would incorporate as many personalities as I could convince to speak publicly.

I talked with various personalities about what they would like to present. The date was set for one month hence.

"They" – I always thought of them that way now – arrived, fresh out of the hospital two days before their part of the presentation. As I prepared a notebook of selected handwriting samples, my excitement grew.

This was their opportunity to speak out.

Realizing that I needed to know who wanted to be seen at the presentation, I pointed to a sheet of paper on the card table, asking who wanted to present and what she/he wanted to share.

Each part answered differently. Each one's handwriting was unique. Each one's art or craft reflected her/his talents.

How wonderfully they all cooperated with me and with one another. I considered preparing each personality for my intended questions but decided to be as relaxed as possible and to go with the flow.

Amy and I practiced piano duets. Esther asked if she could read one of the articles she had written on child abuse. Acknowledging Celeste's fear and the fact that she remained mute, I asked her to put in a nonspeaking appearance. I packed Lee's woodcarvings for display. Lucy, knowing Lillian would be too uptight about the evening, offered to be the one who got dressed and rode with me to the presentation.

When we arrived, we opened their notebooks and placed their craft items on a table at floor level. With each one's permission, I recorded the event. The recording capturing each one's mannerisms, attitudes, voice and behavior still exists today.

I was nervous right along with each of them. Bubbly as always, Lucy started off by telling a joke. She showed her pastel drawing of Fluffy and chatted happily for a few minutes. Then I asked for Julie, who spoke briefly and quietly and read her poem "Six of One."

On down the list they went.

The audience was transfixed.

I knew we were reaching people.

Celeste appeared, quaking and frightened. She removed Lillian's wedding ring and put it into Lillian's purse. I held her hand while I told the audience that Celeste was not married; the wedding ring was Lillian's. Explaining that Celeste was unable to speak because of past trauma, I showed the audience her painting of a girl with a guitar. When I said, "Thank you, Celeste," Lillian replaced her.

Very surprised to find herself sitting at a table in front of a room full of people, Lillian looked to me for an explanation. "Are we here already?"

I knew it had been Lucy with me, but it was so easy to forget that Lillian couldn't see what was going on before she appeared.

She missed her wedding ring and began looking around. The audience members coached her. "It's in your purse. She put it in your purse," they called out.

Replacing her ring, Lillian spoke briefly about her willingness for the "others" to be seen "… Because they are more articulate and better able to demonstrate what can happen because of child abuse."

We showed Lillian's lovely painting of two swans. Then I asked for Lee.

Lee reached into the purse for his cigarettes, lit up after asking my permission, and answered my questions about his age and where he got his name. He smoked while he showed the little shoe that he had carved. There were questions from the audience about how he lived with all the females and how he explained the female body. He told them that Dr. Robinson had promised that if he ended up with the body after everybody else was integrated, the doctor would help him get a sex-change operation. Lee remained during the intermission and circulated among the attendees. He was having a grand time talking to men in the audience and being treated with respect.

Following intermission, I asked for Lizabeth, then Amy. Amy put on quite a show! I held up her finger painting of three pink tulips, green grass, and rain. Amy could hardly contain her excitement – "I am 6," she told us. "Can we play now?"

"Yes. Let's go!" I said.

"Come on, Jean!" she said as she ran over to the stage steps. Walking carefully down two of them, then jumping over the last one, Amy finally leapfrogged onto the piano bench!

The attendees saw the 200-plus-pound body thinking and acting like a small 6-year-old.

If audience members weren't convinced MPD existed before, they were now!

Amy played the melody, and I accompanied her with the chords. "Twinkle, Twinkle, Little Star" was followed by "Jingle Bells."

Amy was captivating. Indicating their newfound belief in MPD, the audience members applauded. They were convinced!

When we finished, I complimented Amy. "You played good, Amy!" I said.

"I know," the happy little voice responded.

Amy looked all around, basking for a few seconds in the attention that she had received, then asked whom I wanted to see next. I called for Sarah Ann.

Sarah Ann reached for the cassette of her music, saying, "You sure you want everybody to hear this, Jean? It's just me playing."

What we heard was a totally acceptable rendition of "Red River Valley." At the end of the number, the listeners applauded. Sarah Ann chatted with me long enough for her to be perceived as a 16-year-old. We talked about makeup, boys, music and her wish for a driver's license.

Introducing Esther, I displayed her splendid embroidery and the macramé purse she made for me as a birthday gift.

Esther's presentation was powerful. She read her article in a strong voice and spoke eloquently of child abuse. Esther was just the right closing for the presentation.

Later most of the personalities wrote positive comments in their journals, but Sarah Ann was disturbed. "I didn't say things the way I wanted," she wrote. "I need to write ideas down. People listened, but I don't know how to say things right."

Lillian's Journal: "Last night, there was a presentation at the National Presbyterian Church in Washington, D.C. There were all kinds of people there in the audience. Some were doctors, and some worked for the government, and Jean and I were there. The subject was 'Child Abuse and its Outcomes.' The other personalities were seen there, and some of the things that were made by them, but the theme was child abuse. Esther spoke of it. Lee was there for a long while. Sarah Ann suggested a minute of advertisement time on television, educating people to the signs of child abuse. A woman who said she worked for the government in the Department of Health, Education and Welfare asked if we would be willing to appear before some professionals to talk about this subject. I hope I got through to people that the reason I felt it was all right for them to see the other 'me's' was because some of the others are more articulate than I. So they can speak of these things much better than I can. I wanted them to give their messages while they are still here and able to do so. Jean says things went well. I hope so. Part of me is feeling helpless in being able to get across to people what needs to be said.

"Amy was there and playing the piano! Lee talked quite a bit and smoked. He answered questions, and Aunt Jean said he didn't beat around the bush.

"Everyone seemed to feel it was okay. I hope so. Two hours went by in about 20 minutes. The people there seemed to care."

Jean as Narrator: In the weeks and months following the presentation, abuse memories seemed to come back with greater ease but still in a piecemeal fashion. Lillian's various parts were out more often, as if readying themselves for direct communication with one another.

One month later, while back in the hospital, Lillian wrote:

What does being a multiple personality disorder mean?

It means lying in bed and having horrible memories and waking up, unable to get your breath because you feel you are 6 or 8 years old, and some old man's tongue is in your mouth.

It means you have no social life then or now because you might say or do something wrong.

It's wishing, longing for a family you never will have.

It's always being the outsider and living with guilt all the time without ever being sure of what you are guilty of.

It's cuts on your body.

It's finding yourself waking up in a hospital from taking too many drugs.

It's finding yourself in school after losing days and having to come to terms with teachers who insist there are seven days in every week.

It's no one listening to you unless it's to tell you, you are weird.

It's being scared at home while being terrified away from home that you will never get back home again.

It's realizing you are still nothing to anyone and no one cares, and when you finally get that through your head, you find a therapist, or rather he/she finds you, and the memory process begins.

It's hating yourself for betraying your so-called family.

It's wanting to kill them without knowing why – and sometimes feeling the same about your own therapist.

It's not understanding why.

It's a therapy of the ongoing hell that is in your head. A hell that invades your doctor's office and invades your home life, if you have any home life.

It is terrifying dreams that leave you breathless and convince you that someone is standing at the end of your bed, again!

It's striking out at those you love the most because the ones you wanted the love from didn't give you any.

It's guilt. It's self-pity.

It's wanting to call and confront an uncaring, sickening family.

It's coming to realize you have to face what they were, that what happened was not a normal childhood upbringing.

It's feeling anger because the wrong people are in therapy.

It's hurting.

It's the inability to cope.

It's not knowing what to do except to escape into "someone else."

It's crying and hurting and devastating memories with you all the time.

It's when your loved ones who have lived through the hell of your memories don't dare approach you.

It's sleeping in the closet or on the floor or wherever it feels safe and seeing your children watch with the fear in their eyes of not knowing what your next reaction will be.

It's having your 6-year-old asking, "Are you Mommy? I want to kiss her goodnight."

It's your child telling you, "I thought you were dead." Or that he threw up when the ambulance came.

It's people at the hospital asking your child, "Why does your mother give us a different name every time we ask?"

It's knowing the toll on your family.

It's feeling the quiet desperation that maybe the therapy won't work, and the tears and anguish will be all for nothing.

It's that horrible barb-wired knot in your throat when you wake up.

It's feeling the bile rise and vomit coming because of someone who sexually hurt you years ago.

It's not knowing what will trigger feelings that will make you lose control.

It's knowing a boy who committed suicide and wondering if you are next.

It's hearing a minister tell you to pray.

It's longing to die.

I am not completely well, but my feelings are real. I wrote this as therapy for me, but also hoping you will at least try to understand how it is for us.

Having purged herself of these feelings, the parts became more aware of one another.

Lillian's Journal: "Doctor's not in today, so I went to my first morning group therapy and ended up crying and having to leave. Some woman was yelling a lot, and I got scared."

Julie Wrote: "Jean, your letters and stamps came at a really good time! Lil had to be in group therapy this morning. Some screaming was done by some woman, first at someone else, then at Lil, and she had to leave crying. They said she didn't do anything wrong, and she stayed herself. Her hospital therapist, Connie, says she did good, and maybe someday she will be able to stay and answer back. I'm so glad I wrote to Lil. I feel like crying for her."

Lillian's Journal: "Talked to Aunt Jean for about half an hour on the telephone. I wrote her a letter today. Feel like I am doing things wrong.

"I'm a little worried that Uncle Walter will think less of me because my mother's name was mentioned. I don't mean to change anyone's feelings about her. It was, is, my problem. Aunt Jean, I hope calling you as much as I do isn't getting to you. Thank you for being there. I can't write anymore right now. Too many memories too close to the surface."

Robin Jean Wrote: "I talked to Dr. Robinson today and said hi. I let him see the things I have drawn. Asked him if he minded me using his name. He said he was flattered. Lil asked out of the group, and the doctor said no.

"Dr. Robinson said he thought it would be good for Lil (and us) to do more writing and speaking."

Chapter 20
Personalities, Personalities, Personalities

With the opening of co-consciousness, dissociation itself is breached, opening the way for the personalities (existing and new) to come out more easily, and out they came.

The reader is now exposed to the workings of the inner mind of the multiple personality disorder patient. A mind that simultaneously manages the thoughts, activities, "appearances" and relationships of 13 or more personalities – personalities who can be suicidal, homicidal, impulsive or hostile at any given time.

Some of them have no last name and only a faint identity.

Others may declare their refusal to integrate.

In addition, Jean herself questions if these personalities are being created in reaction to her curiosity.

Indeed, integration can be a period of great uncertainty.

FA

Jean Wrote: "Dear Joyce, thank you for signing the Valentine card. I really liked the card and will cherish it, especially because it's my first communication from you. I am looking forward to 'getting to know you.' That sounds like a song! I used to play that piece in my organ concerts when I was in a new city. It made a good introduction.

"Joyce, I think there is yellow stationery at your house, and nobody is using yellow. Maybe you would like to have it, or since you draw (print?), if you make your own design and clue me in on your color preference, I will have some stationery made up for you.

"I can't remember your age – 24? Are you right-handed? Amy said you have black hair. I hope to hear from you soon, Joyce. I'd like to be your friend. Jean. P.S. Joyce, do you have a last name?"

Joyce Wrote: "Hello Jean. Tonight we have stamps again so I will write. Yes, my hair is black no matter what you see. Eyes: green. Right-handed. Lefties bungle everything. Yes, 24. I paint some, usually 3x4 pictures with a scripture printed on it. No, I am not religious. Pictures just sell better with scriptures on 'em. I don't believe in miracles or a second coming. Prayer does not change things. Work does. I usually sell my pictures with a miniature easel. Religion is okay if you are weak enough to need it. I like reading mysteries and crime stories. I do not believe in dreams or poetry. I don't have much patience, but I can make kids mind. I don't hit them, but I do threaten some things and would carry out my threats if needed. I believe all people should be treated equal. I don't need friends who are intent on changing me. I won't try to change you.

"I hope the above answers your questions. I don't much want any 'women' friends who give unwanted advice. Perhaps we can chat again next year. I don't need a last name. Joyce."

Jean as Narrator: I sent a second letter to Joyce.

Jean Wrote: "Dear Joyce, isn't this paper pretty? Every time I use it, I think of Esther. I like your stationery too. Thank you for answering me, and you answered so promptly! I really like your letter. I don't know if I could write as good a profile of myself.

"Thank you for writing. We have lots of books you might like. The author who comes to mind for mystery and crime is Agatha Christie. Last night, Walter watched a movie based on her book *Murder on the Orient Express.* He was really engrossed in it.

"I'm sending $5 to order one of the pictures you made. Is that enough? If not, please let me know, and I will send more money.

"I certainly agree that prayer alone doesn't change things.

"I am not pushing religion. I hate having it pushed on me. I have to find out what's right for me.

"I do not want to be thought of as trying to change anyone. We all change, all the time, through our life experiences. I have changed a lot since I have gotten to know Lillian and all of you. I hope you will write again. Jean."

Joyce Wrote: "Jean, I do not take money of yours. You have not seen any of my artwork yet. Next time at your house if I am there, I will bring pictures, and you may have a choice. Do you have favorite Scriptures? Some I have now are:

1. Ephesians 4:26B: 'Let not the sun go down upon your wrath.'
2. Psalms 121:1B: 'I will lift up my eyes unto the Hills from where my help comes.'
3. Psalms 73:28B: 'I have put my trust in the Lord.'
4. Timothy 4:12A: 'Let no men despise thy youth.'

"I have read all of Agatha Christie. I saw the movie *Orient Express* also. Joyce."

Joyce's Journal: "So the great Dr. Robinson told me about my MMPI test results. It said I am a trusting person and resent people in authority. I am seeing myself as a virtuous person. I don't mix in crowds. I put people off by my attitude. I am quick to retaliate when I think I have been wronged. It said this person may have sexual problems. What do they know? I told Dr. Robinson his testing was wrong. I also told him that Lillian could bring James home for Easter, as I could handle him, but Lillian cannot."

Jean as Narrator: During the next visit to my house in Virginia, Rachel Ann and I talked about the variety of interests of all the personalities. We made up a list of symbols; things that reminded us of them. Some symbols were decided from their stationery, e.g., Lucy's cattails, Jackie's mushrooms, Julie's snowflake from her last Christmas card, Robin Jean's robin, etc. Lee's symbol was a miniature work shoe such as he carved. Rachel Ann was trying to find a symbol for herself. We finally decided on a tiny red beetle, which I always called a "ladybug." Rachel Ann thought it could also be a "lovebug."

After they returned home, I received this letter from Joyce.

Joyce Wrote: "Dear Jean, I am concerned about what you are writing (as are the others). A request: Do not give us symbols. Okay? Jackie does not want to be remembered as a mushroom. Let them be people. We are not Eve or Sybil. Lucy is Lucy, not Peggy. Your truth can be different than ours.

"It is frightening to realize that any confidences told are not kept after someone leaves. I do not wish, no one wishes, any ill feelings. Let us be us. I am immeasurably relieved I do not play an important 'persona' in anyone's life. Lucy, of course, considers herself (her truth) to be THE LUCY and wishes to be seen as herself, not the shadow of someone else."

Jean as Narrator: My response followed immediately.

Jean Wrote: "Dear Joyce, I was glad to hear from you. I am not aware of comparing any of you to Eve or Sybil, or anybody else. I don't mean to. I wish you were here! Talking is so much better than writing.

"I am glad you will be coming back for a longer visit in June. I look forward to spending more time with you. Love and regards to all from Jean."

***

Jean as Narrator: One day I received a knock at my front door. Opening it, I was greeted by a familiar body. Lillian? But she said she was Joyce.

Joyce: "I'm Joyce. I needed to get away, and after I started driving to some girl's house, I remembered that her father was dying, and it wouldn't be right for me to go there right now. So I turned the car around and drove all the way to come here. Is it okay?"

Jean as Narrator: "Of course. Come in, Joyce. You are always welcome here. You must be tired," I said.

Joyce visited with me for several hours that day. Asking my usual questions, I learned that Joyce first became a separate personality right after the birth of Lil's first child, Keith.

At that time, Lillian and Jimmy were living at Lillian's mother's. Mother and sister insisted that it was idiocy for Lillian to nurse the baby. They told her that since she was a demon, her milk would poison the baby. "Only animals do that! Your milk is weak. It's much easier to use a bottle. Only poor people nurse their babies."

Lil did not have any money to buy formula. Besides, she wanted to nurse him. Since mother and sister were so set against it, Joyce "came" and nourished Keith. She subsequently took over the entire care of all three babies for the first year of their lives. If a baby cried, she placed him, carefully wrapped, in the bathtub, closed the door, and let him cry until he finally fell asleep, a suggestion made by the doctor for whom Jessica had been working. Rather than being able to lovingly attend to Lillian's babies, Joyce merely tried to keep them from disturbing the adults in the house. Joyce was only around for one year following the birth of each baby. Then she disappeared, and others took over the baby's care.

It was Joyce who explained to me that several of the "others" were having sex with Jimmy.

Changing the subject, Joyce continued, "Jean, when James was born, Lil's mother and sister tried to take him away from her. I was afraid of what they might do to him. They said Lil was crazy and couldn't take care of him. But I could and did until he was a year old!"

Joyce had dinner with me, and later we talked about her hobby. I selected the painting with the verse "Let not the sun go down on your wrath." We went shopping, and while in the craft shop, we purchased additional painting and calligraphy supplies. Later that evening, Joyce left the body, and Lillian looked around, surprised to find herself at my house. The last she remembered, she was at home in New York.

Jean: "Lillian, I am delighted that Joyce came here, and I am happy to see you again. Just call and let Jimmy know you are safe, and stay as long as you like."

Jean as Narrator: The next day, Lillian and I talked about the part of her life that Joyce had taken over. She told me that Joyce was the name of another young mother in the childbirth classes she attended – that Joyce had her baby first, and when Lillian visited her and the new baby, Joyce was doing well, and the baby was contented. So a new personality was made up to care for Keith.

Lillian went on, "Jimmy didn't have a regular job. We had to move back from Florida to be with Mother. Doesn't everyone's mother help with the new baby?" Lillian asked.

"It's not unusual," I answered. "I went to my mother's house after my babies were born. She loved helping me with them."

Lillian: "Jimmy was selling kitchenware door to door, and one day, he came home unexpectedly and heard Jessica using another voice to yell at me. I had told him before we were married that she used a different voice with me, but he had never heard it before. He was shocked but soon forgot about it. We moved out as soon as he got a job. Besides, Letty's husband told Jimmy to keep me away from Letty. We moved three states away."

Jean as Narrator: Lillian related all of that to me in an even, unemotional voice, such that the significance of her sister and Jessica's trying to take the babies away from her escaped me.

Joyce was surprised when I disagreed with her theories regarding child-rearing. She was proud that she never said "shut up" to the boys, only "hush." No laughing was permitted in the house, and no voices dared be raised. No one was allowed to talk away from home about anything that happened at home. And Joyce went one better than what Lillian was taught as a child. Joyce never put anyone in the coal cellar, but if James would be noisy or bothersome, she put him in the closet, "But only till he got quiet and stopped crying. Everybody knows that after 2 years old, you shouldn't cry, but James did."

Joyce didn't know that choosing to have a baby so someone would love you was not right. She thought parents owned their children as property. So many new ideas came to Lillian through Joyce's memories, she wondered aloud to me, "How do I make it right? I didn't know before. I wish I didn't know now. I wish I didn't care."

Joyce told me, "I went out to show the neighbor kids how to play hide-and-seek, and I took a rope. I thought the way to play it was to tie up whoever was 'it,' and the rest of the kids would hide until 'it' got loose."

I said, "No, Joyce. I never heard of playing like that. The way we did it, the one who was 'it' put his or her head on their arm against the tree and counted aloud to 100 while the others ran and hid. At the count of 100, 'it' shouted, 'Ready or not, you shall get caught!' and started hunting. Nobody was ever tied!" I explained.

Another thing: One time, when Letty was visiting, she saw Lillian kiss her small sons and tell them, "I love you" when they were leaving for school. But Lillian stopped doing that when Letty told her that would make them sissies or maybe homosexuals when they grew up. I have seen Lillian's sons when they came home and were all grown up. There is not a sissy among them. Keith and Evan have girlfriends.

Lillian was overwhelmed by guilt as she received Joyce's thoughts and memories. It was hard for Lillian to believe that I meant it when I told her I didn't hold it against her because of her lack of knowledge. But she also readily admitted that she still sometimes felt like hurting James when he was unruly or even when he laughed in the house. Laughter, to Lillian, was indicative of someone being hurt or made fun of – usually her. She expressed feelings of wanting to hurt James, yet knew it would be wrong.

***

Jean as Narrator: The next day, my mail contained a letter from Robin Jean. "Jean, it's time for me to integrate. I sure am going to miss you. St. Patrick's Day is a good day for it – you know how I'm about green." Who but Robin could integrate on the "wearing of the green" day?

Lillian was pleased that Robin Jean was ready to integrate, but the feat was not yet accomplished. She was just waiting for St. Patrick's Day, and Joyce had taken over the body and run away to my house. As Joyce released her secrets, she relinquished control. Lillian and Robin Jean alternated in their conversations with me. I was so curious as to how integration happened, I asked Lillian what was left to be done. She said, "We just have to pick a time and do it."

I asked if I could be there to watch.

"Yes, I would like that," Lillian replied. "I feel very close to Robin Jean, and I know you two were good friends. Today is St. Patrick's Day."

I talked with Robin Jean some more. "I will miss you, Robin Jean. We have had some wonderful times together. I will never forget you. How do you feel right now?"

"My work is done. I came to take care of all of the good sexual feelings that Lillian had denied. I didn't ask for any sexual acts that were forced on her all those years, and I didn't cozy up to anybody for sex. She knows that now, and she is ready to be more loving in bed with Jimmy. When I am part of her, she will have sex feelings, and she won't feel guilty about them. She doesn't need me anymore, and I will always be there, just not separate."

Robin Jean, Lillian and I decided to have lunch together. We celebrated at Ponderosa. As we got out of the car to go into the restaurant, Lillian said, "When you and Robin Jean were talking in the car, I could hear her." Robin Jean chose ribeye steak, baked potato and an all-green salad. We laughed about this being her "last meal," but she said she had no sense of death or impending doom. During lunch, Lillian was exuberant. The conversation alternated between her and Robin Jean. Then Lillian said, "I can see her!"

Her hand reached across the table and covered mine. "I am going now, Jean, and Lillian can be the one to eat dessert. I love Jean. Bye!"

Lillian's voice was the same as always, the same as Robin Jean's, and Julie's, and Esther's and Lee's. "She's gone! That's the strangest feeling! I can't explain it, but it feels right."

I can't explain it either, but I know I never saw Robin Jean again. That afternoon, Lillian and I talked about Robin Jean's part in her life. "Jean, I know Robin Jean was pretty. That means I was pretty once. But I was cheated out of knowing that for all those years. She was still young. I am 20 years older and no longer pretty. Just look at me! Even when I was pretty, I was being told I was ugly. I can never go back. They took something important away from me." The tears slid down her face.

"Yes, they did take away your youthful years, but Lillian, at this moment, you are more beautiful to me than you can imagine. You now have Robin Jean's sense of beauty. You also have the maturity to know that real beauty radiates from the inside. I likewise was denied knowing I was a pretty child. It was important that I not 'let it go to my head.' I was taken completely by surprise once when I overheard a visiting adult comment, 'She's a very pretty girl!' as I left the room. I pretended I didn't hear it, but it made me feel very different about myself. My family never would have said such a thing to me!"

Once more, we shared pain that neither had permitted ourselves to express, and the pain of our shared experiences bound us even tighter.

I noticed that Lillian looked better. She moved faster. She was able to speak up for herself. She could cry, laugh and giggle. And she, Lillian, took more of the time at my house. She told me she was taller. She had more life in her eyes. I began to realize how empty she had been before. Each personality, each part of her life, as it was returned to her, improved her overall appearance and gave her a stronger image. My pride in her swelled.

***

Lillian's Journal: "Joyce gave us a curly permanent. I think it looks nice. Thanks, Joyce. Jimmy wanted to make it okay for Lee to have a head full of curls, so he asked Joyce to give him, Jimmy, a curly permanent. Then James asked Joyce to give him a permanent. She did, but I had to stay away until the house was aired out and all of the chemical odor from the permanents was gone."

Jean as Narrator: Lillian was highly allergic to such smells. Joyce was not. I have trouble picturing Joyce in the body, giving a permanent to Lillian while she was in the body receiving a permanent! Same body. Same hands. One was Lillian, only somehow, not Lillian. It seemed to me she gave herself

196

a permanent. But while she was Joyce, she wasn't allergic to the chemicals. She gave three permanents. I am trying to see how the giver and the receiver could, in this case, be separate.

Joyce made several more Scripture paintings and gave them to Rev. Chris' church for its bazaar.

Jackie wrote to thank me for the line stationery I sent.

Jackie Wrote: "Joyce is an angry person, but she don't know it yet. She wears glasses. I don't and neither does Lucy. Lil is going to see another psychiatrist next week. None of us would be there, but I think I'll watch and see how he operates.

"Do you pray, Jean, other than in church? Do you believe in it for you? Don't answer if my question is too personal. Love, Jackie."

Jean as Narrator: I really just wished I didn't have to sort out my beliefs about prayer and spiritual matters with her. I felt guilty admitting to Jackie that, in truth, I only seriously prayed whenever I got into trouble.

Before Rachel Ann finished her sampler, I received a letter from Lillian in which she seemed to change handwriting halfway through. During our next Friday night phone call, I told Lillian about it. "Do you think there is any possibility that there are two different Lillians? Sometimes you sign your letters 'Lillian' in your smooth handwriting and sometimes 'Lillian' in a different handwriting. The handwritings are very different."

"I don't know," she replied.

During the next visit to Virginia, while sitting together at the dining room table, someone reached up to the saltshaker that sat next to the pepper shaker and the sugar bowl on the table. A small voice asked, "What that?" pointing to the saltshaker.

"That's salt," I replied.

"How you know?"

Realizing now that it was 4-year-old Mary who didn't see the difference between salt and sugar, I shook a little salt onto my hand and offered it to her, saying, "Here, taste it."

But she shook her head and said, "You taste it."

Not wanting her to feel forced, I gave up trying to convince her.

I thought it might be important for her to be able to contact me during some possible future emergencies, so I gave her a fat pencil and lined paper, and we started. "Do you know the alphabet? Your ABCs?"

She made an upside-down A, and I coaxed her, "Now comes B."

"How you make that funny one?"

I had to think a minute. Then it came to me. It was LMNOP. And I realized that she probably knew how to sing the alphabet song but didn't know how to write it. So I started singing it, and Mary joined right in. My dining room, kitchen, hall and living room could be a passageway leading back to the dining room. Mary and I got up and started skipping around that circle and singing. But on the second pass through, the telephone rang when we were in the hall. Doggone it! I didn't want to interrupt what I was doing.

"Mary, please wait for me. I want to play with you some more," I said.

Cutting the phone conversation short, I went through the living room, and I could see Mary hiding under the dining room table. After all, she was a 200-pound woman who saw herself as a little girl. She believed that I couldn't see her if she couldn't see me.

Playing Mary's game, I walked right past her, calling, "Mary, Mary, where are you, Mary?" and passed into the kitchen. I opened the washing machine door, saying, "No, Mary is not in the washing machine."

Opening the refrigerator door, I said, "Mary is not in the refrigerator. I wonder where she could be."

Walking around the other side of the table, I could see her scrambling under the table to that side. As I passed near her, Mary pointed to the studio door, which was closed. She said, "Look in there."

But before I could open that door, I spied her watching. Stooping down to her level, I laughed and said, "Mary, you little rascal! I found you."

She crawled out, laughing and so close to the floor, I couldn't resist playing with her. As she lay on the floor, giggling, I tickled her, and we both had a good laugh. I played with her like I would with any 4-year-old.

Then Mary said, "I go now," and Lillian was there, lying on the floor, noting that she was hot.

"What happened?" Her hair was messed up. Her clothes were disheveled, and why was she on the floor? When I explained it, all she said was, "Oh."

I assured her that Mary was fine, and that Mary and I had been playing.

***

Jean as Narrator: The next time I saw Mary, Lizabeth and I were in a store, shopping for embroidery thread. Before checking out, I asked, "Is there anything anyone wants to see?"

Taking my hand, a tiny voice asked if we could look at ribbons. Recognizing Mary, I took her to the ribbon counter. "What kind of ribbon, big ones or little ones?"

"Little," she said.

"What color, Mary?"

"Blue."

We looked at a narrow blue ribbon. My hand was turned loose, "someone" took over, and Mary never even saw me buy a yard of narrow blue ribbon.

***

Jean as Narrator: One of my friends told me she was greatly concerned because her child's kindergarten teacher reported that little Wendy cried a lot, sometimes in class and often during recess. The mother and teacher patiently and repeatedly asked Wendy what was making her cry, but Wendy herself either didn't know or was unable to articulate the reason for her tears.

Wendy's father had been killed in a motorcycle accident when Wendy was a baby; too young to remember him. Perhaps hearing other children talk about their daddies and seeing so many loving fathers and their children touched something deep inside of her.

Mary was struggling with the death of her father too. When Mary was 7 months old, her father had been killed in a shop accident. While Mary couldn't remember her father either, her pain was different.

I recalled an earlier conversation with Mary when she had said, "I think I make my daddy die."

Shocked, I had asked, "Why do you think that, Mary?"

"She says so. She says I cry at night an' he tired an' got dead."

"Who, Mary? Who told you that?"

"She did. That mother. She cry, cry loud an' say, 'I not want baby, jus' want husband!'"

Pausing for a moment, Mary then continued, "She not like me."

"Oh, Mary, sweet little Mary," I said. Gathering her in my arms, I said, "No, no, you did not make your daddy die. He was working 'way up high in the building, and a great big crane came along and didn't see him. It knocked him down, and he died."

"You sure?" Mary's eyes searched mine for the truth.

"Yes, Mary, I am sure." Her father was Walter's brother, and I had heard about this from his family.

While explaining to Lillian why she lost time, I demonstrated Mary's style of printing on a sheet of yellow lined paper. At that moment, Mary took "Prints" for her last name.

Wendy's mother and I agreed to bring the two little girls together. It was nearing Halloween, so Lucy sketched two copies of some ghosts, bats and pumpkins, along with a few tombstones for them to color. I had heard that it is often easier to talk about deep thoughts and feelings when hands and eyes are otherwise busily occupied.

At the appointed time, Mary opened our front door and said, "Are you Wendy?"

Taking Wendy's hand, Mary led her to where I had laid out the pictures and a box of crayons on the floor.

The two girls sprawled on the floor on their stomachs. I noticed Mary looking around when she took up more space than she expected. Nothing was said about that. Wendy's mother and I sat nearby, nervously hoping and silently praying that we were doing the right thing as they colored away.

I said, "Wendy, Mary's daddy died when she was a baby, just like yours did."

Mary asked Wendy, "You cry 'cause you miss him?"

Never raising her eyes from her coloring, Wendy nodded. "Yes, but I don't remember him."

Then, breaking a long silence, I ventured, "Wendy, your mommy has a picture of your daddy. Would you like her to get another picture, just for you to have?"

Mary said, "Jean say I not make him 'daid.' Jean knows."

"I am afraid I can't find him when I get to heaven. So many people there," Wendy said.

Mary sat up, looked straight at Wendy, and said, "Your daddy will find you."

The two little girls healed each other.

I saw Mary one more time. It was Christmas, and Lillian came to be with us in Virginia while Jimmy, Evan and James went to Ohio to be with Keith at Grandma and Pap's. I knew 11 personalities who were active at the time. I bought 11 simple but thoughtful gifts, wrapped each separately, put each one's name on a gift and put the gifts under the tree. When she (they) arrived, I pointed out that each had a present under the tree. They could open their gifts whenever they wanted to.

The next day, Mary spied her name on a package. "For me?"

Taking my hand, she led me to the Christmas tree, and we sat down on the floor. She reached for and retrieved her package. She couldn't believe she had a Christmas present – the blue ribbon she saw in the store. She was so happy. Then making like a pair of scissors with her fingers, she asked me to "Make two."

I got the scissors and cut the ribbon in half. Then tying one into a small bow, I put a bobby pin in it and put it in Mary's hair. She was so happy!

Watching me while I tied a bow in the other half to put it in her hair, she shook her head. "Put in Jean's hair." So I did, and she was gone. Lillian wondered why she was sitting on the floor!

Chapter 21
Integration: Could It Be This Easy?

Chapter 21 ushers in a period of fast-paced integration, with several personalities integrating at nearly the same time, and in doing so, provides the reader with a glimpse into the process of integration itself.

It is not typical for integration to go smoothly.

In fact, integration can be a period of great instability to the sufferer as well as a period of great uncertainty for the therapist.

Who is ready to integrate? Will it be less dangerous if certain parts remain compartmentalized?

Is the emergence of a "new" personality an artifact of the integration process itself or a desperate attempt to hold on to the familiarity of a personality structure that is rapidly becoming obsolete?

Are there new personalities who have not yet surfaced because Lillian is not yet healthy enough to receive their memories?

Are there personalities who experience integration as the loss of a trusted friend?

Then, there are those integrations that seem almost too easy, as if it is as simple as a personality calmly deciding to integrate, then scheduling a date and time for the integration to take place.

To the trained eye of a psychotherapist, these "almost too easy" integrations do not seem authentic.

In the nomenclature of psychotherapy, they represent a "flight into health."

The medical dictionary defines "flight into health" as "... the early but only temporary disappearance of symptoms ... a defense against anxiety engendered by the prospect of further psychoanalytic exploration of the patient's conflicts."

This psychological phenomenon occurs unconsciously, serving to protect the patient from knowing the deepest of the traumas. Even the patients consciously believe they are nearing the end of treatment.

In reality, "flight into health" suggests the presence of additional unrevealed traumas.

Faced with these possibilities, therapists often find themselves beset with uncertainty.

Not so with Jean.

Jean does what Jean had always done. She continues to accept unconditionally, continues to remain curious, continues to welcome each new part, no matter how frightening that personality might be.

Often, it is the last of the personalities to integrate who are the ones who have been most traumatized. With them comes the deepest fear, unrelenting rage, intense despair and the greatest risk of suicide.

Many multiple personality disorder patients report integration fears.

Does Lillian becoming "one" mean that there will be no more Esther to take over when a strong and decisive self is needed?

Will an integrated Lillian have Esther's determination and conviction?

What about Amy, Lucy, Rachel Ann, Sarah Ann, Celeste, Pat, Lizabeth, Robin Jean, Terri Beth, Jackie, Buddy and the others?

What painful memories do they still hold? What will the pain of reliving their traumas bring?

FA

Jean as Narrator: As Rachel Ann neared integration, she wanted to make something for people to keep and remember her by. I suggested putting her family on a sampler. She said, "I don't have a family."

"Yes, Rachel, you do have a very special family," I explained. "You have Lucy and Julie, Lee, Sarah Ann and all of the others. A sampler like that would be most useful, and you certainly would be remembered by such a sampler."

The design of the sampler was Rachel Ann's. She was excited about it and brought it to me to see her progress on her next visit.

She made a sampler for Dr. Robinson, one for Jimmy and another one for me. I cherish mine to this day. (Thank you, Rachel Ann. You taught me patience.)

With that, Rachel Ann said she was ready to leave and thought she had to stay until the sampler was done. But some of the others told her that they would finish it for her, and Rachel Ann Robinson was no more.

Julie: "Jean, it's really going to happen. When Lillian wakes up tomorrow, I will be gone but not far and will always be close. I love you always. Julie Zannoni."

Jean as Narrator: A few weeks later came two letters – one from Lillian, one from Esther. I was reminded of Julie's perfect typing as I read Lillian's page-long, perfectly typed letter. She said she wished she could be more like Esther. Lillian wrote that she would like Esther's qualities – confidence and the ability to make decisions. Lillian was convinced that she could never be like Esther. Dr. Robinson asked her if she was ready for Esther to integrate. Expressing uncertainty, Lillian said she was unsure.

As I read Lillian's letter, I tried to picture this – Lillian, in Lillian's body, is in the doctor's office, but sometimes her body is occupied by Esther. One asks a question, and the same body answers it – sort of like talking to herself (her selves).

Lillian was not the only one who was unsure. Jimmy discussed the possibility of Esther's integration and was against it. Esther had been the one he could count on to tell him like it is.

Lillian Wrote: "I feel scared. This isn't like Julie's integration. I cried – well, I feel like crying now, but not for the same reason. Esther has always been there. This is scary. What if I lose Esther? What if something comes up? What if I need her? I hope this is right! Esther wrote in my journal, 'This will be great! – you, Julie and me.'

"Aunt Jean, I was in Dr. Robinson's waiting room, just before James came out of his therapy with Dr. Alabiso. I felt okay just knowing that Esther wasn't separate. I really felt self-assured. I know that I won't be able to go away and have Esther be there. What if I need her?! Esther is so strong. Can I be like that? Will I be, someday? If she is strong, why don't I feel brave now? I am frightened. Even Jimmy doesn't think that I can make it without her. It was easier to let her talk and make decisions. Now I have to be in on it too.

"Oh, Aunt Jean, I am scared. This doesn't sound like Esther at all. I can just hear Dr. Robinson or Rev. Chris or you say, 'Give it time.' I hate the word 'patience.' This will be all right – won't it? Lillian."

Jean as Narrator: The other letter, on yellow stationery, was from Esther herself (herself?).

Esther Wrote: "Jean – unexpected good news. Lillian and I will be integrated in a little while, even before you get this letter. I think this will be great! You are superb. (I am not going too far.) I am not much at letters, but next time we meet, I will be part of Lil. Thank you. Esther Winslow."

Celeste Wrote: "To my Jean, the day has come for me to say au revoir. You say, 'What it means?' It means I hope you miss me and remember Celeste with affection. You are a beautiful lady. I am happy, Jean. I wish you also much happiness! I do not have words to know how to say all my feelings. I cannot say to you in person on the telephone. I have no words of enough love to express to you. I hope for you to think of Celeste some time. Goodbye, Jean. So much goodness and graciousness inside! I am happy to know you. Celeste."

From the desk of CELESTE   AUGUST 28, 1981

TO MY JEAN

TODAY HAVE COME FOR ME TO SAY au revoir – like you SAY WHAT IT MEANS? IT, MEAN I AM HOPE YOU TO MISS ME AND REMEMBER Celeste WITH AFFECTION. YOU ARE SO – LIKE ANY SAY BEAUTIFUL LADY. I AM HAPPY, MY JEAN. I WISH YOU ALSO MUCH HAPPINESS!

I DO NOT HAVE WORDS TO KNOW HOW TO SAY ALL MY FEELINGS. I CAN NOT SAY TO YOU IN PERSON ON TELEPHONE. I HAVE NOT WORDS OF ENOUGH LOVE TO EXPRESS TO YOU. I HOPE FOR YOU TO THINK OF Celeste some Time.

GOODBYE MY JEAN SO MUCH GOODNESS AND GRACIOUSNESS INSIDE! I AM HAPPY TO KNOW YOU.

Celeste

Lee's Journal: "Hey, Lillian. This is Lee. So now I don't take up no more of your time. I wrote to Doc, Rev. Chris, and Jean, Jim, James and Evan. How about all that writing? Man, I am glad life is over for me being responsible. I am going to clear out. Don't expect much. No pot. No pills. No fake anything.

No guns. I am going out clean and square. Thanks, Jean. Hey, the sex thing turned out to be no big deal, thanks to Doc. Hang with it. Ciao. Lee."

Buddy Wrote: "8/11/15. This is Buddy. Me and Mary are leaving and we won't be separate from Lillian any more. I wrote to Chris. I told him he can have my pipe. It didn't cost nothing and besides, I never used it. I wrote to Col. Bussy good bye. Well, goodbye forever. Buddy."

Jean as Narrator: And so it went; one personality at a time. All of those whom I had come to care about seemed to vanish.

What would become of those who had not yet integrated?

Was it too easy?

Chapter 22
Amy's Sweet Goodbye

Bye I make will to James. have my stuf Amy Oct 28 1981

While each integration is unique, some are more memorable than others.

This is the case with Amy's integration. Present from 1978 until 1981, Amy is the personality most loved by all the others, including Lillian.

From Amy's integration, the reader comes to understand that the integration of a young-child personality is qualitatively different from that of older ego states.

While the personality characteristics of the "others" will likely be reflected in Lillian after integration, it is improbable that Amy's characteristics will be manifested in an adult, integrated Lillian.

We are not likely to see Amy's playfulness, innocence, naivete, excitement about Christmas and interests reflected in an integrated Lillian.

In this sense, young-child personality parts are more "gone" than the others.

For this reason, Amy's integration has been given its own chapter.

FA

Jean as Narrator: When I answered the phone, Lillian was first to speak. "Aunt Jean, Amy almost changed her mind about integrating when she saw

James crying. It was nip and tuck for a while, but she is gone now. She wanted to talk to you for the very last thing she did. I feel like crying. I wonder why."

I felt like crying too, and as soon as I hung up the phone, the tears came. Amy had been such a special child, and I had come to love her more than I could have believed possible. After all, she wasn't even real. Or was she? Oh, yes, Amy was real.

I reflected on our time together. When I first tried to establish communication with Amy, she could neither read nor write, as Julie wrote in her poem "Six of One." She printed her name from right to left, but she trusted me enough to believe I wouldn't force her to use her right hand. However, once she had permission to write left-handed, she made some letters with her left hand and some with her right hand, but all were eventually correct.

Amy was created when Lillian was very young. The memories, the secrets she held, centered around being bad, being hit, having her hands tied and burned, and being dirty. Thinking she would like a doll, she was given a small doll in a box. Amy said, "Closets are where you put babies."

When I sent her a small tube of hand lotion that first Christmas, along with Big Bird, she questioned me over and over as to who was going to burn her hands.

Persuading her that neither Dr. Robinson nor I would punish her was not too difficult, but she never gave up her idea. She thought I was being good to her for giving her the lotion and that the lotion proved to her that I knew someone was going to burn her.

I gave Amy a newborn baby doll in 1980. She thought it was very pretty and immediately snatched its bottle, hid the doll under a chair, pulled the ribbon from its hair and threw it in the wastebasket, "Now what we goin' do to it? Cut? Tie? Burn?"

I was horrified, and I frankly had no idea what to do. Taking the baby in my arms, I said all the sweet things I could think of to her. Then, cradling baby, I began to sing to her. Amy looked on, completely confused – "No. No. That not what you s'posed to do with babies!"

"That's what I do with babies, and that's what I did with mine," I said firmly. "That's the way babies should be treated." But Amy could not comprehend. Knowing I was in deep water and in over my head again, I simply said, "She is a box baby. This is her bed." I put the box lid under the box.

I couldn't figure out what might need to be done to get Amy to integrate. We colored, read, played the organ, wrote letters and enjoyed one another's company. One incident was hilarious to me.

Amy and I were on the floor, coloring. Lillian, or whoever dressed that morning, had put on a low-cut blouse that kept flopping out when Amy leaned forward. I said, "What's in there?" We both peaked down her blouse. "Boobs. Not mine. Lil's," Amy said. I started laughing. Amy laughed too, but I'm not sure she knew why that was funny.

One day I had Amy stand beside me in front of a full-length mirror in my mother's room. Pointing out that she was almost as tall as I and no longer a little girl, she studied our reflection for a minute and said, "But we are bigger across than you. That's 'cause there's so many of us in there!"

I used Amy's trust in me to find out if there were more personalities. She looked at me and grinned, "Do you think there is more?"

I have a fond memory of Amy sitting beside me in church. When Rev. Chris invited children to the front of the church for the children's service, Amy asked me, "Can I go?" I nodded yes. Rev. Chris was happy and said, "Come on, Amy." Like any other 6-year-old, Amy half walked, half ran to the front of the church to join the other children. When she came back, she, as Lillian, sighed and sat down beside me, wondering what had just happened. I told her. She sighed a special sigh.

At that moment, I knew that Amy would be a forever-remembered child.

Amy had been "out" for three years when Lillian finally asked the doctor why she was still there. Upon questioning, Dr. Robinson learned that Amy was still waiting for someone to burn her hands. She still had the tube of hand lotion I had given her nearly two years before. When Dr. Robinson convinced her that no one would ever burn her or Lillian's hands again, Amy's mission was ended. She was integrated the next day, but before she left, Lillian called to say Amy wanted to talk to me. "I can see her, Aunt Jean. She is ready to be integrated."

"Jean, Jean, it's me, Amy. Dr. Robinson say I can go now. Don't be mad. James cry when I tell him. I will be Lil's shadow just like you and me played. I love you, Jean."

"Oh, Amy, I am so proud of you, and I am so happy today for Lillian. I will always remember my Amy. You are beautiful! Bye, sweetheart!"

Lillian Wrote: "Aunt Jean, I have accepted that there is no more Amy. She got what was enough for her."

Chapter 23
Anger

Whereas, in the past, amnesia and dissociation served the function of counterbalancing the impulse to act out on negative emotions, a newly integrated personality is more likely to be disinhibited.

Often, the first and strongest emotion of a newly integrated individual is anger.

No longer the self-doubting, self-deprecating Lillian of previous chapters, Lillian's anger surfaces full force and head on.

Lillian's personality becomes that of an anger state, a state lacking the self-discipline of Esther, the outgoing good-naturedness of Lucy or the sweet innocence of Amy.

It is as if Lillian feels all of her anger all at once – anger at Jessica and Herbert, at God, at the church, at evil, at Rev. Chris, at Dr. Robinson, at Jimmy and even at Aunt Jean.

During this rage state, the impulse to act out is not easily constrained.

Calling on dissociation itself as a tool for managing Lillian's rage, Dr. Robinson uses clinical hypnosis to compartmentalize Rose's fury. However, rage contained is not rage resolved.

FA

Lillian Wrote: "I woke up crying in the hospital again. I had a dream about when I was in restraints that time I was in the hospital in Niagara Falls. Rose has been out, and she is violent. No one had heard from her since it took five hospital staff and a hypodermic needle to subdue her. Now Rose is back. The hospital aide told me Dr. Robinson anticipated me, saying I was there when it was really Rose. So I was to be kept in restraints on doctor's orders. I asked the aide to please check because Dr. Robinson wouldn't have me tied for Rose. I know he wouldn't, but he did. I couldn't stop crying. If Dr. Robinson lets

Rose come back, I am going to leave. I can't stay here in this area where anyone can hurt me to get even with Rose. No way! I will go!

"I talked with Dr. Robinson about the dream, and he had been with me for two hours that day in the hospital. Rose had been there – or came back and tried to leave. Dr. Robinson grabbed her to keep her from leaving, and he said it took five or six people to hold her down. He said she was biting, scratching, hitting, kicking and yelling obscenities. They gave her a shot, and she still fought. I can't relate that to me at all. If I didn't know Dr. Robinson, I would think he was making it up. He told me he did not change the orders that day. I thought he decided he would have me in restraints to hurt me because he couldn't hurt Rose. He said, 'No!'"

***

Lillian Wrote: "The next week after I was discharged, Dr. Robinson and I talked about Rose being so violent. But Dr. Robinson had a plan. He showed me an empty pill bottle. The doctor hypnotized me, called Rose out, ordered her into the bottle, put the cap on it, and set it on his desk. Then he asked Jackie to 'look around in Lillian's head to see if Rose was gone.' She was. At later appointments, there sat the bottle on his desk with Rose in it."

***

Lillian Wrote: "I am in Virginia at Aunt Jean's. It's Thursday. So much has happened. Jimmy took Monday off work. The whole day was wrong for him. We were at a mall. He asked me to go to a show. I didn't want to. On the way home, the car began smoking. So now we had two cars, neither of which were working. The lawnmower broke. He turned the furnace on to check it, and it wasn't working right. He got a bottle of vodka. I refused to drink any. So he drank and drank. The next thing I was aware of was trying to figure out what hit me! Jim! He made a mockery of me; said things that I need to try to forget, and he hit me. He said, 'She hit me first,' as if that justified him hitting me. I am so thankful that I have Jackie. Whenever I don't know what just happened, I can ask her, and she will tell me. Lucy wrote a letter to the doctor and wrote on the outside, 'For Dr. Robinson – No One Else.' Yet, Jimmy opened it and then still didn't give it to the doctor. When she found out that

Jim opened her letter, she hit him. He was drunk from the vodka. Jimmy wanted to hurt Lucy. He did. He hit her, but it was me that he hit. He said so many awful things. He hurt me, inside and out."

***

Lillian Wrote: "Jim called. He acts like all is okay, so why am I crying? Aunt Jean says Rev. Chris has time for me after services Sunday. I really don't want to talk to him. I don't want to talk about Jim to anyone. I don't want to talk about Lucy either."

Jackie Wrote: "We are at Jean's. I told her about it all being my fault because I knew it was Lucy who got angry. I'm scared Jim will hurt Lil again and maybe Rev. Chris will now too because I wrote him, and he is big like Jimmy. I never thought Jim would hit Lillian. So how do I know that Rev. Chris won't do the same? Why do all men have to be like that?!"

Lillian Wrote: "Jimmy called. He went with James to see Dr. Alabiso. Dr. Alabiso said Rose can't come back until Jim gets his head straightened out some. It seems like Jimmy wants some help. Ribs hurt, neck hurts, face hurts from Jimmy."

Jackie Wrote: "I talked to Rev. Chris today. He said my last letter scared him! I just wanted to say goodbye to someone! If Rev. Chris didn't get mad at me last summer, he must not ever get angry enough to hit anyone like Jim did to Lil. It's scary to go back there to Jim and Lil's home."

Lucy Wrote: "I was thinking about killing myself. Then I told Rev. Chris what I done wrong, and he said it wasn't bad enough to kill myself over."

Lillian Wrote: "Jimmy called. I told him I still hurt from the bruised places in my ribs. It hurt so bad. I don't know how to get past it. I trusted Jim completely, and he made a mockery of me on purpose. Life sure isn't much fun. Aunt Jean took me to Rev. Chris' office today, and I stayed from 2:30 until 4:30! And poor Aunt Jean stayed in her car all that time! I told Rev. Chris a lot more than I intended to! Found myself saying things I didn't mean to say, like, I'm scared Jim will do this again, and if he does, I will have to leave him. I don't want to leave, but I can't let him hit me or hurt me on purpose and do nothing. I am scared. I am not like Lucy. I won't fight back, ever. Jim thinks he was justified because Lucy hit him first. She just hit him and left, so the one standing there to get hit was me! Is it okay for him to hit me because Lucy hit him? He hurt me. I wanted Jimmy to be stronger than that. He has things all out of whack."

Jean as Narrator: Jimmy sometimes called just to talk. When I asked him how he could stand all the unhappiness at home, he said that when things get too bad, he gets a six-pack, drives to a lonely rest stop and drinks it all. He said that was the only way he could get to the tears.

In reviewing Lillian's journals, I came across this:

"Aunt Jean took me to Rev. Chris' today. Rev. Chris talked with me. He is really good at counseling. He said, 'Don't be a co-alcoholic and try to fix things up for Jimmy.' Rev. Chris said this isn't the first time in my life when someone hurt me, and I could express my anger and could feel like hurting back."

Lucy Wrote: "Lil, Dr. Robinson says I owe you an apology. I left you, and Jim hit you, and I started it all by hitting him first. I am not sorry for hitting him. He was wrong to open up the letter I wrote to Dr. Robinson! I am sorry you got hurt. P.S. Maybe I should tell Jim he didn't hurt any of us, just you."

***

Lillian Wrote: "Saw Dr. Robinson Friday. He sees Jimmy next Friday. Jim says he doesn't remember hitting me more than once. Seems like he spent all day Friday swearing at everything but not at me. If I (or someone else) makes Jimmy angry, will he drink and then get even with me? Jim came in this morning, saying something about him giving me permission to hit him so many times. I couldn't believe that he was serious! If he feels he needs to be punished, let him do it.

"James is home. He is eating us bare. He's been busy painting a green St. Patrick's Day hat black so he can use it as Dracula for Halloween. James put a Halloween ghost and pumpkin in the window.

"Jimmy and I have been doing a lot of talking. I am finding out I feel so much anger. Jimmy shut me out when he quit going to church, and now I find I am angry at him for not letting me know what was happening in his life. Today, I wrote Rev. Chris. I feel like I have so much anger in me against religion, God, the church, demon beliefs, sect churches with their rules, me taking the blame for things I didn't do, and me having to stand up in front of the church and ask for the church's forgiveness. I feel like I have so much anger and hate. I want to go back and hurt each individual separately – twist the knife. I wrote Rev. Chris, 'Please help me with this. Give me a starting place. I didn't know anger was there. I don't want this. What do I do?'"

Lucy Wrote: "Lillian is so angry about religion."

Lillian Wrote: "I am trying to memorize the 91st Psalm. Can't allow myself to think about church. Where is God? I'm so angry at so many things – God, religion. My throat aches from the weight of it. God, where were you? What kind of seminary teaches reverends to tell children they were destined to be bad before they were born. They can't change it! I believed God expected me to be used. I wasn't any good. I didn't want to be thought of as a demon. It was God's people who told me I was possessed, and when they sang, they sounded like they were happy. I was so evil!

"I was a child! Is no one ever innocent? When does the dirt start to collect on a baby to make it dirty? Who picks out the kid who is the sinner? Who gave the church people the power to judge? Who taught the church to kick you when you are down? Seminary school? The Bible? God?

"Now we are at Aunt Jean's. I drove down last night and got here at 2 a.m., and we talked for about an hour before going to bed.

"Jackie and I went to see Rev. Chris. I saw him for half an hour. He told me to go home to Aunt Jean's and write how I feel about him and his church. So I did. He said to read the Psalms. I haven't. Talked about anger but only a little."

Joyce Wrote: "Lil came home and started reading Psalms and tore them out of the Bible! I didn't think Lillian would ever do that! She was reading the Psalms that 'God heals,' and she wrote in big letters, 'NOT TRUE!' The Psalms said that He will deliver us from evil. But He didn't! Then she wrote, 'Maybe I am the wicked one.'"

Lillian Wrote: "Dr. Robinson, I am at Aunt Jean's. During our appointment with Rev. Chris today, he asked me to write a letter to him about the church. I came back to Aunt Jean's and wrote the letter he asked for. Then on Thursday, I started reading Psalms and got angry. I tore the Book of Psalms out of the Bible. I told Aunt Jean I was going home, and I went to get gas. Anyway, the next minute I was in Rev. Chris' office, and by my watch, it was a half-hour earlier! I had changed clothes. Rev. Chris had my Bible and what I had written, and I got it figured out that it was Friday, and I hadn't gained time at all. I had lost 23-1/2 hours! Rev. Chris showed me he had my Bible, torn pages and all! He also had a note I had thrown in the wastebasket. Then he asked me about the so-called Rev. Kane. Rev. Chris said he knew about Rev. Kane. He asked if when Rev. Kane did the things he did to me, did I think God violated me. He sure didn't mince words! I got up to leave a few times. I told Rev. Chris I hated God! I told Rev. Chris I hated Rev. Kane. I lost a day. Rev. Chris helped me a lot. I felt that I did not need Lil anymore."

Jean as Narrator: Lil visited me after Lillian returned from talking with Rev. Chris. Then Lillian told me she could see Lil and know what Lil was thinking. Lil told me that Lillian does not need her anymore, and she is ready to be integrated.

I told Lillian that if Lil was going to leave, I would like a note from her. I didn't have anything in her handwriting except her signature on a ceramic dish she made for me.

Lil spoke up, "Do you have something I can write on?"

Sensing the urgency of the moment, I grabbed the nearest paper and handed it to her.

Lil Wrote: "Dear Jean, Lillian is going to be okay. She will follow things through now without me. Thanks for your love. Lil."

Lillian Wrote: "I talked to Rev. Chris again today. I told him I felt hate, really deep hate, for the first time when he worked with me last Friday. I have said the words before, 'I hate Mother,' but never before felt the depth of feeling I got last Friday. Isn't it ironic that the first time I was able to get in touch with the hate I felt, my hatred was directed at God because Chris is a reverend?"

***

Lillian Wrote: "Dr. Robinson, I just spent a session with Rev. Chris again. I told him I was angry with him because it was his fault I got so angry the other day. Dr. Robinson, when I said to Rev. Chris that I hated God, I meant **I hated God**! I never before remember feeling hate like that. I have said I hated different people, but this was really deep hate, like when I realized I was angry at Aunt Jean that time. I was really angry at her for telling me to 'Go home and tell your mother.' It was the same with this feeling of hating God. I didn't realize feelings could reach that sort of intensity. I guess that's the first real deep feeling of hate I have ever had.

"Anyway, when I saw Rev. Chris today, somehow, I ended up saying I was mad at him for actually pushing me to get angry. I didn't want Rev. Chris to

216

make me angry. Then he pushed me again by telling me that the Bible had not been proven to be 'God-inspired.' I told Rev. Chris I hated him. He was supposed to be a friend, and he didn't help me in the way I thought he would, and I told him so. Then he hit me (verbally) with being a reverend like Rev. Kane, and I was really angry at him. I don't want a God who allows evil to happen. I don't want a God who lets a man like Rev. Kane become a reverend. I know now that when things are rough, the only one I can rely on is me, not God! Rev. Chris says now that I have really felt hate, Rose will be coming back soon."

***

Lillian Wrote: "Aunt Jean reached her limit with me today and let me know it. And I didn't come through for her. I told her I didn't trust her or Rev. Chris or Dr. Robinson. Nobody! She says it's about time I did, and she said she was 'upset' that I can't. But when Aunt Jean admits to being 'upset,' that means she is angry, really angry! I'm not coming through for anyone, am I? Does anyone completely trust another person, ever? I don't know. Found myself not being able to talk. What if I ever said I hated Aunt Jean? I'd never be able to forgive myself. I'd rather never speak again. My emotions are out of whack. Aunt Jean is like Jim. They think, 'Oh, Lillian doesn't have any feelings except good ones.' Sorry, I'm not like that now. Well, it's 3 a.m. I lost a whole day. It was 9 p.m. when I became me. I was hating God, hating Rev. Chris, even angry at Aunt Jean."

***

Jackie Wrote: "Lil is not the only one who is angry. I have found a way out. I wrote a couple of places and got an answer today. I can go to Florida or California by driving someone's car there who can't drive for themselves. I can make enough money to stay in another state as Jackie! I was going to say goodbye to Dr. Robinson next week, but now we won't have an appointment, so I will be leaving before I see him. I called Rev. Chris. He said to call him when I get wherever I am going. I guess I will, but I sure ain't coming back! I am going as me!"

217

Jean as Narrator: Lillian called and asked me to talk to Jackie. I asked a lot of questions, trying to convince Jackie to change her mind. What will James do for a mother? The ad said you'd be driving an elderly lady. Did you find out if the lady is crippled? Maybe you have to get her in and out of a wheelchair. What would you do for friends? I will miss you. How will you get a driver's license in another state? Do you even have an ID?

Lillian Wrote: "We went to Ohio for Thanksgiving and spent Saturday at Letty's house. James played with Letty's children all day. Keith came over too. He says he is getting married before Christmas. Letty told me Aunt Pearl died from starvation. She took her insulin as usual but didn't eat for two weeks. Letty says her mother has been 'out of it' for a long time and believes Jehovah's Witnesses are after her.

"James' appointment with Dr. Alabiso was today. He has a meeting with Gateway in two weeks. Dr. Alabiso said, 'Since you have decided to wait till after the holidays for Rose to come back, I can't recommend that James come home until after Rose is integrated.' That means resolving her anger."

***

Lillian Wrote: "I remembered today that the day I started menstruating, he met me in the hallway and said, 'I am glad you are a woman now.' I was embarrassed. I hate him. Dr. Robinson says we have enough other areas to work on; we are not going to have Rose come back until later."

***

Jean as Narrator: I received a card of farewell from Jackie. On its outside was printed, "Sowing seeds of kindness reaps a rich harvest of happiness." Inside was written, "Jean, I have decided to write a few just-in-case letters. If Lil changes her mind and says yes to integration, I'm not going to stay around and write. Not being at all would be easier for me than knowing I am giving control over to Lil. I prefer to believe we will share, and I will always be. Integration is not for me."

Lillian Wrote: "I feel awfully alone without Jackie. Guess I relied on her too much. I get panicky when I become me and can't ask Jackie who is there. Somehow, though, I don't feel like she is really gone. I went to church with

218

James at Gateway. I am so confused. Why would I go to church? I hate God. It is awful to be afraid of doing things and going places by myself. Maybe, Jackie being part of me will help that. Only, I don't feel she is part of me. Severe headaches again, after a long time without them. James called this evening. He said he broke another window; one in his bedroom. James said the other kids were calling him names; swear words, and he went up to his room and pounded on the window. He has cuts and scratches on his hand and up his arm. The nurse will keep an eye on it every day to watch for glass splinters. I told James he is going to get something for Christmas that he doesn't know he wants, but when he sees it, it will be just what he wanted. He tried, but he couldn't guess it. I wrapped fudge tonight and put ribbons on the packages. Jackie said that Joyce made the fudge.

"Doctor's appointment today. I had told him Jackie was still around – no integration. He said I was trying to please other people. Jackie, Anne, Joyce, Lucy, Rose and me – that's all who are left. I am getting well. Keith called from Pap's and said he and his fiancée couldn't get here for Christmas. James cried, and Jim said, 'Let's go down to Pap and Grandma's.' So we did. Gateway let James be with us for Christmas, but only if Jimmy was there at all times. Letty, Jim and I talked quite a bit today. Letty said her son told her that James said I told him he should hate Rosalind and Jessica. I didn't! What I told him was that I never wanted him to ever live with them if Jim and I were to die. Letty said that Keith, Evan and James will maybe hate me someday for the way I treated them. I tried to tell her that my sons have already expressed their feelings to me of how they resented me, and they are talking about their feelings and not holding them in. Letty said I was the reason Evan was into drugs. I guess I knew that. But Evan got help. James is getting help. They are learning to express their feelings."

Jean as Narrator: When Lillian told me the above, I thought it probably meant that Letty did, in fact, know something of the abuse heaped upon Lillian. Was Letty herself abused?

Lillian's Journal: "Jimmy took James back to Gateway on his way to work today. I'm alone except for Jackie, Joyce, Lucy and Anne."

Lizabeth Wrote: "My lovely, caring Jean, goodbye letters are so awful, aren't they? So, I'm not leaving. I am joining forces with Lillian. I still feel like I am going to die, but it don't scare me, so it has to be right. I wonder if

Lillian will be right-handed. It's four minutes till 1981. Happy New Year. Thanks and love. Lizabeth."

Chapter 24
Rose's Secret

It is common for individuals with multiple personality disorder to regress before facing the worst of their traumatic memories and the rage that follows.

Lillian's self-loathing returns. Like an omen, it is a predictor of what is to come.

In the face of Rose's return, Lillian reverts to feelings of the past – "I am dirty. I wish I could bleed to death to become pure and clean."

Rose's trauma explains why Lillian is angry at God for not preventing the "sacrifice of babies."

Weeks of rage marked by suicide attempts and assaults on hospital staff continue before co-consciousness leads to integration.

Is Rose's trauma the link connecting Rachel Ann's fear of dogs, Amy's rejection of baby dolls, Lillian's anger toward a god that allows children to die and Jackie's determination to have a baby?

FA

Jean as Narrator: Lillian took James to see Dr. Alabiso. The psychiatrist at Gateway and Dr. Alabiso agreed that Rose must be integrated before James could go home. Lillian wanted James home. She was determined to have Rose dealt with once and for all.

Lillian Wrote: "I tried to see James. Gateway said he was sick, and I caused it. They refused to let him see me. I am not his mother anymore. I am just a monster who causes disease to everyone around. Here is Lillian, the monster. I feel dirty; I don't want to be."

Chrissy Wrote: "I wrote Jean and just said I am not as dumb as everyone else thinks I am. I told her I describe myself as just being acceptable. Annie said all preachers preach hellfire and a whole bunch of stuff I don't agree with. Annie told me there were men who stand in the back of the church with sticks to hit people who fall asleep. There was a box up front where they put bad people, and they make them wear prison clothes and make them sing in front of everybody, and Jean was up there about every week because she is bad. I don't believe it for a minute, but that is Annie."

Lillian Wrote: "I wish that I could bleed to death so I'd be pure and clean. It is in the Bible. Cleansing evil out of your system by bleeding works for me. It doesn't for Aunt Jean or Rev. Chris because they weren't taught that. It doesn't hurt that much, and I have blood to spare. I hate life. I am so sick of so many things and always wondering if I let someone down. James thinks I am a freak. Jim is tired of a wife who doesn't come through for him. Being a multiple, I can't help it. It is not like having a cold. It doesn't go away in seven days. I need to take my pills. I was okay when I took them regularly. Shit on life!

"I went to see Dr. Robinson and told him I hadn't been taking my medication, but I take sleeping pills as soon as Jim goes to work; two to three in the evening, and I'd been going on eating binges and then putting my finger down my throat to make myself throw up and then bleeding myself (blood from my arms) because I felt dirty and the awful dreams and the wanting to deal with Rose, I felt I needed help in the hospital, but just for a short time, and he agreed. I am going into the hospital on Sunday so work can begin on Monday. Dr. Robinson didn't put me down. I saw my family doctor, and he put me on antibiotics for the infected places where I used a hat pin to hit a vein to bleed myself. Dr. Robinson said Aunt Jean had called, worried about the bleeding. Jimmy promised he'd call, and he didn't.

"I am frightened of the hospital – not Dr. Robinson, but the staff. I am terrified of being kept tied down by a staff that misreads Dr. Robinson's orders or has some other excuse for hurting me in the pretext of helping control Rose's behavior, not mine. Dr. Robinson, please be on my side."

***

Jean as Narrator: The long-awaited time arrived. Rose had been in a pill bottle for over a year, put there by hypnosis. Dr. Robinson and Lillian met in a conference room in the hospital. Staff members were alerted. Dr. Robinson handed the bottle to Lillian. Lillian was as ready as she would ever be. Lillian opened the bottle, and all hell broke loose! Rose hurled the bottle across the room.

"You son of a bitch! You kept me locked in there for two hours! Bastard!" Rose shrieked. Her shrill voice pierced the relative quietness of the ward, and her obscenities filled the air. Staff rushed into the room. They were incredulous! Just seconds earlier, they had spoken to calm, soft-spoken Lillian.

"Shit ass! Cocksucker! Pig!" Rose spat. She tore wildly out of the room, screeching. "You aren't lockin' me in there again!"

The instant Rose sprang from the bottle, Dr. Robinson damned himself for not planting a posthypnotic suggestion that could return her to the bottle upon command. He made a mental note to do that as he made a mad dash to retrieve the bottle. Thank heaven it didn't break when Rose threw it.

She ducked into the lounge, twisting and dodging Dr. Robinson and his assistants. Dr. Robinson landed a flying tackle as Rose headed for the elevator. They grabbed her and wrestled her to the floor. She was a fighter! Arms and legs were flailing at her would-be subduers. Rose aimed at groins, faces and eyes, spitting, scratching, biting and kicking savagely. She was clearly intent on inflicting injury.

At last, people were summoned to pin down Rose, and a hypodermic was administered.

Dr. Robinson talked to calm her down until, at last, the injection took effect. They took her to the "dangerous" floor and put her in the psychiatric intensive care room to sleep it off.

Lillian Wrote: "Rose was brought back today in the conference room. I think she tried to leave because a shot was mentioned by Dr. Robinson, and the next thing I knew was that I was in a PIC room.

"I am afraid here, afraid of being locked up or put in restraints. Dr. Robinson left orders to not let that happen. Oh, I hope they follow his orders!

"Rose made two attempts to leave today, and I am back in this awful room with just my nightclothes. They locked the door, but as soon as they knew it was me, they unlocked it. Thank you. One of the nurses has been in a couple of times to see if I am okay. I hope that Dr. Robinson can hypnotize Rose tomorrow so no one can be hurt. I feel so ashamed."

Jean as Narrator: The next day, the doctor hypnotized Lillian and asked for Rose. Rose came out yelling, "I am getting out of this fucking place!" She ran, but Dr. Robinson had anticipated her actions, and they placed her in restraints more quickly this time.

Rose screamed that she hates kids. Rose said she did not believe she had been in a bottle for over a year – "No way, it's 1982!" she screamed.

Dr. Robinson lost a lot of sleep that night trying to figure out a safe way to conduct therapy with Rose. He hit upon a plan.

The next day he told Lillian she would be in the hypnotic state to watch the whole time he'd be in hypnotherapy with Rose. At the outset of hypnosis, Dr. Robinson implanted the suggestion that when he snapped his fingers twice, Rose would instantly be gone.

Lillian's Journal: "Dr. Robinson was here for hypnotherapy. Rose threw one of those so-called call bells at him and broke a pencil several times and threw a bottle. She said she killed a bunch of people: some in an airplane crash, some with hepatitis and a grandfather. She said she could just wish them dead. Rose said she wasn't afraid of locked doors or restraints. When Dr. Robinson mentioned a hypodermic, she said she wasn't afraid but acted like she was. She said people have control when you are unconscious and can cut you up. She tried leaving. Four or five staff members had her pinned down, and when Dr. Robinson snapped his fingers, just as quick as that, she was gone! It's incredible! No one got her hurt! Then Dr. Robinson brought me out of hypnosis by counting back from 10. He doesn't seem scared of her. Even gave her a hug! I hope he sticks with me through this. He says Rose sounds angry but looks sad. Also, I will be here longer than I thought.

"James ran away from Gateway to come see me, but he didn't make it. Now they will probably restrict him even more."

Chrissy Wrote: "Today, I tried to kill Rose, but it didn't work. Instead, I almost got me and Lil and Annie. I put a silk scarf around her neck – real tight and tied it in knots, and nobody could breathe or talk, not even Lil, and she fell and hit the floor. Everybody here helped. She got a few neck burns, and her throat bled a little. I guess I didn't help any. I promised to check things out in the future before I do things to help anymore."

Lillian Wrote: "Session with Dr. Robinson. He hypnotizes me every time for Rose to be there for therapy. I am scared. When she tried to leave, and he put her in the bottle, I screamed, 'No!' I was scared. Dr. Robinson said Chrissy wanted to leave the hospital but promised not to. I think he asked me to promise, but I am not sure. They gave me a hypo. Later I wrote Dr. Robinson a note about the dogs, but I didn't remember what I said. I'm scared of trying to leave and being locked or tied, and I don't want him to work with Rose anymore. The alarm went off, and they gave me another shot. I'm so afraid that no one will like me if they find out what happened to Rose. I don't want her to tell. But I know what she has to tell."

***

Lillian Wrote: "Still in the hospital. Dr. Robinson was in, I guess. I remember him walking in, but I don't remember anything under hypnosis today. Isn't that strange? I feel like I have a few things mixed up."

Chrissy Wrote: "I called Dr. Robinson today to ask if I could just tell Lil what she does not remember, but he said no; that he gave her a choice. He didn't get mad that I called and asked neither. Lil, if you want to ask anything from me, doctor said it was okay when I called him as long as it's your choice."

Lillian Wrote: "This is Tuesday, I think. The doctor went over what Rose told him yesterday and what I remember of it. He didn't talk to Rose at all. I thought it was all a dream, and I get so sick inside thinking about it. Dad used to bring home what I thought were packages of raw meat (garbage, he said) once in a while, and he had me throw the meat to the dogs that came around. But once I noticed it wasn't just cut up meat. He was involved in abortions, and I was letting them be eaten instead of buried. And the awful part is that even after I knew, I still did it. I was too scared of him not to! It was me who wasn't wanted. I should have been cut up and fed to the dogs. I feel so dirty. I am so ashamed that I did that four or five times after I knew. I need to be cut up. Bleeding isn't enough, and besides, Dr. Robinson made me promise not to cut myself up like I deserve. My whole insides hurt. I threw up. There is no way to make it right. No way to undo. Why couldn't I have refused? I can't think about it. I don't dare. When I leave here, I have to cut me up to even things out. James wanted a puppy, and I couldn't let him. I just can't be around dogs now. What will everyone think of me? God can't forgive that! How could I do that? Why couldn't I say no? There is no way to make it okay."

Rose Wrote: "Today, I am here, and Dr. Robinson thinks it's okay. He told Lil's favorite nurse, and I told three other nurses what I did, and they still treat me like a human."

Lillian Wrote: "So now Rose is out of the bottle. Free to be around. She promised not to cut herself or me up. It is hard to keep from doing that. I feel like it is right for me to be cut up in pieces. I guess Dad did that years ago by all the things he forced on me, and me afraid to not obey. How can God forgive me? Yet Dr. Robinson was so kind.

"There is just Rose, Annie, Chrissy and me. I wonder if I'm afraid of getting well. Then no one will care for me. It's not true. I need to learn to be a stronger person. I don't want to die, but I feel that's the only way to make things even out with God. I don't want my children to hate me, even if they read of what my life has been. I try not to judge. I hope God helps them not to judge me harshly. It's 12 midnight in the hospital. It's so hard, and I feel so alone.

"Dr. Robinson suggested James come in here and meet Rose. So Jimmy brought him in. That was a nice surprise. I think Rose told James that what she was scared of was if anybody found out what she did, they wouldn't like her, and also that she didn't want James to be afraid of her, but she didn't tell James what it was that she did. I guess it went okay. It seems funny to think of the name Rose and not have a scared feeling. I don't know how to get past this feeling that I should be cut up in pieces. Maybe Rev. Chris can help. Jim said Rose called and asked Rev. Chris for an appointment to see him. She sure seems to have changed a lot.

"I took a light bulb from the shower room and broke it. I hid it in a drawer to use to cut myself. When I went to get it, it was gone. So I had to tell the staff this morning because I was afraid another person/patient might be suicidal, and I'd be responsible. We found it. Chrissy had hidden it from me. Every time I think about what Dad made me do, my whole insides hurt. How can God forgive something like that? But I don't think Rose had a choice. Life was awful then. So scared all the time and afraid to say no to anything.

"Dad said he was going to take care of me. He'd make sure there wasn't any baby. He said, 'I have to tie your hands. You understand, don't you? I wouldn't hurt my little girl unless I had to. It's for you, honey. Dad will take care of you. You know. Give me your arm. Come on. Trust Dad. This has to be. Just us two will be here. No one will know. If you fight, Dad will have to hurt you, and you know Dad doesn't want his pet hurt. Do you want your mother here? Should I tell her you have a baby inside? Are you going to make any noise? I will say this once: One sound, one sound, and I will have to gag you. We don't want the neighbors coming, do we? I have to tie you up. No! Don't struggle! No marks, no bruises! How would we explain that to anyone? Stop, baby! Do you think I want to kill you? Don't move! Leeyun, listen to Dad! You die if you move! Got to save that sweet pussy for paying customers, don't we?! Do you want a cover over you, baby? If you don't make a sound, Dad will cover you. Dad loves his pet, don't he? Can't you speak? Tell me yes. Tell me you love Dad! I can't hear you. No! No tears! Not my girl! Dad had to hit you. You understand Dad had to do that. Say you understand! I can't hear you! Tell Dad you're sorry!'"

Jean as Narrator: The letter was never mailed, but the very writing of it freed Lillian of her fear of telling family secrets and released her anger. The horror of it all was unspeakable until the words were written down. From there, it was a small step to verbalize the memory. It had taken years for Lillian to feel safe and trusting enough to tell anyone. She had overwhelming feelings of guilt and rage, which Rose had secreted from her for so long. Lillian could feel the guilt Rose felt, but it took several more days for her to admit to the rage. Dr. Robinson worked alternately with Rose and Lillian.

Rose bought a can of Coke from the machine, emptied it and broke the can in half to cut herself up. She started on her wrist but stopped abruptly, went to the head nurse and said she promised she wouldn't do that. "But promises are hard to keep." In a few days, Lillian was released from the hospital to come and visit Rev. Chris and me. Dr. Robinson never dealt with any of the many religious themes that kept cropping up in Lillian's therapy. It always seemed to Rev. Chris and me that Dr. Robinson seemed to have an abundance of faith in us! He and Rev. Chris conferred by telephone from time to time, but Dr. Robinson seldom called me. Lillian didn't want him to.

During the first day of Lillian's visit, Lillian said to me, "Rose – she is what's making me so sick. She wants integration. I'd like her dead – no part of me."

And with her eyes staring at her hands, twisting in her lap, Lillian went on, remembering and telling me, her Aunt Jean, whom she knows loves her "… and Dad gets a hanger out, twists it, and I think he doesn't mean 'care for' me. He means to kill me. And unexpectedly, I find I'm still alive afterward. I figure out I had a baby inside, and I see Dad's baby, Letty, a little princess, and I think, 'Dad has his baby. I want one of my own to love me and have everybody love it like they do Letty.'

"And then he pulls me outside. He has the newspaper bundle. I already know what's inside. I cry, 'Please, Dad, don't feed it to the dogs! I will dig a hole for that.'

"Then he comes with a soft cloth and warm water! 'I will keep your secret. Only me and you know it. It's our secret,' was what he said.

"I hugged him. I told him I loved him, and I think I hate him the most for making me such a disgusting object who forgave all for the comfort of a warm washcloth. There is my shame; being so sickly grateful for nothing."

Lillian's voice rose, and she looked at me straight in the eye. "I kept my trust. I lived with what I am, and Rose kept my secret. She has betrayed herself and me!"

Lillian was sure nobody would like her once we learned what Rose had done. I wrapped her again in my arms, sheltering her with my love while she cried.

Lillian Wrote: "Rev. Chris came out to Aunt Jean's. He talked to me a little and then to Rose, and she told him what she had done. I guess Rose got scared and left, and I felt like throwing up. Rev. Chris thinks all my cutting myself in the past was really, in my mind, me cutting myself up, and he said I don't ever have to do that again. My stomach had hurt for weeks, and suddenly it stopped and doesn't hurt anymore. I feel like I'm free! I don't feel like cutting myself anymore.

"I am so angry. I never want anyone else to know. Dad was such a bastard. Rev. Chris heard me say Dad handed me the washcloth, so I washed my face. I was the one who made me feel better. Not Dad!"

Rose's last entry in her journal was this quotation from St. Augustine: "He loves each one of us as if there were only one of us."

Jean as Narrator: Rev. Chris baptized Lillian two days later. Rose was integrated; so was Anne.

Chapter 25
Betrayal

During the period in which the personalities give over their memories to the host personality, many individuals with multiple personality disorder feel betrayed by God.

Often, there is no forward movement until the individuals resolve this deepest of angers – the anger toward a god who did not rescue them from child abuse.

In Chapter 25, the process of resolving this deepest of angers begins.

Jean, as she has done so many times in the past, finds a path to healing.

FA

Jean as Narrator: The day after Christmas, I had driven to Ohio alone to see my mother. When I started home, it was dark, and the roads were clear. I thought I could be home by early morning, but as I crossed Pennsylvania, snow began falling. After I exited the tunnel of the turnpike, the weather deteriorated rapidly. By the time I reached Breezewood, several inches of snow lay on the ground, and it was snowing heavily.

Stopping for food and fuel, I inquired of a trucker about the weather toward Virginia.

When he said the highways were covered, and 4 inches of additional snow were expected by morning, I called Walter. He reported there was no snow, rain or ice at home in Virginia, and none predicted. He suggested my staying overnight at Breezewood if I had doubts about the wisdom of continuing.

Thinking about the possibility of being snowed in at Breezewood for a day or two, I cleaned the snow off the car and started out. The minute I turned away from the lights of the town, I knew I had made a grave error in judgment. It was snowing heavily. If I got stuck, it would be dangerous to be walking back to Breezewood. Leaning forward and holding the steering wheel in a death grip, I could barely make out tire tracks to follow! And I couldn't turn around!

The sound of my own voice shocked me. "God help me!" I could hear panic in my voice.

Watching in my rearview mirror, I saw two cars behind me. I was creeping along! My eye was drawn to a highway patrol car's blinking lights. The patrolman drove silently past me and pulled his cruiser directly in front of my car. I fought back thankful tears and heaved a sigh of relief.

The patrolman turned off his whirling lights and proceeded very slowly. A long parade formed behind me. Each time some car in the lineup pulled out to pass the lot of us, the patrolman turned on his lights, and the inpatient driver dropped back in line. We drove that way for about 20 minutes, when flashing lights in the opposing lane drew our pilot away.

Cars began passing me immediately. I held my pace, benefiting from their wide tire tracks to follow. What a surprise, when less than 10 miles down the highway, the road was clear; no snow, no ice.

Alone in the now-clear, starry night, I reflected on what I had just experienced.

I thought, "God helped me." I felt compelled to share my experience and called Lillian and Jimmy. Lillian was fascinated. Jimmy was noncommittal. The others heard that conversation too.

Jackie Wrote: "Dear Jean, this is from Jackie. I need to ask you some things, and I don't want you to get angry. I am not going to say anything to you that I think you wouldn't like on purpose. I just want to ask you some questions. Dr. Robinson said I could say anything to you, and you wouldn't take offense. Okay? Do you feel warned? Honest, this is because I want your answers. It's religious, so if you ask Rev. Chris, that's okay; only I want your feelings. I hope you take me serious and think about your answer and not just say something to put me off.

"Jean, I listened to you talking to Lil and Jimmy about God taking you through the snow safely to get you home. I heard you talk about how God works things out in your life. Jean, why do you think God helps you, and that same God lets someone else die? How come God helped you when God lets children be scalded to death by their mother and doesn't interfere? Isn't a child more important?

"Don't be mad, Jean, but don't you wonder? Who told you God will help you every day, and I only asked for his help once or twice in my whole life, and he didn't come through for me? Why does he help you? Even if I wasn't good enough, the baby that I would have had would have been innocent. It wouldn't have been bad. Sarah Ann wasn't bad, but God ignored her, and she was asking for help.

"I would guess that all of us were as sincere as you are when we talked to God. Do you think he just talks to certain people? Are you special? Do you think you believe in God more than I do? What is God like? God either treats us all alike and helps all of us every day (which God doesn't), or God treats us all alike and doesn't help anyone!

"I think you really believe God follows you around all the time running interference, but Jean, why doesn't God do that for everyone who wants help? I really needed God to help me when I was 11. God didn't come through. Don't God like kids? If I remember right, God didn't exactly keep you safe when you were 11 either. So why do you think that God is so great now? I think of more things God hasn't done than things that God has done for me.

"Jean, do you have any answers? No, forget I asked that 'cause you'll just say no, and I won't have gotten any help at all. How can God cope with all these everyday things for you when the world is falling apart, and God doesn't interfere? Do you know something no one else does? I mean, Jean, if God was going to allow someone to die, wouldn't an auto accident be more merciful than being scalded to death?

"I want no part of God! God is no better than those parents who know their kids are being abused and do nothing! What good is God if he only takes care of his favorite ones and none of the ones who are dirty like me?

"That's all.

"I love you, dear Jean. Jackie."

Jean as Narrator: Wow! What a load! It took me a week to brazen myself enough to answer Jackie. Then I just turned my pen loose.

Jean Wrote: "My dearest Jackie, I have been thinking a great deal about your letter and the questions you raised. That's a lot of good, sincere, probing thought. I don't know where or how to begin, so I will plunge in.

"As we dilute the unpleasant happenings with positive people in our lives, we become like those we associate with.

"I believe Herbert and Jessica inflicted horrible abuse on Lillian and all of you. Unfortunately, Sarah Ann or you could not escape.

"I think, Jackie, that God sent me and Sarah Ann and you to help Lillian. And so, we are here to help her to work out these deep feelings of resentment and anger.

"I wish God could take away all child abuse and pain. Sometimes evil wins. I know that when evil wins, God suffers too.

"The way God interceded was by giving Lillian other parts of her mind. I love you, dear Jackie. As always, Jean."

***

Jean as Narrator: The National Weather Service issued a blizzard warning from Niagara Falls to Syracuse. Schools were closed. The thruway was closed down from Eastern Pennsylvania to Rochester. Jimmy was holed up in a motel, waiting for the storm to end. Driving an 18-wheeler on ice and snow was too treacherous. James was at Gateway.

Lillian was home alone – meaning only one body was there.

Lillian stood watching out the window. More than 2 feet of snow had already accumulated. It was snowing hard, and the wind was blowing. An erratic movement caught her eye. The roof blew off their storage shed, and its walls collapsed crazily. Lillian's first instinct was to run out and salvage whatever she could, but she couldn't even get the door open, because heavy snow drifted against it.

Back at the window, Lillian watched helplessly. Plastic storage bags blew open, scattered their contents, flip-flopped around on the snow, then filled with wind and sailed away. Summer clothes lost their protective bags and flaunted themselves ridiculously in the snow and in the air. It was an absurd and laughable scene, except for the sadness Lillian felt. Somehow, it was like her life – first all contained and "put away," then piece by piece, personality by personality, exposed briefly before blowing away forever. Lillian wondered if anything would be left so she could pick up the pieces when the storm was over. For her, the storm was symbolic.

Lillian was caught in the storm of her own anger.

Just then, James' bicycle caught her eye. She ran to the door and tried to open it. Failing again, she watched as the bicycle twisted about foolishly, finally making a rest for itself in the unforgiving snow. For a moment, she felt that she could not save it. Would she be there when her storm was over? Or would she be blown away like the other pieces, to become melted snow, then mud, then nothing?

Integration? Anger? Death? Peace?

Lillian turned away. It was 2 degrees below zero. The temperature was dropping by the hour. Inside their home, it was 12 degrees. Jimmy had meant to get the skirting replaced around the bottom of the trailer after he moved it, but there just never seemed to be enough time.

Lillian called to tell James she had canceled his next-day appointment with Dr. Alabiso.

James cried.

Now the only time James was permitted to be with his mother was when she took him to Dr. Alabiso's office.

Dejected and alone in what seemed to be a godless world, Lillian crawled under the electric blanket she had bought for Jim for Christmas, knowing full well that if the electricity went out, she could freeze to death. Lillian couldn't get out, and nobody could get in. It was so desolate there! Not a single neighbor's house could be seen from Lillian's home, even on a clear day. Lillian sank into a troubled sleep.

The next afternoon, Lillian called me. "It's 2 o'clock in the afternoon, and it's still snowing so hard I can't see across the road. Our water pipes are frozen. Water I left in a couple of drinking glasses is frozen too! The scariest part is the wind blowing. It was 7 below last night with 50-mile-an-hour winds. The wind chill factor makes it feel like 50 below zero.

"You should see the snowdrifts! There is one out back that must be 20 feet high! It sort of falls over itself at the top, like whipped cream. It's higher than our roof, but then the roof on a trailer home isn't very high.

"We are really broke, Jean. I made myself some instant cocoa and ate the last six peanut butter crackers in the house. My big meal of the day! I found a candy cane from Christmas, and that will have to be supper. Maybe I will lose some weight before the blizzard is over! A blizzard isn't fun when you are alone, and you can't count on your God for help."

Chapter 26
Could It Get Any Worse?

The period between integration and the development of an intact self is often lonely.

The personality parts are no longer experienced as separate individuals. At the same time, the "host" personality has only an embryonic sense of self.

During this period, "multiples" often experience an intense sense of isolation.

It is during this vulnerable period that "Ellen" releases memories to Lillian of her mother's twisted, demonic thinking and her stepfather's penchant for vile, sadistic abuse.

Will Lillian be strong enough to face the pain?

Could it get any worse?

FA

Jean as Narrator: A letter addressed to me, Aunt Jean, in care of Rev. Chris, arrived at the church. I read it over and over, trying to understand it. As always, when a new handwriting appeared, I thought it was from a yet-unknown personality.

I showed it to Lillian, and we studied it together. We determined that Lillian had no access to a car at the time the letter was postmarked from Alabama.

So thinking further, Lillian's maternal family would have been gathered at a recent funeral, and the only address the family had for me was Rev. Chris' address. Some of Lillian's maternal family knew who I was.

The handwriting looked like that of an old person and read as follows: "Lillian's mother had a difficult labor with her firstborn, causing her to be deathly afraid when she was found again in that condition. The first child looked just like her – red hair, light skin. They called her Rosalind. Lillian's mother had not desired the second babe at all. When the child birthed an easy birthing, she, I believe, would accept it, but unfortunately, the child was found to have not formed completely right in the girl child area where the hole is in front. She took pains to conceal it even from her husband. Since I visited with her and her aunt for a spell, I knew some of her feelings about this babe. She did believe the deformity was caused by the way she thought before it was born. Later, she changed her thinking to feel that the babe itself was a demon. The babe was found borne without there being big enof place in the babes front to have a man when she came to be full-grown, though the deformity did not cause her problems going to pee. A doctor made to repair the deformity when the babe not yet one year. Her mother was constant to admonish her to keep her hands away from herself. She did not treat her well at all, believing her to be dirty down there and did not allow her to cry. In that time, she was caused to tie the babes hands for her. I am too old to have anyone's anger, so I wish her mother not to know I write. I do not know if this is useful. If it is not, then you can let it go from your hands. I have heard you are good to her. That is good. I will rest easy from this now. Aunt Gladys."

Lucy Wrote: "Oh, Dr. Robinson! She made it hurt! When she climbed into bed with me after Herbert died, I thought it was 'cause she was lonely. But then she put her fingers inside of me. It felt good at first, but she did it till it hurt, just like she did when my real daddy died."

"She said, 'You have to do this till it hurts! That's what men like.' Then she put my hand on her. She had hair! She said some mommies put candy there for little girls to lick. She asked, 'What kind of candy do you like best, honey? Licorice? Horehound? Maybe a candy cane?'

"I was real little. She always came at night after Sister and me was asleep. I never saw her do it to Sister.

"This happened after Lillian's father died and again after Herbert died. I got to throw up!"

Lillian Wrote: "I learned that my mother's sister, Aunt Pearl, died and was already buried back in Ohio. I loved her as much as I knew how to love anyone. She was more a mother to me than Jessica. Why couldn't it have been Jessica that died? I wish I could have gone to the funeral. No one will think I cared. I called Aunt Jean tonight. She says write about how I feel about Aunt Pearl. I can't. I'd probably cry, and Jimmy wouldn't like that. He wants a Lillian with no feelings.

"I have burns on my arms. I didn't do it, and I don't know who would do it or why. This is happening now. But when I saw Dr. Robinson, I ended up crying about Aunt Pearl. The doctor said the burns were because I didn't deal with my feelings. I think he is right."

Lillian's Journal: "When I talked to the doctor today, the roaring in my head was there, and the room was foggy. I kept thinking dumb things. He asked about 'lessons' Dad gave me. I tried to talk about something else, but he kept asking me about the 'lessons.' Then he showed me a letter from 'Ellen.' Then I got a roaring in my head, and the room was foggy. I wish there was someone to take over."

Ellen Wrote: "Hi, I'm Ellen. I told Dr. Robinson that I did the burns so he'd understand, but he didn't. Dr. Robinson said I shouldn't do that anymore. Don't be mad, all right?"

Jean as Narrator: This was Ellen's first visit. Ellen introduced herself to me. She didn't understand why I asked what color her hair and eyes were. Couldn't I see for myself? I mumbled something about different shades of hair being called various names, and she bought it. Blonde hair and blue eyes. Ellen was 25 years old. She first came to Lillian's rescue when Lillian was 8 or 9 years old. Ellen had a tremendous down-country twang. Ellen released additional memories for which Lillian had complete amnesia.

Ellen's Journal: "Dad gave me speech lessons. 'Say-It Time,' he would announce. Say-It Time usually began at the kitchen table with Lillian seated on a stool. Dad would pronounce the word and say, 'You say it after me.' Even though he was unable to pronounce words with a letter in the middle, I was expected to speak as demanded.

"I tried to match his voice, but he grew increasingly exasperated. 'Stupid! Dumb! Can't do right!'

"He also held Say-It Time with Letty, though she was just 3 years old. As Dad grew angrier, he eventually said, 'We're goin' t' the basement.'

"I knew that anytime he wanted to play in the basement, it would be bad.

"In the basement, nobody else could see or hear what he did or said, but at least there was no one to watch.

"'Now, brat, say what I say – I am a dog!'

"Crying fearfully, I repeated it.

"'Get down on all fours like a dog and say, 'I love you, bitch!' Eventually, he would make me say, 'Punish me, 'cause I want to be good.'

"The punishment was a frayed electric cord that got plugged into a wall to make me jump. The water on the floor made it all the more frightening. I was sure I was going to be electrocuted. It's a wonder that I survived."

Lillian Wrote: "It is lightning and thundering away outside. I just pulled the plug out of the wall for the TV. For the first time in my life, I am by myself! Keith and Evan won't believe it! I feel so mixed up in my head. It seems like my life doesn't have any direction. I want to be Jackie and go to college, and Lucy loving Jimmy. I don't seem to be anybody at all. I am afraid I am going to live through all of this therapy and end up with one person who doesn't know how to do anything at all, and I am going to be alone. I want a friend, someone who isn't just nice or kind to poor Lillian. I think I will never be good enough to deserve having my own friend. I never learned to take care of me.

"It is lightning and thundering and raining, and I am alone. My life is a storm. The lights will go out; then what? I am scared, but I won't tell if you won't. Lying is a safety precaution. So, it is okay in emergencies."

Jean as Narrator: Knowing of the abuse endured by Ellen and feeling completely alone, Lillian felt empty, as if there were nothing holding her together.

Chapter 27
Foreboding

Always shy, always hesitant, with a body language that suggests shame, Lillian accompanies James to his sessions.

The unpredictability of Lillian's ever-changing personality leaves James feeling insecure, fearful and emotionally cast adrift.

While it is hoped that the predictability of life at the Gateway Home and the kindness of the staff would create a secure "holding environment" for James, the fear of separation from his mother is more powerful.

Instead of bonding at Gateway, James' anxiety increases. All he can think of is how he can get back home.

James is a sad and overwhelmed child.

FA

Dr. Alabiso as Narrator: I first met James when he was 10 years old. Big in stature and gentle of heart, James was a kindhearted child.

Over the next two years, we developed a deep bond as James learned to navigate the world of multiplicity.

These were the loneliest of times for James – times when Esther took over, stranding Lillian far away from home while leaving James at home alone.

Often finding himself at home with no adult around, James and Amy kept each other company.

Losing themselves in play, they became best friends. For Amy, it was like having an older brother and best playmate all in one.

Lillian was sometimes in the hospital for weeks at a time. James was alone again.

Each week in play therapy, James shared his experiences at home. During these sessions, I entered James' world. We talked about Amy as if she actually was another child. I joined James in making cards for Amy's birthday and in searching the crevices of the office couch in the hope of finding left-behind change for Amy's Christmas present.

In one session, when Lillian brought James to therapy, it was Amy who greeted me at the door of my office. Two hundred pounds, 5 feet, 4 inches tall, Amy couldn't contain her excitement about meeting "James' doctor."

Once in the room and settled, James and Amy talked of life at home. It was clear that Amy had come to rely on James to feel safe.

During another session, expecting to see James and Lillian in the waiting room, Lee paid a visit. I expected Lee to look as I had envisioned him in my mind's eye – dressed in jeans rolled up at the ankles, wearing a wide black belt, flannel shirt and a barn coat with his hair cropped and slicked back. The person who stood before me looked like Lillian, except that he wore black pants and black tennis shoes.

Although quite a presence, Lee was actually shy – "Only can stay a minute. James and me been carv'n. We thought you'd like to see our work."

From his pocket, Lee pulled out a beautifully carved pair of gazelles sanded smooth and hand-rubbed, giving them a soft and oily finish.

"James did them with a little help from me." James beamed. "They are for you. Got any wood?" And then Lee was gone.

I have those carvings at home to this day.

James was growing increasingly sad and unhappy. His placement at Gateway strained our relationship. After all, I was the one who said it was no longer safe for him to live at home.

The predictability of life at Gateway and the kindness of the staff were not enough to offset James' fear of separation from Lillian.

Faced with periods of being left alone at home and with the possibility of physical abuse by Esther, James nonetheless longed to return home.

At age 10, James was soiling himself both day and night. To compound matters, James could barely read.

While at Gateway, James was often found crying at night.

In a moment of panic and desperation, James put his arm through a window. He attempted to run away twice. In therapy, James explained he was trying to get to Lillian.

Following one therapy visit in which Lillian brought James to a session, Chrissy took over and "made a break for it" on the way back to Gateway.

Jean as Narrator: Later, Chrissy revealed the following story in her own words: "This is gonna be a story. The Great Escape from Gateway by Chrissy and James Mason.

Chrissy: "Monday, right after seein' Dr. Alabiso, we didn't say nothin' ta' him 'bout it. On the way back, I said, 'James, are you okay if we go see some friends on the way back to Gateway?'

"James said, 'Mmm hmm.'

"So we headed down the road. About an hour later, James said, 'Who are we seein'? Where are we goin' anyhow?'

"I said, 'We gonna go see Rev. Chris an' Jean.' I said, 'Et's jes' a little ways, et's jes' a little ways on the way home.'

"James said, 'I don't think we better do that. We better call.'

"I said, 'You call.'

"James called Rev. Chris. Rev. Chris wasn't home. I called Tamora . Jean said, 'Chrissy honey, you better go home and take James back Tamora. Et's very late, and you are vera far away. I will call Gateway and tell them you are all right.'

"I said, 'Wayell, tell 'em we had a flyat tahr. But then you sayid you wanted to call Dr. Alabiso.'

"So James called Dr. Alabiso.

"James said Dr. Alabiso said to come raht back raht now, and we might be there by 10 or 11 tonight. Dr. Alabiso said he'd call Gateway, and we won't get inta no trouble. It wasn't nobody's fault.

"James had a McDonald spaceship meal.

"And then we headed back up the road, and ever'body lived happily ever mower, and thayt's the end of the story."

Jean as Narrator: When it was over, James was back at Gateway – safe (safe?) but even more unhappy.

James was separated from Lee, Amy, Jimmy, Evan and the others.

He was now living in a world where everybody was who he/she was – no people with more than one personality.

In addition, given that one or more of the personalities "posing" as Lillian could take him away again, Dr. Alabiso could not recommend that Lillian bring him to his therapy sessions any longer.

After that, James was brought to therapy by Evan, but for him, it was not the same.

Dr. Alabiso as Narrator: Over time, James became sad and dejected.

Would he ever see his mother again? What was his future? Where would he live? How would he cope?

James was losing hope.

Chapter 28
Faith Renewal

Jean addresses Lillian's God anger in a most unconventional way – a way that no therapist could have thought of, much less implemented.
Jean simply arranges for Lillian to be inspired by God.

FA

Jean as Narrator: Rev. Chris was leading a group to the Holy Land. I urged Lillian to accompany me on the trip.

Various of the personalities had talked about it. They all knew that they could go only if I took responsibility for them. So when Jackie asked me if she could go, I set out the rules. "Yes, Jackie. I'd love for you to go. Anybody who wants to go is welcome. I have just a few requests. One: I need to know who is going. Two: I need to be told whenever there is a change and who is with me. It is important for me to know who is with me at all times. Three: Everybody who goes must agree to stay right with me. No running away or wandering off. We will be in a strange land, and I could get lost hunting for one of you. I will be your partner. If someone gets teed off at me, we have to talk about it and work it out. I am so happy that you can all go. We are going to have a wonderful time!"

Joyce Wrote: "I don't want to go. I don't need to be looking for a God who isn't there when you need him!"

Jean as Narrator: I wondered what Joyce would do for a body! I knew Lucy wanted to go. Now Jackie, then Annie and, of course, Lillian. Naturally, our tour would be flying out of Washington National Airport to New York. Lucy became fearful of flying and told me so. She also told me that Lillian had never flown before. Even though "they" had flown to Washington dozens of times, someone else always boarded and departed the airplane. Jackie told me she liked to fly, and she would be the one who got on the plane with me.

Rev. Chris wanted to see Lillian the night before we left on our trip to ascertain her state of mind. Then he asked for Lucy. Someone anonymously had sent money to Rev. Chris for Lucy to use on the trip. Lucy had stayed up all night in the hospital once with the girl who lost a baby resulting from rape. The girl wanted to repay Lucy. When she was in the hospital, she got Rev. Chris' address from Lucy and sent money to Rev. Chris to give to her. At least someone wanted to help her!!

Lillian didn't even know the girl's name. She was thankful for her kindness, but there was still a separateness between Lillian and God.

Early the next morning, we joined a convoy to our bus. Our total group was comprised of 45 in all.

Jackie took over for Lillian as we approached the airport. Later, settling down for a long flight from New York, Jackie and I conversed for over an hour. Then Annie asked, "Is it okay for me to be here now?"

Her accent always gave her away. "Annie?" I asked though I knew who she was.

"Yes, can I be here?"

"Sure, Annie. Did you see that takeoff?"

"No. I didn't watch. I never been in an airplane before. It's really big, isn't it? I never thought they made any of them so big."

Annie was impressed. I was always surprised at how young and naive Annie was. She brought out all of my motherly instincts.

After what seemed like hours of flying over the ocean, Annie said, "I'm tired," and Lucy ventured out. The three of them alternated. Lucy was always there at mealtime. I sense that others in our tour were discussing having a multiple personality in our group. I am sure they were anxious and uneasy about her. Everyone seemed to know that the two of us were not to be separated. I wondered if they were afraid of us.

***

We arrived in Amman, Jordan, and went to our room, which was next to the room where Rev. Chris and his wife were staying. After a few minutes' rest, Lillian and I explored the bathroom, where we discovered a bidet. Neither Lillian nor I had ever seen a bidet before, and we didn't know its purpose. Talk about naive! As we stood side by side, trying to figure it out, I turned on the faucet. Surprise! We were hit with a shocking spray of cold water! "Turn it off, turn it off!" Lillian shouted.

I turned the faucet off, and the two of us giggled hysterically, as people sometimes do when they are very tired. We rolled on our beds, consumed with uncontrollable laughter. Every time one of us would begin to regain composure, we would look at each other and start all over again. We laughed until our sides hurt. We had been "baptized" even before we got to the Holy Land! We tried to guess what guests in nearby rooms must be thinking of our hilarity. It felt so good to hear Lillian laugh with such abandon.

The next day, Rev. Chris asked what happened in our room the night before. Lillian and I looked at each other and told him that we were just a couple of country bumpkins who had never seen a bidet before. There was no way to explain how funny it was to us.

We boarded our buses for the trip into Petra, remains of an ancient city carved from solid rock. The buses could only go partway. The final 2-mile descent was to be taken by horseback. Departing the buses and following our leaders, we rounded a corner and came upon a breathtaking sight! Into our vision came hundreds of Arabian horses, many of them saddled. They were scattered over the valley floor directly below us. Mixed among the horses were men dressed in native garb. I couldn't pry my eyes off the sight! It soon became apparent that we were going to ride horses down into the valley before us.

We scrambled up on a huge rock, each in turn, and mounted horses for our journey. We could choose to ride horses or have the horses led by Jordanian guides. I watched as others in our party proceeded. Knowing that I had to be behind Lillian in case she became frightened, I watched her mount her horse. I heard a resonating slap on the flank of Lillian's horse, a slap administered by the man we thought was going to gently lead her horse. I was dumbfounded as I watched her become smaller and smaller as she and her horse disappeared into the canyon. Being nothing of a horsewoman myself, I literally begged my guide to lead my horse, and he did. When we reached the bottom, Jackie was waiting for me. "I didn't know you could ride like that!" I said.

"Neither did I! That's the first time I have ever been on a horse!" Jackie was laughing. Later Jackie said it was Lil part of the time and her part of the time. I was amazed.

The next morning, we headed for Israel. It was cloudy, overcast and raining lightly. Our guide asked us to rejoice in the rain, for their average annual rainfall was less than an inch. The guide detailed Moses' wandering in the wilderness for so long in the area we were passing through. The bus wound through valleys, over mountains and rocky terrain. It was interesting territory because of its desolation and history, but visibility was limited. As the bus climbed a winding mountain road, our guide apologized for the weather. "If it were not so overcast, you would be able, just around the next bend, to see Mount Sinai off to your left, where Moses received the Ten Commandments."

Jackie was the one who was with me. She was explaining that nothing in her experience made her believe in God. Her presence on the trip was part of her search for proof. A proof that Lillian desperately needed in order to heal. As she spoke, the sun came up brilliantly, and there in the sky was the most brilliant rainbow I have ever seen in my life! Jackie said, "Oh, look!" Speechless, we gazed in astonishment at the unbelievable sight. Rounding the bend and looking to the left, we could see Mount Sinai. The whole bus seemed to reverberate with a great unspoken "Hallelujah!" that soon gave way to excited verbal celebration.

"If I ever had any doubts, Jackie, that rainbow at this instant dispelled them! What a wonderful sign!" I wanted to believe that the rainbow was just for Jackie.

Jackie and I oohed and aahed over the grandeur and the mystique of what we had just seen. She grew silent, obviously deep in thought. About an hour later, Jackie said, "Okay, Jean, I get it. I have to believe in God before I can forgive God."

We passed into the Promised Land. The fields were irrigated and produced giant vegetables. It seemed to me that there was no other world than what was before us right then and there. It filled my eyes, my ears and my memory. Jackie would be with me, then Lillian, Lucy or Annie. They were overwhelmed with what they were experiencing too. All of them needed to come to terms with their anger at God.

The bus was equipped with a small table with a seat reversed so that four people could play cards or converse around the table. We had met a young preacher name Rev. Lloyd Thomas, who had accompanied his parents. His father was also a preacher. Apparently these clergy had been briefed that there was a multiple personality and her aunt in the group. Lloyd and his mother were sitting across the table from us, and we struck up a conversation. Lloyd asked me what it was like to be a multiple. Lloyd thought I was the multiple!

He later told us that his mother kicked him under the table twice. Isn't that intriguing? Who is normal? Lillian or me?

Lloyd became friends with Annie, and each evening on the trip, Lloyd invited Annie to accompany him for a walk, and they would go out to buy doughnuts. Sometimes they just walked outside of the hotel, taking in the sights. It offered me a brief respite from my responsibility for her, and it was interesting to watch how quickly she became Annie whenever Lloyd appeared.

***

As we stood at the top of Masada, looking out over the Dead Sea, I asked "her" if she would like a picture taken with Rev. Chris and his wife. She said no and immediately handed me her camera. Now she was Annie, and she did want her picture taken with them. I took Annie's picture, and she continued to tour with me for the next several minutes before she gave the body back to Lillian.

***

Lillian's Journal: "We are in Israel at the Hotel Tiberias. We went to Masada today. It was such an experience! I am in awe. The mountains there are so different from what I expected. The desolation felt in Jordan's hills was different from the mountains full of caves in Israel. Masada – the cisterns, the storerooms, the bathhouse. Mosaics 2,000 years old! Beyond comprehension! I feel so privileged to be part of this group, but I do not feel God's presence yet.

"The story of Masada told today by our guide was that the people wanted to serve God and chose to give up their lives rather than be slaves. By dying for their strong beliefs, they won.

"Has my life been a Masada?

"I think I am beginning to pray."

***

Jean as Narrator: When we reached "The Source," the tunnel through which the city's water is carried, it was Lucy who was with me. Following other members of our group down the steps into the tunnel, Lucy became frightened. I held her hand and reassured her that Rev. Chris would not lead us into danger. There was a small amount of water, just a small puddle, on the floor at one spot, and boards had been laid across the water there. Lucy just couldn't move. I coaxed her. "Take just one step, Lucy. Now one more. Look ahead at the other people. We are all right." But Lucy, remembering the basement where "Dad" took Ellen for a "Say-It," finally said to me, "Jean, I can't do it. I will have to let Lil come back. She is stronger than me now anyway."

And Lillian was with me, frightened; wondering where she was, how she got there and whether she could get out. By this time, Rev. Chris, ever watchful Rev. Chris, who had gone ahead, came back and told her, "It's not very much farther. You can do it."

When we at last came near the exiting stairs, we could see daylight through a small window cut through the rock to signify the end of the tunnel and to light the stairs. It reminded me of windows in a basement.

Suddenly Lillian stopped, frozen in her tracks. Perhaps she was getting Ellen's memories of being in the basement, with its puddles of water, and could not move. Rev. Chris asked softly, "What's she scared of, Jean?" I shrugged my shoulders. I still held her hand. Rev. Chris tried to take her other hand, but she pulled away. The other ministers and fellow travelers silently and patiently waited for Rev. Chris or me to tell them how to help.

At last, I began climbing up the steps, and Rev. Chris told Lillian to look at me and keep watching me. The others stayed close enough behind to catch her if she fell or if she turned and ran. When we were all finally safely out in the sunshine again, Lillian made a sarcastic-sounding comment to me, but when I asked her to repeat what she said, I only got, "Never mind." She was upset with me and lagged behind for a short distance. My guess is that she might have been embarrassed. In a few minutes, Lucy reappeared and said, "Boy, that was scary. I didn't think I would be afraid down there, but I was."

We stayed at the Hotel Tiberias that night. Our room contained two single beds. Tired as we were, we soon dropped off to sleep. Sometime later, I was awakened by a blood-curdling scream. I had never heard such a shrill and frightened scream. Jumping out of bed, I ran to Lillian's bedside and shook her awake. "Lillian, Lillian, I am right here! It's Aunt Jean! You are safe! What's wrong?"

When at last she could speak, she sobbed, "I was back there! It was so real! I was locked in the coal cellar again. I was always afraid to go to sleep until daylight. One time, when I was sleeping, someone stuck a coal chute in the window and down onto the coal pile. Then the coal started coming down on me. I kept moving around in the coal trying to keep from being buried. Some chunks of coal were big and they bounced. I was so scared! I kept scrambling higher and higher. The dust! I couldn't breathe! I was afraid the room would get clear full, and I would be crushed against the ceiling!"

"Didn't you tell them to stop, or couldn't they hear you?"

"I didn't make a sound. If anybody found out I was locked in the coal cellar, they'd have known I was bad. I didn't want anybody to know how bad I was! I kept quiet," Lillian said.

"How did you ever get out?" I asked.

"When everybody else sat down to eat the next meal, I was missed. Mother finally remembered where she put me. When she opened the door, coal spilled out, and she backed up quick so it wouldn't hit her. She told me to stop shoving coal at her and come down from up there. I had to stoop down and duck under the top of the door. She yelled at me. 'Look at you! You are filthy!'"

Lillian was trembling, "When I looked up and saw that window today, I was right back there in the coal cellar!" I held her until she calmed down. It was quite a while before we could settle to sleep again. I was sure people would be knocking on our door, asking what was wrong. That scream had been long and piercing. Once in the past, Amy had tried to tell me about the coal cellar, but the scream I heard on that night in Tiberias said more than any words could have possibly conveyed. It was like a primal scream that had been suppressed for over 30 years.

We saw so much in our nine days, it was overwhelming. Lillian suddenly realized that she could make her own decisions! It didn't matter what anyone else thought. Her half-beliefs, half-truths and mixed-up feelings clashed in battle. I could tell she was struggling. She linked her arm in mine.

"I found God here!" she said.

***

Jean as Narrator: That evening I was the one who was awestruck. We got into our hotel room overlooking the Sea of Galilee at sunset. I gasped and hurried close to the window, for there was truly the most magnificent sunset I have ever seen. I wanted to take pictures but needed to put fresh film in my camera. What a dilemma! If I took time to load film, I would miss part of the beauty stretching across the sky as far as I could see, but I might be able to capture it on film. I opted to just watch and lock the memory in my heart. It was the right decision. I can recall the feelings that welled up in me these many years later.

The next morning, we took a boat across the Sea of Galilee.

Lillian dipped her hand in the water and picked up a few tiny pebbles for James. She was touching the Holy Land.

Riding along in our bus, Lillian and I alternately babbled excitedly and withdrew into ourselves. Certain things called to her, and different sights affected me. Each time we passed shepherds on hillsides, I was ecstatic! They looked exactly like pictures of shepherds I had seen in the Bible. The shepherds were dressed the same. They held a staff or crook in one hand. Even their headgear matched the pictures. They were either young boys and girls or old men. And the sheep! They didn't look like the sheep I was accustomed to seeing back home. They had very long wool. I thought of Angora. Some were white, some even black, and there was every shade of gray and beige. It seemed that nothing had changed here in 2,000 years! I had expected blue jeans, but I was wrong. This was another world.

Reluctantly, Lillian decided it would be okay to purchase a Bible. She bought one for me; I selected one for her.

I was lagging behind with Rev. Chris when our group left the bus. All at once, a figure came toward us from a side street; a figure dressed completely in white. His face and head were covered in what looked like white gauze. Even his hands and feet were wrapped in white. He met our eyes briefly, then looked away. "Chris," I whispered, "a leper?"

In this day of antibiotics and modern medicines, I wouldn't have thought it could still be.

How could all these scenes be exactly as the Bible described them? The leper, the woman in native dress carrying a tall water jar on her head, a donkey pulling a cart loaded with pita bread.

Stepping outside again, we saw our friends quickly taking snapshots of one another.

"Lillian, don't you want me to take your picture here?" I asked.

Shaking her head "no" didn't count. The head that shook "no" was connected to a hand that simultaneously extended her camera. "Take mine, Jean." Lucy? Jackie? I didn't know.

We were at the tomb where Jesus was buried and arose.

I took one shot, then asked, "Anybody else?" and got another affirmative, so I snapped again. She came to join me, and we stood together, glued to the spot, oblivious to everyone around us.

Lillian began crying softly. Again I put my arm around her. Someone seated behind me whispered in my ear, "Can I help?" I placed her hand on Lillian's back, along with mine. Two more loving hands appeared and rested on Lillian's back and shoulder. Someone else tucked a fresh tissue in Lillian's hand. We didn't know what was going through her mind, but there was no doubt of its power.

Lillian Wrote: "I was really there. I know. No doubts. So can I believe? I do believe! I felt the strong love that flowed through the hands of others on my back and shoulder."

Jean as Narrator: The following day, we left the Holy Land, crossing into Egypt on our way to the Cairo airport. Transformed by her experiences in the Holy Land, Lillian was different. She was changing almost by the minute – taking charge. In our room, Lillian began writing in her journal – writing, writing, writing. The next morning, she was first up and coaxing me to get up. She went to a souvenir store by herself to spend the last of her money on picture postcards and gifts for Jimmy and James. When we lined up to board the plane, Lillian said she had never been on a plane before. Someone always did the flying to my place. Lillian was taking over her life.

***

Lucy Wrote: "Well, Lil was going to write, but she can some other time. We are on our way home. Lil got on the plane and stayed herself. I guess that shows it's time for me to not be separate anymore. Dr. Robinson is going to miss me. It will get dull without me around! The only question I can't come up with any answer for yet is how come a God who was supposed to be a loving God allows for human sacrifice."

Lillian Wrote: "I can't believe we were in Egypt only yesterday. I went through customs. I did! Me! Not Lucy! Not Jackie or anyone else! Me! I'm not sure how I know, but I know now that God cares. I sure hope that I can teach or help James learn that. Neither Keith nor Evan has that. Right now I need to concentrate on how I can keep James safe. I wish there was someone who could do that."

Jean as Narrator: Scribbled out in blue ink on a yellow napkin was a note. "Lil, we got to talk. Chrissy."

A few hours after getting back to Virginia, I was handed a yellow paper napkin with this message written on it: "Jean, I am atryin' to get your attention. It ain't aworkin'. Can I make a 'pointment with you in the next room? Chrissy."

Chrissy said she would be the one to take care of James and keep him safe. She said that she liked kids, and she wouldn't let "nobody" hurt James. She promised to take James directly back to Gateway after his visits with Dr. Alabiso. No more taking him on trips."

What an accent she had! Her speech pattern was that of a country Kentuckian. She had named herself after Rev. Chris.

***

Jean as Narrator: Rev. Chris talked to Lucy and Jackie. They were ready to become part of Lillian. He said goodbye to them both. Jackie was integrated in the church parking lot on her way to my car, where I was waiting. Opening the door, Lillian said, "Jackie's gone! Just now! I feel like I will really be only me and soon. God made me stronger in Israel."

The next day, Lucy appeared to say, "Let me talk to Rev. Chris about my friend who committed suicide. Rev. Chris says that God understands when someone commits suicide. How does Rev. Chris always know what we need to hear? He gave me a hug when I told him, 'I just need to see Dr. Robinson one more time before I leave.'"

Lillian was ready to leave my house and return to New York. It was a different Lucy who came to me and said, sadly, "Jean, this is the last time I will ever see you as THE LUCY. Lillian has become stronger and doesn't need me now. I wish it didn't have to be. I always liked you. You were my friend, and you always came through for me. As soon as we get home, I will see Dr. Robinson and tell him goodbye."

Lucy's tears, her demeanor and her words took me by surprise. I hadn't realized she was close to integration. I had tears in my eyes as I hugged her and said, "I love you, Lucy. THE LUCY!" We shared a weak laugh, and she said to me, for the very first time, "I love you too, Jean."

***

Lillian Wrote: "I saw Dr. Robinson. Lucy did too. She was integrated today. I guess she was just waiting for a hug from Dr. Robinson. She told him all about coming back to God. We talked about the time coming when there would be just ME – no 'others.' He said I didn't need Joyce and Annie. They don't take time very much. It's mostly me all the time now. Only what if James comes home and I can't handle it? I better keep someone to take over so I don't get angry with him. Dr. Robinson says stop wanting to be perfect. It's scary thinking I have to be responsible for me all the hours, all the time. Lucy is gone and Jackie too. Just me, Joyce and Annie."

Joyce Wrote: "Dr. Robinson thinks it would be all right for me to leave; so let's. Lillian, you still have Annie."

Lillian Wrote: "Okay, but I need someone."

Jean as Narrator: It was an excited Lillian who called me with the news. She had learned that Joyce had been having sex with Jimmy out of a sense of duty, and Lillian, herself, could do that and more now that Lucy, Robin Jean and Lizabeth were part of her. It fascinated me that I knew there was a Chrissy, but Lillian still didn't.

Several days later, I received a letter from Lillian that read, "I HAVE STOPPED HATING GOD."

Part 2

Chapter 29
New Doctor: New Rules

Chaos rules.

Lillian and Jimmy move to Pennsylvania. James is placed with Pap and Grandma in Ohio. Lillian begins a one-year admission to a state psychiatric hospital. Contact with Dr. Robinson and Rev. Chris is broken. A new psychiatrist is assigned. Restrictions are placed on contact between Jean and Lillian.

The system of relationships that has kept Lillian moving forward is put asunder.

What's more, Lillian is now generating new personalities as she comes in touch with trauma memories that she has never had before.

Lillian becomes more depressed, more dejected. Jean agonizes over the restrictions on her contact with Lillian.

Neither Jean nor Lillian understands the reason for restricting Jean's contact with Lillian. What had worked so well before, Jean's loving acceptance of each personality, is no longer permitted. Perhaps Lillian's new psychiatrist imposes the rule in order to protect Jean from a dangerous personality, or possibly it was the belief among psychiatrists at the time that the personalities should not be encouraged in their separate identities.

The days become darker. The nights become longer. Lillian is losing hope.

FA

Jean as Narrator: During the summer of 1983, Jimmy's job was in jeopardy. He was required to relocate to Pennsylvania. Lillian and James had to change doctors. The psychiatrist recommended by Dr. Robinson was Dr. Richard Kluft, who specialized in treating multiples. The Masons moved again, for the fourth time in three years. The truck terminal Jimmy worked out of was over 100 miles from Dr. Kluft, so they moved halfway between.

As Dr. Kluft began working with Lillian, other personalities started showing up. Fearing for her life, Dr. Kluft asked Lillian to consider a voluntary admission to the psychiatric hospital in Philadelphia. He could work more intensely with Lillian and keep her safe, believing that she could be fully integrated in about a year's time. Jimmy consulted with his insurance company and was told insurance would pay 80 percent of the hospital expenses and doctor's bills. (They had gone through a medical bankruptcy the previous year.) James went to live with Pap and Grandma in Ohio. Lillian signed the admission papers.

I called Dr. Kluft and offered my help. His response was anything but warm. I did not understand. About a month later, I planned to visit Lillian. Dr. Kluft had to give permission.

During the four-hour drive to Philadelphia, I kept wondering what it would be like to visit someone in a state hospital. Portions of movies flashed through my mind, and I shuddered.

Arriving at last, I entered the specific building and approached the receptionist. Asking my name and Lillian's, she checked her list, issued a visitor's pass and directed me to the fifth floor, where I was guided to a locked ward. Lillian was pointed out to me. She was sitting, head down, on a bench. I went quickly to her and gave her a hug. She hadn't let herself believe I would really come, even though I had told her on the phone when I was coming.

She was in terrible shape! Neither of us seemed able to converse. We sat side by side on that bench, so close, our bodies touched. She quietly pointed out one patient who never spoke and another who talked to himself, one who had been kind to her and one who swore at her. She had great compassion for them and equally strong fear for herself.

Lillian was painfully aware that staff members were demonstrating their omnipotence. She was at their mercy. They had all the control. They could be gentle, or they could be harsh. They could be fair or not. Lillian didn't know anymore what was fair. She felt their intent was to break her down; to destroy her personalities, reducing her to a nothing – one personality with no parts.

We sat there against each other, soaking up one another's warmth. For the first time in my life, I was at a loss for words. I couldn't stay there for even an hour. The pain was intolerable, seeing her like that. She didn't ask me to stay any longer. Her pain must have been excruciating. Promising to call her and to come again, I took my leave.

I did write to her, but not as often as in the past. I also telephoned her, and she called me occasionally, but Dr. Kluft had us confused. I wondered why he seemed so reluctant to have me help him. Nearly two months passed before I visited Lillian again. She always had to have Dr. Kluft's permission.

This time I was sent to a different building and to the second floor. As I exited the elevator, I faced a hallway with wire-covered windows to my right. I could see patients inside but walked quickly ahead to a locked door, trying not to see those sad faces. I was expected. My pass was viewed and the door unlocked, then relocked behind me. A second locked door was unlocked, then relocked. It was like something out of a horror movie. I was apprehensive and frightened. My hands were clammy, and my heart refused to behave.

The contents of my purse were examined, and my pens and pencils were held at a desk for later retrieval. I was told that Lillian could not have pencil and paper. This time she was seated near the nurses' station. In a very low voice, she told me how some of the orderlies and nurses were treating her and how very frightened she was. She had to sit in front of the nurses' station for punishment. When I asked the reason for the punishment, she said, "I guess I deserve it. I lost time. Then, when I became me, I asked for a pencil and paper so I could write and ask one of the personalities if she knew why another patient was tied to his chair. They gave me a crayon and a tiny slip of paper, not big enough for anything. I threw the paper at them.

"They said I was violent, and for two days I had to sit within arm's length of a nurse who was assigned to me. They called it 'one-on-one.' Even when I had to go to the bathroom, she or he had to stand right there. It was humiliating!

Finally, on the second day, I was crying, and a girl gave me a tissue. When the nurse watching me looked away, I stuffed the tissue down my throat, shoving it down as far as my finger could go. I must have passed out. The next thing I knew, my hands and feet were being tied to a chair, and my friend was in tears."

Lillian requested and received permission to show me her room. "Ten minutes" was the limiting reply.

The room was clean and neat. Lillian was provided with a window seat, where she spent many listless hours. Gesturing behind the drape, she showed me her drawing of a girl pointing a gun. "I had that facing the door at first, but it spooked some of the staff, and they tried to make me take it down. We compromised. I put it on the side of the window seat, where only I can see it. I'm not ready to give it up yet. I told them they would know when I was ready."

On the wall were drawings obviously produced by small children. Lillian told me, "There are two more children, Jean and Paula. Dr. Kluft says they are 4 and 7 years old. I don't know which is which. Dr. Kluft doesn't want you to ask for any personalities, and he told me they were not to talk to you."

She pulled out more drawings done by the children and showed them to me. Studying seven stick figures, we tried to figure out whom they represented. One was Dr. Kluft. One was Lillian's assigned therapist, Lynda Reed, Ph.D. One was Aunt Pearl, another appeared to be Aunt Mary. The other three were Dr. Alabiso, Jimmy and me, Jean! I ached for those two children, but all I could do was say to Lillian, "I hope Jean and Paula know that I care about them." But Dr. Kluft was in charge, and he could keep me from seeing Lillian or even talking to her if he chose to do so. I was forced to comply.

When my hour was up, I prepared to leave. Lillian apologized for my having to see her in this awful place. I promised to come back. I signaled the orderly; he unlocked the door, walked me through, relocked it, and we proceeded to the next door. As I passed through, he relocked the gate behind me. I glanced through the thick plate glass windows to see Lillian walking beside me. We looked longingly into each other's eyes. She pressed her open palm against the inside of the glass, and I matched her with my open palm on the outside of the glass. We were both crying.

It was a depressing drive home. I felt so hopeless. What did Dr. Kluft have against me? How could he lock Lillian up there and lock me out? I couldn't figure it out.

A few days after our visit, I received a card. It seems that little Paula did, in fact, know me, and knew that I cared for her. She signed the card thanking me for coming to visit. She misspelled her name. She printed it "Puala."

I called Dr. Kluft's office and offered to move to Philadelphia to help him with Lillian. Since I had helped Dr. Robinson, I thought I could do the same for him. I offered to help him with other patients or work elsewhere in the hospital to earn enough to rent a nearby room. He said no. I felt so bad. Jimmy only visited her once every week or two and stayed only 15 to 30 minutes each time. She couldn't tell him about her treatment for fear he would take up "her cause" and make waves with the staff. That would only have resulted in more trouble for her. She, too, had to comply. She had to work things out on her own. When she was not communicative with Jimmy, he would leave. He was as supportive as he knew how to be. He kept in touch with Dr. Kluft, just as he had with Dr. Robinson. She had not seen Evan or Keith in nearly a year.

And just as before, whenever Lillian became suicidal, Jimmy confronted her with, "If you're going to commit suicide, get a divorce first and take your old name back. Don't darken the Mason name with a suicide." Likewise, when she wanted to discuss her plans to kill "them," Jim, knowing she would be killed or jailed if she made an attempt, told her to get a divorce first. It was a sobering thought to Lillian and an effective deterrent. "If you love us, don't leave us!" Jimmy requested.

A letter from Lillian told me how she was getting double messages. One from Dr. Kluft and Lynda, her therapist, was that it was important for her to "express your feelings." The other one, from the staff, was to tie her up whenever she shed a tear or expressed anger. The way she saw it, if she showed any emotion, she would be punished.

There were times when she could not eat. Staff would fill her plate and put it before her. There she would sit obediently, day after day. She was reminded of how, as a child, her uneaten plate of food had been refrigerated and placed before her at the next meal, and at the next, and at the next, until she ate it.

Her condition became critical. She couldn't stand anything in her mouth, not even water. Her weight dropped by 12 pounds. Dr. Kluft was working with Lillian in therapy, but his fellow psychiatrists began exerting pressure on him. They wanted Lillian hydrated intravenously. Five doctors stood watching as Dr. Kluft gently coaxed her. She couldn't let her doctor down, but it was so hard. At last she said, "How about a piece of ice?" And Lillian managed to get it into her mouth. Later that day, she drank some Pepsi, but she nevertheless had to have an IV for several days.

Bit by bit, or rather bite by bite, Lillian eventually began eating again. When she was finally able to speak of it, Lillian divulged another memory. It was of her stepfather's penis in her mouth. Lillian had recovered Ellen's memory from before Herbert's death, when Lillian was only 12.

Lillian Wrote: "I didn't understand Dr. Kluft at first. Every other word that came out of his mouth was a swear word. He complained that I wasn't working with him. I finally wrote him a note asking how I could work with anybody who swears like that. It reminded me of just the way it was at home when I was growing up. After he got my note, he stopped all swearing. It's so hard here, Aunt Jean, and I miss you so much. I know I'm here voluntarily, but last week I called Jimmy and asked him to bring my clothes and take me home. He said okay, and I signed myself out, but the agreement is that I have to wait 48 hours, and Dr. Kluft has to be notified. By the time Jimmy got here with my clothes, Dr. Kluft had come in especially for me and talked me into staying. But I am glad to know that Jimmy would come for me, even though we both know I need to be here. I am doing this for James, so he can have a regular mom and for Jimmy too."

Jean as Narrator: Between Thanksgiving and Christmas, I went to see Lillian again. She was permitted to leave the hospital with me for two hours. What a joy to get her out of there and to myself! We drove downtown to a shopping center, ate junk food at the food court and sat there and talked until our time was up.

James had written me a letter, asking me to buy a Christmas present for his mom. He enclosed two dollars. Everything I considered buying for her became unwise. A brooch? No, it has a pin. Earrings? No, she might swallow them. A scarf? No, she might strangle herself. I finally bought slippers from James and a robe from me – a robe without a belt.

I left the gifts with a staff member. She put them on the shelf in the storage room with Lillian's name on them, promising to deliver them Christmas Eve. Jim had given his gift to her two days before my visit.

When I called Lillian the day after Christmas, she had gone through a terrible holiday.

Jimmy was with James at Pap and Grandma's, thinking Lillian would be taken care of. But on December 24, Lillian had been moved to a different floor, and the presents were forgotten about. She was miserable. She had been forgotten and alone on Christmas Day! Many patients were permitted to go home for the day, and she was on a new floor with patients she didn't even know.

I told her about the gifts I had left. She checked with the staff and called me back. They were found. She liked them, but I will never forget how bad I felt for her.

***

Lillian Journal: "I was around 4 years old. We were going to move to another house. She took me to the attic where there was a crate and made me get in it. Then she nailed the crate shut. I heard her go down the steps. I could see out through the slats. Everything was quiet. Time passed. Later, I heard someone in the house. I was so thirsty, and I cried for a drink. A man who had come to paint the house for the new tenants heard me and came up the attic stairs. When he saw me, he pried the crate open and took me out. I was stinking and filthy, but most of all, I was scared. Scared that Mother forgot where she put me again.

"The painter took me to his house, where he and his nice wife cleaned me up. I remember that she put me in the sink and washed me while he washed my clothes. They doctored all the nail scratches and removed all the splinters. It hurt, but I didn't cry. It took a very long time for them to find out who I was and where my family was. Finally they learned my Aunt Pearl's telephone number and called her. She came to get me, and when she called my mother at work, Mother said she thought I was with Aunt Pearl all that time.

"Later, when I was growing up, someone said my mother was psychotic."

***

Lillian Wrote: "Movement therapy didn't go. The therapist came and got me. Cried from the very beginning. She was trying to be nice. It struck me with such force: When you know someone hates you, and you know they will do things to you, you never know for sure when or what the hurt will be, but you know you are going to be hurt. It is worse when another person is present. She, Jessica, would be kind in front of people. Then sometimes, for no reason, she'd

263

hurt me. 'Come,' she motions me to come to her or to go past her to get something, and you know she will trip you or punch you or pull your hair or bend your fingers back, but she is acting nice. I cried, and I got up and left therapy, yelling, 'This group is awful. They are never going to be any good. It will never get better!' and I cried and cried and couldn't stop. I can't believe I yelled for the first time in my life! I guess I finally found my voice. It was after 1 p.m. before I got myself stopped crying. Movement therapy was over at 11:30 this morning!"

***

Lillian: "I talked to Dr. Kluft about child abuse, Keith and Evan, and being angry at them, wanting to put them in the closet and not doing it. Instead, going out into our shed and using a knife to hit into a block of wood, wishing it was who? Me? Mother? Them? He said I got the idea someplace. Today in art therapy, I am going to sculpt a hand holding a knife.

"Aunt Pearl didn't have a great life either. Whenever her husband got angry, he beat her. One time, she dropped to her knees and began praying loudly, and he stopped. He was religious? After that time, Aunt Pearl repeatedly ended his frequent violent attacks the same way. Was there incest there too?

"I'm trying to sculpt a hand holding a knife. Jean is bringing my woodcarvings. I have been asked if I would give a woodcarving demonstration. Tired. Cannot sleep in bed. I asked Dr. Kluft about integrating me."

Chapter 30
Still More?

In the past, the integration of the personalities seemed almost too easy. They decided to integrate, set a date, took care of loose ends and became integrated, or were they?

Ordinarily, the process of integrating personalities is painful and confusing, and it takes place over an extended period of time. Often it is excruciating.

While in the state hospital, Lillian finds out that she has seven more personalities. She also discovers that Lucy and some of the others were never fully integrated. They only appeared to be in order to please Dr. Robinson.

Lillian finds that the principle "Sometimes you have to take something apart before you can put it back together" applies to integration as well.

At its core, dissociation is a primitive psychological defense.

Why do some abused children develop multiple personality disorder and others do not?

Generally speaking, the more vulnerable the child and the more invasive the abuse, the more likely the child is to develop the disorder. This is especially true for children under the age of 5. Children at this age are completely defenseless against abuse. They do not have the language development – much less the language skills needed – to protect themselves.

Dissociation becomes their primary defense. Knowing this, Dr. Kluft pushes harder to recover memories of trauma before the age of 5.

When dissociating, adults who were severely abused at these early ages think in the same manner as a 3- or 4-year-old child. They draw false conclusions, are unable to separate cause from effect, fact from fiction. Indeed, children so afflicted lack the ability to recognize when their thinking is irrational, fragmented or psychotic.

As such, the reader likely will find Lillian's thinking in this chapter difficult to follow.

FA

Lillian's Journal: "Slept a little bit last night. I feel like scum sewage. Shame. Jessica pushed me out of the upstairs window. Pushed me! My own mother! I fell but caught the tree branches and slowed my fall. Looked up. She was watching and laughing! I hurt, so I lay there a little bit. Miracle. Nothing broke. Just aches. I could have been killed. Well, maybe not. Only a two-story house. I deserved it. Always doing everything wrong!

"That evening I found myself on the stairs at the hospital. Dr. Kluft was holding my wrists. He said something about Jessie (Jessie??), letters, someone running after me – who?"

Jessie Wrote: "Dr. Kluft wanted to talk to me today. No way can anyone speak with someone named after Jessica. He asked if there were other personalities. How could he do that? Heard someone say, 'Seven, come 11. Throw the dice.'

"Dr. Kluft says maybe there were eleven and now there are seven. He says Jessica did a lot more things to me than I ever realized. I don't want this. I do not need any therapy about Jessica. He says he will not let me go home."

***

Lillian's Journal: "Saw Dr. Kluft. He said there were seven. Names were written on my hand: Ginger, Torrey, Carla, Kathleen, Doddy, Bonnie, Diana and Jessie. That's eight. Seven plus 11, he said 18. God! I really hate this.

"I am so depressed. Someone watched a TV show with me. I felt frozen when it was over. It was about incest, a stepfather and a mother with daughters. The nurse told me I came in my room and cried and banged my head against the wall for two hours. Not me. I wonder who. Am I losing time again? Lots. Will tell Dr. Kluft, 'Let's get this over and let me go home. I haven't the guts to go on.'"

Chrissy Wrote: "Dr. Kluft asked me to talk to Doddy. But Jessie thought *he* wanted her and got up to run. Dr. Kluft said, 'You cause a crisis on this floor right now, and to North building you go!' I was afraid. Jessie said, 'Jessica's dad hit Jessica, and Jessica hit her mom on the head, and her mom died, so Jessica was going to kill Lillian, hit her on the head till she died.' Jessie didn't want to be found."

Jean Wrote: "I had to read the above paragraph repeatedly in order to fully grasp the importance of Jessie's brief statement. When at last I fully understood, I realized that Jessica had, indeed, intended and attempted to kill Lillian. What a sick woman!"

Lillian Wrote: "If I could, I'd stay in bed all day. Woke up in the closet. What kind of life is this? Blow this place. Who the H is Dr. Kluft that he needs to know my mind anyways? Everything seems out of place. Feel like I need to hide somewhere and regroup. I cry and cry. Jim called.

"I saw Dr. Kluft. He said what I wrote to him is all about Mother. He said we have to keep on working. I said I just can't. He said he tried hypnosis and it didn't seem to work. He said I was blocking. Somehow a scene flashed – 'If you don't do it, I warn, you will be hurt.' When my mother's father lived with us, I was told to stay away from his bedroom door, but I thought he was hurting Mother. She brought me in. She was undressed."

Chrissy Wrote: "Somebody went out the fire door and tried to hide in the bushes and cried and cried. Then somebody tried to get back in but couldn't. Door was locked. They banged on the door for a long time. Found another door to ring the bell and someone came and showed her where to go, and a doctor met her and brought her back. She said she was hiding from someone. Told her address and her telephone number same as Mother's. Her last name, the same as my real father's. 'Don't call Mother, she will be mad,' she said. Remember the hitting was because somebody was talking about bad stuff. Didn't remember her name. Oh yes, 'Lillian' answers to Lillian too."

***

Jean as Narrator: It became harder and harder to understand Lillian. She seemed confused. Her sentences didn't always make sense. She seemed as if she were in a different world.

This time, when I asked permission to see Lillian and take her out to eat, I was restricted. I could see her, but she could not leave the floor. We visited in her room. Chrissy just had to talk to me. Dr. Kluft said no. Lillian told me about the girl who walked out of the hospital the night before. Lillian was so frightened. "Aunt Jean, do you think there is another Lillian? Look at this writing in the journal."

I studied the writing. She made her capital "L" open at the top. The "other Lillian" had made hers closed. The writing *was* different. I had seen it before. It was the same one who had written months ago, when Lillian was terribly suicidal. I thought someone was writing "Be sure, Lillian," but she meant "Be sure. Lillian." One with a comma and one with a period (Ah, yes, she was the one who drew the picture of the girl aiming a gun.)

Her signature had an open top to the capital "L."

Two Lillians?! Without Chrissy, I didn't know who was there! Oh, it was just too confusing. Lillian became extremely agitated and talkative. What I did, mostly, was listen. What I thought was, "Dr. Kluft had better know what he is doing!" She expressed her feelings of isolation and the fear that her mother might find her and hurt her, even here in the hospital.

Lillian told me, "It's so hard, this going back, this dredging up, this talking out loud, this awful fear; afraid Dr. Kluft will laugh at the things I'm afraid of and feeling sick because Jessica used me. She told me lies, and I believed her!"

Lillian Wrote: "As of now, I refuse to write anyone else's words going on in my head, little girls included. Writing down is sickening. Telling someone else is worse. One of these nights, the feelings will be too much, and I will tie a plastic bag over my head. I hate pretending it doesn't bother me. Stay in control. Say I'm okay no matter what.

"How can they talk out loud? I hate them. I hate me worse. Dr. Kluft has too many other patients in crisis. Don't make waves. Don't feel. Sit in the corner and cry, and say I'm okay. Go ahead everyone. Say your piece. I will buy drain cleaner and drink it. No one will talk again. I lose my voice once in a while. The drain cleaner will make all of you lose your voices too! I feel so, so sick. Went to church with the group. Should've known better. The fool, me, Lil can't be there and not cry. I should have been dead years ago. Why does Dr. Kluft think it's okay to use their language? Why does he think it's okay to call them names, yet think it is wrong for me to cut them with a knife? They tore my guts out years ago. Dr. Kluft wants to have it done again. The talking, bringing the memories and feelings to the surface, it doesn't make me better or well. It is tearing me into pieces, and I have to keep pretending I'm okay. Here is Lillian trying to please again! How many times must I be physically and emotionally raped in my head 'for my own good?' It's therapeutic? For whom? Kill the children parts of me, and I will be free. Dead but free. No more humiliation. No more shame. No more laughter.

"I saw Dr. Kluft. Felt so tired. He didn't press me on anything. Talked about not talking and Chrissy mentioned the drain cleaner. He says it would kill us. I don't think so. Just make it so no one could talk. My stomach goes in circles. Jessica wrote to me. Again. Same letter as Rosalind's. I asked her to stop. She ignored it. I am so sick inside. I feel crazy. No reason for tears, ever. I feel like I am going to die.

"Dr. Kluft saw two other patients who are friends of mine this morning but no time for me. I guess 'cause I don't need it. One of the friends told me that if I lived closer, Dr. Kluft wouldn't have me in the hospital. That he just has patients in the hospital who are in crisis. Anyway, why stay where my doctor is too busy? Too many people to help that want it. (The handwriting now looks like Lucy's). I miss Jim and I want to go home, wherever the hell home is!

"Lucy and some of the others were not completely integrated with Dr. Robinson. They just wanted to please him."

Chrissy Wrote: "Dr. Kluft don't want us as a patient. I thought he cared. Nobody does. I going to go home. This is lonely here. No one cares about me or anyone of us."

Lillian Wrote: "Can't go see Dr. Robinson anymore. Doing everything wrong, not thinking right. I am going to die here in this room."

Jean as Narrator: One by one, the "new" personalities took over.

Erica's Journal: "I said it wrong. I said it was all her and not us, and now Dianna, Doddy and Torre say I can't see the doctor anymore. None of us, 'cause I said it's not us, it's her, and nobody's allowed to say that. Doctor says I have to stop thinking of us as us and think of us as Lillian. I have to punish myself. I will bang my head against the wall in the closet again, where no one will hear. I want to die or call James, maybe. He is 13 too."

Dianna's First Journal: "You are bad, Erica. Don't ever think she was wrong again. Jessica is very powerful. Don't forget that, Erica. Never talk about her, or some fortuneteller will show her where we are."

Lillian Wrote: "Crazy night. Crazy day. Saw Dr. Kluft. Will not try to take drain cleaner or anything so I can't talk. I just have to make the doctor realize I really can't. I need to get those who might talk blocked. Memories seemed to be everywhere. Can't hide from myself. I want control but not memories. I think I have to die. I feel diseased. How will I be able to face myself if anyone ever knows all that happened, all that was done to me? I let it happen. When I was old enough to refuse, I didn't.

"Every time Dr. Kluft says Jessica is crazy, he means me too. I didn't get away from it all. I have to die. I am dying of shame. Erase Lillian from life. I am scared of me, of Dr. Kluft, of Jessica. My insides and my head hurt. Too many thoughts too fast. I want someone to care about me, and I can't care about me. Everything is leading up to me having to kill me. Will I when the time comes, when there is no other way out?

"Days are awful. Nights are worse. I see images of things in the past. I try to turn away from some terrible feelings rising out of nowhere, and another image comes from another direction, just as horrible. I go to sleep feeling like a disease and dream I have become one. There is no safe place.

"Dr. Kluft says he can help me. I think he can if I could let him. It is too much. I am a failure. I don't believe I can get well. I want to not be worthless, animal sewage, scum. I want to see my sons. James, I am losing him. Maybe it's best. I don't deserve him. Can James handle my death? Must ask Jim to help James in case it comes up. Dr. Kluft is an expert. Must remember he knows I want to be home with James and Jim. He will get me well. Nice dream, huh?"

***

Jean as Narrator: Received a stunning card in the mail. The handwritten capital "L" open at the top. The other Lillian? Yes. No. I don't think so. Probably.

The card portrayed a boy in a top hat, bow tie, yellow shirt and knee-length pants with striped stockings. He was standing in water almost knee deep. Tears were in his eyes. His right hand was over his heart, Pledge of Allegiance style. In his left arm was a large heart-shaped box hinged across the middle and with the top flipped up. Stars were falling from the box. A cat sat on a straight chair, peering down at the rising water. A dead goldfish lay in the bottom of a goldfish bowl, and another fish raced around the top of the water, wild-eyed and frightened. Clouds outside a window dumped a waterfall.

The caption was: "His heart broke open, and all the tears that had been hidden inside it spilled out like thousands of tiny stars. His heart must have been sadder than he suspected because it cried and cried till he floated out the door and away down the road on a river of tears."

Inside was a brief handwritten note. "This card is about me. Sometimes, I feel so like it says. Lillian."

Was she the one I met only once who called herself LILL? No, I didn't think so.

My tears mixed with profound amazement as I studied the card. The card helped me understand that it was the personality of Lillian who had given back all those tears to Lillian. That is why my Lillian had written, "Why do I cry all the time?"

How did every part of her know the intensity of my love and my curiosity? When had I met this Lillian? The names Lillian and Lillian were interchangeable. I wondered how much more she could survive, and I breathed yet another prayer for her.

Lillian Wrote: "Lillian is fused; also Ginger, Torrey, Carla, Kathleen, Doddy, Dianna and Ella. That leaves me, Chrissy, Storm, Herbert, Jessie and Erica. I told Dr. Kluft that was it. No more. I don't want him to talk to anyone now. No more personalities. It's a fake anyway. I am all this to myself. Other people are only one person. Aren't I just one person? I can finish it myself without any help. I better save money to leave here on my own.

"Jessie integrated today. I wrote Dr. Kluft a mostly angry letter. Jim says I shouldn't talk about wanting to kill someone. That there shouldn't be any question. Either I love Jimmy and the kids, or I don't. 'If you love us, then don't think about revenge!' Why not? She hurt me! No one did anything to stop her. Why stop me? Let's be fair about this. Let me kill her!! Stab her to death and past death!"

Chapter 31
James

It was a cold and damp March morning. The sky broke gray on my way into the office.

I was working at my desk when the call came in.

"Hello. Dr. Alabiso?"

"Yes."

"This is Dr. Raymond Martin, Stark County medical examiner."

In the moment between breaths, my heart sank – had Lillian succeeded? Were they all gone, the ones I had come to have such deep empathy for – all of them? Even little Amy?

Breaking into my thoughts, Dr. Martin continued, "The law requires that the circumstances at the time of death be determined and that suicide be ruled out."

That moment hung frozen in time.

Dr. Martin continued once again.

*"**James Mason Is Dead**. Was James depressed? Did he ever mention suicide?"*

Ultimately, James' death was ruled accidental. But I was troubled.

The move to Ohio ended James' weekly therapy sessions. These sessions were James' connection to the world outside of multiplicity. James was living with Mr. Mason's parents. Mr. Mason's job had taken him away from home for days at a time. Lillian was hospitalized six hours away in Philadelphia. Children were not allowed to visit. Evan did not move with the family. But James had never mentioned thoughts of suicide.

I wrote to Lillian and Jimmy, sharing my memories of James. I closed the letter, letting them know that I had accepted another child into therapy, assuring them that I would see this child without charge until he was emotionally safe and healthy.

Looking back, I suppose it was my way of keeping James alive.

In reading Chapter 31, I realized that I had never resolved my grief. On the way back from my final meeting with Jean at her home in Virginia, I drove to the Mason family cemetery in West Virginia – James' final resting place.

It was exactly as Jean had described it.

The white church was set against a stark landscape. James' grave was on the hill that rose up across from the church.

I stood there, silently remembering a sad and sweet little boy. I grieved now for Lillian and Jimmy's loss so many years ago. I grieved for Amy, who lost her playmate, and even for Esther, who must have regretted her sternness with James.

I grieved for Lucy's, Sarah Ann's, Julie's and Lee's pain.

I was quiet inside on the five-hour drive back to Niagara Falls.

James was gone.

FA

Lillian's Journal: "I see death beside me sitting down. Weird! Whoever heard of death sitting or standing? It doesn't frighten me. I am not afraid of death. Let it be mine. Someone is going to die. Back home? Pap? He is 71. I feel death. It's close. I am not close to Pap. Mine? Staff would think I'm crazy if I say these feelings. Will the doctor laugh? Strange feelings. Ignore. But this feeling is strong. Lillian is going crazy?"

Jean as Narrator: When Lillian told Dr. Kluft about her feelings, he said, "Let's wait and see what develops. I believe you."

After she left his office, she told two friends who were also patients at the hospital. Later, Lillian got out her hair dryer, cut off the cord, and took the cord down the hall to one of the patient community shower rooms. Wrapping a cord around her neck, she then looped it over the shower bar. But she flung it off, thinking, "Why am I doing this? I'm not suicidal." Lillian threw the cord into the trash. She didn't understand.

The next morning, Jimmy and Evan showed up unexpectedly with Dr. Kluft. The instant Jimmy saw Lillian, he groaned aloud and grabbed her to him. He was sobbing. Lillian couldn't believe what he was saying. She had never seen him cry like that, so she knew it must be true!

Their James was dead! Their baby!

***

Jean as Narrator: How can it be that the telephone ring sounds the same, whether the news is good or bad?

"Aunt Jean, Aunt Jean, James is dead! Please don't let it be true! Jimmy drove all night to get here to tell me! Oh, Aunt Jean, what am I going to do?"

"What? Lillian? What are you saying?!"

"James is dead!"

"Dead? Where is he?"

"James, dead? It can't be! He is only 13 years old!" I thought. I tore myself back to the anguish coming through the telephone.

"Wasn't he at Jimmy's parents' house?"

"Yes, but not now. James is dead! I thought it couldn't be, but Jimmy was crying so hard that I knew it was true!"

"You are telling me James, your little James, is dead? How did it happen? When?"

No wonder Lillian couldn't believe it. I couldn't either.

"Pap found him next to a chair and hanging by his neck up in his bedroom! Oh, God! I don't want Jessica to find out. Please don't let anyone call her or my sister either. I don't want Jessica there. What can we do?"

"I won't call Jessica, and I won't call your sister."

Back to the telephone, I had to hear it one more time. This time I heard her say, "They don't know all the details. Will you come?"

"Of course. I will leave for Ohio as soon as I can pack a few things."

I left soon after Lillian called, and during the long drive, I kept trying to remember all that she had told me on the telephone. I knew she needed me. I remembered many, many attempts by Lillian and various personalities to take her life (or theirs), but never had it occurred to me that she would make it and James would not. The idea that he might have to face life without his mother was omnipresent, but the reversal of roles never crossed my mind.

Jimmy and Lillian went directly to the funeral home and asked to see James. They were refused at first and told he was not ready. Lillian said, "We will wait."

When they finally saw James, Lillian ran her fingers through his shiny, clean, slightly damp hair. Jimmy started to put his arms around her, but Lillian, in her grief, was too bound together with James to allow anyone else in. "No. Don't touch me," Lillian said. Jimmy backed off.

They went from there to select a coffin and to get a new suit for James.

***

Jean as Narrator: At Pap and Grandma's, Lillian found the necklace James had been wearing, the one she made for him for St. Patrick's Day. Also in his room were two notes James had written. One note said, "Today is Valentine's Day. It isn't the same without Mom here." On the other side, "Today is St. Pat's Day. I miss Mom."

Lillian told me, "I wouldn't have found those precious notes if I hadn't been cleaning up."

Lillian called Rosalind to tell her. "I have some terrible news. James is dead!" she said.

Rosalind's response was as cold as ice. Lillian was so shocked, she dropped the phone. Lillian was crying. She didn't in her wildest dream anticipate such a response!

Jimmy grabbed the phone from Lillian, "Don't bother coming to the funeral! We don't want you or your mother here!" He slammed the receiver down. He was furious!

Letty called a little later to find out about funeral arrangements, but they hadn't decided the day and time. Lillian told her so, but Letty never called back. Since Letty had an unlisted telephone number, Lillian could not call her.

Letty blamed Lillian and Jimmy for not informing her when the services were. Later, we learned that Rosalind had told all their relatives that none of them were wanted at James' funeral. So not one of Lillian's many cousins, aunts, uncles or friends came to the funeral or even sent cards. I was glad I could be there for her.

Lillian stood by the side of James' coffin all evening. She draped the necklace with the copper four-leaf clover over his hands.

Lillian's mother did not show up, nor did her sisters. I was relieved, for I knew that they would have found a way to blame Lillian and hurt her. They always did. They apparently didn't see the obituary column in the newspaper until the visitation was over. The funeral and burial were to be held many miles away in West Virginia at the Mason Family Cemetery.

I was accepted as part of Jimmy's family, perhaps because they all knew how much I loved Jimmy and Lillian. Many times his family expressed appreciation for my affection and support for Lillian. I slept at their house that night.

James' grandparents' house was modest and even boasted an indoor bathroom added about five years earlier. It was a homey little house, and the hand-crocheted afghan on the back of the well-worn sofa and the doilies on the end tables made it seem even warmer. On the coffee table was a delicate starched and ruffled doily that was all the rage in the '60s.

We were all worried about how Grandma would cope with James' death. She prepared a big country breakfast Saturday morning. When we finished eating, she asked if I wanted to see where James had died. Leading me through the kitchen to the corner door, which went up to James' room, she admonished me to be careful on the spiral stairs.

"We had steps shaped like this at the house where I lived as a small child," I reminisced, trying to make conversation. I was really at a loss to know what to say. What must this dear lady be feeling? How could she be so calm? She didn't even look like she had been crying. How should I act? What could I do? But even as she showed me where James died, she maintained her composure.

The room, as with most attics, had a sharply slanted ceiling. "This is James' room, where Pap found him," she said. She began pointing things out to me. "That captain's chair was on its back, and here, see this bar? We put it between the rafters so that James could have a place to hang his shirts. He put his belt over the bar. When the chair went over, he was hanging by his neck and couldn't unfasten the belt."

I looked around the room, noticing how clean and neat everything was. On James' bed was a worn handmade quilt.

James' teacher told Jimmy that when she told the class about James, one boy became ill. The teacher gently probed for whatever knowledge he had about James. The young friend had told James not to do what he was doing.

I slept on the sofa at Jimmy's parents' house. We prepared ourselves as best we could for the sad day that dawn would bring.

At daybreak, Jimmy's brother left to ride in the hearse to the church in West Virginia. We left about an hour later. Jimmy drove my car with Lillian seated beside him and me in the back seat. There was little conversation. Although three carloads of us left at the same time, we did not form a cortege. Each car proceeded at its own speed; its occupants concentrating more upon their grief than the driving.

It seemed as though we drove for days. In reality, it was a three-hour drive. After we crossed the Ohio River into West Virginia, the hills grew steeper as the roads became narrower. It was cold, but the grass was greening; a sure sign of spring. The trees were full of little fat buds, announcing, with promise, the reawakening of the earth. Trickles of water from freshly melted snow and thawing ground tumbled down the mountainsides. We passed through canyons, over hills and through valleys dotted with tiny homes.

The road became little more than a cow path with one set of tire tracks for vehicles going both ways. Jimmy slowed to a crawl and shifted into low gear to drive through a meandering creek, which allowed itself to be momentarily interrupted by our car. I asked Jimmy what would happen if he met a vehicle, and he said, "One or the other of us would back up until we found a wide enough place to pass."

Now the trees stretched their roots under and on top of the road, slowing our pace even more. Insistent rocks pleaded unsuccessfully to deter us from our painful but necessary journey.

Jimmy's voice broke the stillness inside the car. "We are almost there." His heart was heavy as he passed his shirtsleeve across his eyes to dry the tears one more time. It had been many months since they had been able to visit with this part of Jimmy's family because of repeated hospitalizations and medical costs. But their bond with relatives here was secure, and they knew it. Returning to these hills of West Virginia, the home of Jimmy's childhood, usually gave Jimmy a thrill of elation and joy. He and Lillian owned a few acres here and planned to build a log cabin on the land. But today, sadness flooded his soul and overwhelmed his eyes with tears.

People began appearing along the road, having learned of the tragedy. Some waved in recognition. The lines etched on their faces spoke of hard work, hard times and hard living, but I saw more there. I saw compassion.

Finally passing through a second creek, this one wider and deeper than the first, and rounding one more curve, we came to a little church.

There were a couple of cars, the hearse and three people outside. A man who lived near the church was the gravedigger. He had completed his task, and we watched him dismount from the tractor and disappear into his house to wash up for the services.

I took my cues from Jimmy. We got out of the car to find a bathroom. It was a typical outhouse, similar to the "outdoor plumbing" of my youth. This one had a quarter moon cut out above the door to let light in. Opening the door, I discovered a "two-holer," and thank goodness, a roll of bathroom tissue, unlike the Sears catalogs we used back on the farm!

Even from the outside, the little church was somewhat foreboding. It was cold inside too, and nothing in or about the church spelled warmth. There was no piano or organ, no decorations, no padding on the seats, no vestments on the pulpit, but most notably, no people. All in all, nothing about the room felt like "sanctuary."

In the front of the church, to the right side, was the casket holding James' body. It stood open. Lillian walked to the side of the coffin and straightened James' shirt, smoothed the covers, tucking him in for the last time. Then, standing with one hand on the edge of the final resting place of her beloved son, she looked down at his inert body with all the tenderness and love any mother could possibly have for her child. Jimmy and I stood on either side of her, helpless to ease her pain.

Silence. Jim blew his nose. More silence. At last, growing bold, I began speaking in a voice that seemed unlike my own. "James, dear little James, you have been such a good boy. I know you didn't want to leave us. Do you see God? God loves you, James. I remember all those times when you called me on the telephone, James, and I will never forget you. You helped your mom, and you helped me to keep your mom alive. I will stay with your mom, James, I promise you. I will always be her friend. She will never have to be alone. I love you, James. Goodbye. I love you."

I saw myself searching the sparse one-room country church nervously, thinking surely someone would come to be with them soon. But as seconds stretched into minutes, we merely seated ourselves in the front pew nearest James. I wondered how people (whoever those 'people' were) could just leave Jimmy and Lillian alone there like that.

I had touched my own grief, and my tears began.

Everything was quiet again. Then Lillian began speaking softly to James. I was relieved to hear her expressing her love to him and giving voice to her feelings. I wondered if there were other personalities who wished for a chance to say their goodbyes. Several of them had shared in his care, and others had played with him. All of them cared about James, even though he was "Lil's kid."

Jimmy and Lillian turned to each other and embraced. Still no tears from Lillian. Some other people began collecting in the church – about 35 in all. Four men in suits walked to the front of the church and began singing without accompaniment. Their suits seemed quite out of place among these flannel-shirted, blue-jeaned mourners. Their gospel music was unfamiliar to me, but well-sung. Musical instruments were prohibited in this church.

A young preacher stood and read the obituary and gave the usual platitudes. He spoke of death as a good resting place. It seemed so inappropriate to say those words about James. He was young. YOUNG, NOT OLD! He still had years of living to do. It all felt so cold. It was obvious that the "preacher" hadn't known James, or Lillian or Jimmy either.

Family and friends passed by the open casket and moved on out. Evan tearfully tucked a bit of fur from James' pet rabbit into the pocket of his little brother's suit. Jimmy placed James' sword in the coffin to guard his little son. When James had learned that the samurai's sword symbolized his soul, he had asked for one for his birthday. Keith's contribution was dice from a board game enjoyed by the two brothers. Remembering James' note about missing her on St. Patrick's Day, Lillian removed the pressed four-leaf clover she carried in her wallet and slipped it into the casket. One lingering glance at James, and we left the church.

The cemetery was across the narrow, soggy dirt road from the church and up a severely steep incline. While the gravedigger went home to change his clothes again and returned to the tractor, the family gathered outside, where, with very little talking, they invited us to Jimmy's aunt's for a family meal after the burial. We agreed to go.

Jimmy had warned me to bring old shoes or boots, so I was prepared. As I stepped to my car to change, I heard the tractor being started and saw several men dragging great chains toward the tractor. I watched in amazement as the men attached the tractor to the hearse, then lined up behind the hearse and began to push. Slowly, slowly, the hearse began to move up the steep hill.

We started up the hill on foot, following the tracks the tractor and hearse had just made. It was a difficult hike, and it left me panting for breath at the top. Very few of the mourners attempted the climb.

We gathered around the hearse. The casket was carried by relatives, including James' two brothers, and placed over the open grave. The cemetery was so high that it was hidden from the view of any casual passersby. It was a family cemetery, and only about 20 grave markers could be seen. James' grave was at the far corner, bordered on two sides by a barbed-wire fence, beyond which the terrain suddenly plunged to a valley, where a swollen creek snaked its way to the river. The words to a favorite song recorded by Tennessee Ernie Ford sprang uninvited into my mind. "There will be peace in the valley for me." For James, peace overlooked that valley.

After a brief committal by the preacher, most of the people left, but Lillian wanted to stay.

She went to her first son, Keith, who informed her that he and Evan were going to fill their brother's grave. They had discussed it ahead of time, and "would she just leave them alone!"

Oh, he was angry! Years later, they discussed that anger. He was afraid his mom was going to try to stop them. "No way!" Lillian wrote, "I was concerned for them both, but also very proud."

We moved a short distance away and watched as Keith and Evan took up shovels and began replacing the freshly dug dirt, first with gentle sprinkles, then with more deliberate action, and finally, removing their shirts, they slung the shovelfuls of dirt down. It was the last thing they would ever do for their brother, letting their actions give them a release where words and tears had failed.

Evan called his mother over as he dug out a sweatband and put it on his head. "Mom, it will be better if you just please leave us alone. We'll come in when we're done."

"You are sure you're all right, Evan? Keith?" Lillian asked. Still no tears from Lillian.

"Yeah, Mom, we will be okay," Evan answered.

As we carefully descended the steep hill, Lillian said, "I am glad they have each other."

In the car again, Jimmy drove a mile or two to his Aunt Mary's home, where great thought and loving hands had prepared a meal for the family and friends gathering there. The house seemed very small as we walked through the meadow to the door, and I wondered if it could hold the number of people descending upon it. Several folks were on the front porch, some occupied chairs and some sat on the edge of the porch with their legs dangling.

We were greeted by friends and relatives who spoke words of welcome to us and comforted Lillian and Jimmy. They seemed to know of my involvement with Lillian, and some expressed their relief that I was there with her. We shared a meal of meatloaf, potatoes, vegetables, homemade bread and elderberry pies; all prepared on wood or coal stoves. We thanked them for their hospitality and departed.

Lillian was expected back in Philadelphia the same night, and since her safe return had been entrusted to me, the two of us began our arduous and pain-filled journey back East. Jimmy led us in his brother's car to a major highway, where he gave me directions to the turnpike. As we drove by the cemetery, Keith and Evan appeared by the side of the road. They had been watching for us. They had finished filling the grave. "Mom, we covered the grave all over, like a blanket, with the flowers people sent to the funeral home, so it looked pretty," Evan said. They hugged their mother and me, and we left. Jimmy remained with his sons.

It was a long, quiet drive. We kept watching the map and soon became frightfully aware of the shortage of time. After I had driven a couple of hours, we estimated the time of arrival at the hospital. Clearly, we would not reach Philadelphia before gates and doors were locked, and "lights out" was announced.

We decided to call Dr. Kluft and request an extension of time. He agreed that we should stop overnight and rest before pressing on. We signed in at the next motel.

How good it was to have the time pressure taken off! I knew Lillian must have been exhausted, but as we prepared for bed, I realized how little I knew about Lillian and/or any personalities at the present time. Wondering if Lillian had, in fact, been with me all through this trauma, I became apprehensive. I wish I could have done as I did so often in the past and ask Julie or Lucy, Esther or Jackie to tell me who she was, and what Lillian was thinking and feeling. Someone was always able to tell me exactly what to do for Lillian to keep her safe. But this new doctor had a totally different approach that minimized my interaction with Lillian and denied me information regarding the personalities. I felt helpless and angry again at Dr. Kluft for shutting me out.

An overwhelming sense of responsibility seized me. How could I stop her if she decided to leave? She could simply slip the bolt on the door and be gone. She wasn't talking about her feelings, and I wasn't smart enough to ask what she was feeling. "She has just lost her son – her baby!" I thought. "And I haven't seen or heard any crying. Not a tear! How can she stand it!? What would I be doing if I had lost one of my children?"

Lillian and I had not slept in the same house, let alone the same room, for a long time. Is this Lillian? If so, will someone else gain control of the body? Someone who doesn't know me? We are in a strange town where nobody knows me, and I know nobody. I slept lightly that night and with one eye open, tired though I was.

Resuming our journey the next day, we talked about shared incidents involving James.

"James always knew when Amy was there. Other people couldn't tell, but James seemed to have some way to know when she was there that was only his," she recalled.

"Yes, and James had a lot of common sense. He seemed to understand when it was important to call for help. I remember when he and Amy called to tell me he had taught her to dial my telephone number. And he was the first one to meet several new personalities. They were an accepted part of life for him."

"He saved my life more than once," she responded. "He called you. You called Dr. Alabiso, and Dr. Alabiso told James what to do that time I passed out on the floor. I would have died."

I could only guess at her unspoken thoughts.

She could have been thinking about how many times she wanted to die and had failed in her attempts to kill herself. Was she wishing she could be dead too? Or dead in his place?

Miles slid past our windows, and Lillian told me some of her thoughts. "All the way to West Virginia, I kept thinking, it's April 1. Please, God, let it just be an April Fools' Day joke. But God didn't. He let it be Easter." And that was a shock to me because I hadn't thought about it being Easter all weekend.

It was still many miles to Philadelphia, and we stopped at noon and called Dr. Kluft. We would just barely make the deadline on the second day, and I had given no thought to the fact that I would have driven eight or nine hours and was still a good four hours away from my home.

As I parked my car in the lighted parking lot nearest the hospital, I had the fleeting thought that I could, if necessary, sleep in the car by reclining the passenger seat, perhaps in a restaurant parking lot, on my way home. I mentally ruled out hunting for a motel, for I had been here many times before and was afraid of the area and leery of getting lost trying to find a motel. Having lived my life in the country, the city – any big city – held too many unknowns for me.

Entering the hospital, we were immediately caught up in its daily activities. Nothing had changed. Didn't anyone see the pain Lillian was bringing back with her? I had to sign in and wear an identification badge. Dr. Kluft must have given my name, or I could have never gotten past the lobby.

We proceeded to her floor, and the staff, having been advised of the tragedy, warmly expressed their condolences. Then they resumed their routine, calling her to the medication station and taking her blood pressure.

At Lillian's request, I stayed with her for a while. She showed me some needlework she was doing and some drawings. The longer I stayed, the more impossible it became for me to leave. When she said softly, "Aunt Jean, can you stay just tonight? I never sleep in my bed. I sleep on the floor in the closet. I feel safer there and more comfortable. Please? I know you are tired."

I thought to myself, "Keep talking. I am a pushover." I was exhausted.

We briefly explored possible ways for me to stay. None was feasible. But all the talking we didn't do in the car insisted on being done now. We talked about everything, it seemed, and the clock kept ticking away. I fully expected a staff member to arrive and order me to leave, but none did. In fact, a staffer spoke to me, saying she was glad I was able to go with Lillian to her son's funeral. I was certain she would report me, and I would have to leave, but no one appeared.

Ten o'clock came and went. I sat on the bed with my back against the headboard and my stocking feet stretched out before me. Lillian sat in the easy chair. We just needed to be together.

An 11 o'clock bed check was made, and the staffer seemed not to require my planned plea for time. Perhaps she had phoned the doctor and received permission for me to stay. At any rate, Lillian and I took that to be tacit approval, and I stretched out fully on the bed in my clothes and slept fitfully. Each time I roused, I could see Lillian quietly sitting against the wall in the closet. Finally by morning, she curled up on the carpeted floor of the closet with her pillow and slept a little.

As soon as we heard the sounds of the new day's activities in the hall, I put my shoes on and washed my face. I couldn't brush my teeth. I hadn't carried my suitcase in. I prepared to leave. Lillian had an appointment with Dr. Kluft that morning, and she wanted me to wait long enough to meet him. To the best of my senses, Lillian remained herself throughout the entire ordeal of James' death and burial.

I sat in the doctor's waiting room through their hourlong consultation, then met Dr. Kluft for the first time. Afterward, the two of us returned to Lillian's room to say goodbye. We held each other for a very long time. It was one of those times when no words are needed. I promised to call her when I got home and promised to visit her again as soon as I could. I left the floor quickly, making certain that at least one staffer had observed my leaving. Going down the steps into the huge main lobby, my eyes filled with tears. What a woman! I can't imagine how I would begin to handle all that she has endured. Now she must grieve the loss of her son in this terrible place. Alone! Dear God, help her!

Chapter 32
Grieving and Healing: It Was All Me

Paradoxically, Lillian's grieving for James signals a turning point in her healing.

Memories are now coming quickly. With each memory comes the signs of true integration – facts, body memories and feelings; and with them, the most deeply buried traumas are revealed.

Well enough to leave the hospital, Lillian takes up her new life as one integrated person.

Then, once again, sadness returns.

FA

Jean as Narrator: Lillian's next weeks and months in the hospital were well documented in her journal. Her improving mental health and her growing spiritual strength pulled her back from the depths of despair. Her first journal entry after burying James brought forth the depth of her pain.

"My son is dead – my James: 13 years old. Oh, God, I can't make it without him! Oh, James! I don't dare to think. Nothing makes sense. So much I want to write. Proud of Evan and Keith. How deeply love hurts! God, help Jim to bear this. Help Evan and my firstborn, Keith! I can't write. I throw up. Later maybe."

And in another handwriting in pencil, an unknown personality tried to comfort her. She wrote, "So sorry, Lillian."

A few days later, Lillian wrote, "One week today, my son has been dead. I wish I was with him. Must go to him."

She was so intensely suicidal that she was moved again to North building, where she had to be placed in restraints. It reminded her of the tying up she experienced as a child. Her mother had tied her up and locked her in a closet repeatedly. She had been tied on a bed with legs spread apart at home for

Herbert to do the abortion before she was 12. Those friends of her dad tied her all kinds of ways. But one day, one of the male nurses, as he gently fastened the restraints around her, said, "I am doing this to help you until you can help yourself. I am sorry. I don't want you to be hurt." Lillian was touched by his caring.

Six days later, Lillian wrote, "I wish I could die. I wish I didn't love Jimmy or Evan or Keith. People get in my way. I want to be dead, and I can't."

Desperately wanting revenge on family members responsible for the illness that kept James from her, Lillian talked to her doctor about her plan.

Lillian's Journal: "Doctor is threatening to tell the authorities of my plans for murder. Maybe if I get committed for life, that will be punishment enough for me to make up a little for my James being dead. I never would have believed anything could hurt so much inside. A child's death! If Jessica and Herbert had killed me, no one would be hurting like this now; not Jimmy or Evan, Keith, Pap and Grandma. No one would have missed me or even cared. If I hadn't gotten sick, my James would be alive. I know that beyond any doubt! How can I stay alive knowing I didn't come through for James?"

Jean as Narrator: Lillian read and reread the condolence letters that Dr. Robinson and Dr. Alabiso sent her. She was very moved by such loving tributes. She cherished those two letters and wrote in her journal, "Dr. Alabiso and Dr. Robinson know how I loved him. I want my James back. I want to shake him and then hold him close. Easter is gone. Christmas, any holiday are gone. James is gone. I want to be dead, but Jim and Jean think I should love them enough to want to stay alive. But they have no guilt! It was me who let James down. If I'm going to die, why not kill Jessica in the process? And maybe someone will kill me, so I won't have to!"

Later that same day, Debra, a patient, gave Lillian a quilt that she had spent six months making while in the hospital. Lillian was overwhelmed with Debra's kindness. Another patient, Bridget, bought her a book on lace sewing. Lillian thought, "People are being kind to me, and I don't understand. There is no way to repay."

Lillian's Journal: "Oh, my James, only 13 years old! I just want to hold him once more, and I can't. My heart is broken into hundreds of pieces being held together by barbed wire. I want to be dead. Someone do it for me – another personality? Chrissy? Kill me for James. Maybe Chrissy. Please!"

Jean as Narrator: Chills went down my spine at the response that Lillian received back.

Chrissy Wrote: "I can do it for you."

Jean as Narrator: Then, the anonymous personality who wrote in pencil warned, "Be sure, Lillian."

That handwriting had not been seen before, but hers was the still, small voice of life and hope that refused to be quieted or ignored.

A whole month passed before another entry was made in the journal. In that dark time, Lillian was fixated on revenge. She found herself trying to get through "the valley of the shadow of death." Her wish to survive was dark. She violently fought for her death, and with each passing day of grief, she began to fight for her life.

***

Lillian's Journal: "The doctor is away this week. I should have written in this journal every day, but I hadn't even picked it up until a nurse mentioned that I ought to at least look to see if anyone else had written anything. I wonder who wrote in pencil, calling me Lillian? If there is 'another,' that will be letting a lot of people down. Besides, there has to be a reason, and there aren't any reasons for 'anyone else' anymore. I am my mother's and father's daughter – the bad seed, and this is appropriate for a member of my family. I am just like a violent person. It is fitting that I be what my heritage shows me to be. The doctor says I will get well and go home and do what I have to do. I have the right. I don't expect anyone to understand, so there is no reason to speak of it. I already know it's unacceptable to anyone else. It's my right! No one else will be involved. No other 'self' is being asked. In fact, that would cheat me from what I need to do for me."

***

Lillian's Journal: "I find great peace settling over me. Isn't it funny? Dr. Kluft has turned into someone who cares. Lynda, my therapist, treats me like I'm real. Have I changed? Or have they? I need to back away from trusting so much. Being around people will only cause more hurt. People hurt. Being here on this floor while the doctor is gone, I have been punished when I have done

287

nothing wrong. Except I still exist. I want to live. I feel good to be alive sometimes. Other times, I want to hide from the world, not need anyone, not take up the staff's time. One member of the staff especially makes me feel like sewage. I don't need to be here. I wish I could leave. I don't fit anywhere. I want to live! How can I feel like that when James can't be here to see me feeling good? I am writing too much. I wish I had a private room, someplace to cry. Stupid to think I am worthy. Are people real when they tell me I'm okay? Is life a farce? I wish I could tell people about child abuse and incest."

***

Jean as Narrator: But the good days were few and far between. On one of the bad days, Lillian very nearly succeeded in a suicide attempt. At the nurses' station, an unintelligible voice came over the always-open intercom from Lillian's room. The two nurses looked at each other and took off running. Just then, Lillian fell into the hall from the doorway, unconscious. The nurses dropped to the floor and found a thready pulse at the carotid artery. But one nurse's fingers found something else at the neck ... swelling. She realized something was tied there. "Help me! I can't get the scissors under it! It's a string of some kind!"

Forcing the scissors down into the rapidly swelling flesh, she cut. The ends flew loose. Dental floss! They had to spread the skin in order to remove the offending floss around her neck. "Breathe, Lillian! Come on, breathe!" Her body betrayed her mind, and Lillian began to breathe. She was sent to North building, back again to the "violent ward."

Ever so slowly, Lillian began to heal. Rev. Chris called her often, and I called and visited her as frequently as possible. She was usually given special permission for me to take her "out of that place" for a few hours, and we would invariably drive downtown, eat fast food, and talk, talk, talk. On one occasion, Rev. Chris went with me to Philadelphia to visit Lillian. I remember her telling me that Dr. Kluft ordered pottery therapy. Her therapist, Lynda Reed, suggested a statue of a boy sitting.

One of my visits to Lillian in the hospital was particularly memorable. She was expressing feelings by working with clay. After explaining to me how good it could feel to pound the clay, slam it down on the table or cut it up, she showed me a perfectly stunning statue she made of James. He was sitting on a rock, with his eyes cast downward, and the detail of the denim outfit he wore was exquisite! Every stitch of the jean jacket's topstitching was distinct. I asked her how she made it so perfect, and she told me she did it with a straight pin. The double rows of topstitching went around the bottom of the jacket, up the front, around the collar, and even around the upturned cuffs and sleeves. There was a pocket on the jacket, and it too, was double topstitched. Down the side seams of the pants, more miniature "stitches" followed the wrinkles of the garment in its natural yet unnatural perfection.

The head was wonderfully formed, and every hair was depicted as a single strand by those wonderfully loving and talented hands of Lillian's. It had been fired one time, and the realism was absolutely stunning! Lillian reached for the statue as I studied it and suddenly became violent and snatched it from me. Fortunately, she was not allowed in the art room without Dr. Reed. Instantly sensing a change of personalities, Dr. Reed yelled for help, grabbed Lillian and restrained her.

"What can I do?" I shouted.

"Pick up the statue! Set it high up on the cabinet there!" Dr. Reed shouted again for help. Her help arrived, and the "other" personality, realizing that she was outnumbered, returned the body to Lillian. Dr. Reed ushered us out of the therapy department. Lillian was returned to her room. It had frightened me terribly at the time, and now I marvel at how quickly I got over it. Lillian had to make a hole in the bottom of the statue in order for it to be fired. That triggered a memory of her mother coming to her home to sexually violate her and 2-year-old James, rupturing his sphincter muscle. No wonder he soiled himself so often. This was part of Lucy's secret. Dr. Alabiso had told Lillian and Jimmy that James' soiling was an expression of his anger. Now, for the first time, she found that it was from abuse inflicted on him by Lillian's own mother.

***

Jean as Narrator: Lillian's feelings of guilt over James' death were profound! She walked out of the hospital, headed for the train tracks just a couple of blocks away. Her plan was to throw herself in front of the next train. A nurse driving to work stopped her car beside Lillian and asked, "Where are you going?"

"To the El."

The nurse tried to dissuade Lillian but to no avail. She proceeded to the hospital and alerted the staff. Before the staff had time to respond, Lillian reached the tracks. At the spot where her path intersected the train tracks, the rail bed was some 5 feet below street level. People were waiting on the platform. She paused, looked down and jumped! Somebody yelled, "Yeah! Do it!" Someone else shouted, "Lady, you're gonna make me late for work!" As she looked down the tracks and at the trains passing two tracks away, the heckler urged her on. "Go ahead! Jump over there!"

A man wearing a cross around his neck jumped down beside her. "You don't want to do this! Whatever it is that's bothering you can be worked out!"

"Get out of my way!"

Two burly policemen ran down the tracks to Lillian, along with some railroad men. With one determined motion, they lifted and boosted her up to where two more officers miraculously appeared above her. The four of them overpowered her, handcuffed her hands behind her back and lifted her into a paddy wagon, which appeared from nowhere.

Lillian asked to be returned to the hospital but instead was taken to the emergency room of another mental hospital, where she sat all night under guard. The next morning, other patients were offered showers, but not Lillian. When her guard was distracted, Lillian went to the shower, laid her clothes on a chair and entered the shower stall. When she reached for her clothes, they were gone! They gave her a sheet to wrap herself in and took her back to the state hospital admitting office wearing only a sheet! She finally was sent back to her room. Dr. Kluft was furious about the way she was treated and made several angry phone calls.

***

Jean as Narrator: One day Lillian called to tell me that Dr. Kluft had been working with the memory tracer. Her name was Pearl. By tracing Lillian's memories, Pearl and Dr. Kluft uncovered a personality they called "The Sleeping One." She, an infant, had been put to sleep for surgery required by Jessica's savagery and just never awakened. Dr. Kluft found out that Lillian believed that "The Sleeping One" had her soul. She believed that she could not get well until it was returned to her.

Again, I called Dr. Kluft's office to express my deep desire to be involved. I thought being a woman, I could help with that "baby," but when he told Lillian about my call, she accused me of wanting to help the doctor kill her! She thought that she, an adult, would have to be integrated into the infant, and she wouldn't know how to talk, walk or eat. As it turned out, "The Sleeping One" was integrated into Lillian.

***

Jean as Narrator: As Lillian's healing progressed, my own needs began making demands on me. My whole life seemed to be one of caretaking, teaching and pleasing others. I had neglected myself, and the time had come for some extended grieving and healing for me. I entered therapy. It was very hard work. I had buried anger and pain from childhood, as had Lillian. The therapist helped me to identify various "parts" of me and to bring my life into balance. Relearning self-confidence in my office skills, I worked part-time jobs for a year and a half. While I rebuilt my self-esteem, I learned to live alone and finally landed a good full-time job.

Since it appeared that Dr. Kluft didn't wish for me to be close to Lillian, my contact with her diminished, and my visits to Philadelphia ended. In August, she sent me a card. "Wish I could see you! We'd take a walk and talk and talk and talk and talk and talk ...."

Lillian Wrote: "To my Aunt Jean, I miss you! This card just reminded me of us. Just think, I am now an ex-multiple personality. Jim bought me a pin that says Lillian on it to celebrate. He said he could afford it now that there was just one of me! I hope you are okay. I think of you often. Really, I do. Take care. I love you. Lillian."

Lillian's Journal: "I feel more depressed than I have ever felt in my life. Am I feeling everyone's depression? I'd like to be dead, but more than that, as I wrote to Dr. Kluft, I have felt rage lately more intensely than I ever imagined possible, and I want to work to bring out that rage at Jessica (and others) so that when I stab and stab and stab, I will feel what I am doing instead of just this 'head knowledge' of knowing that I want people dead and how to do it. Right now, it's mechanical. I don't want to be a robot when I do what I want."

Jean as Narrator: The return address on the envelope demonstrated that Lillian's sense of humor was intact. It read, "L. Mason, PA Insane Asylum, Philadelphia PA."

Lillian's road stretched endlessly before her as she, as one person, contained all the feelings her personalities had kept secret for so many years. She remained in Philadelphia for several more months, struggling with rage and her desire for revenge.

Later I found out that after her discharge from the hospital, her half-sister, Letty, disclosed that their mother, Jessica, was in a nursing home, but Lillian was not permitted to go there. Lillian drove to the nursing home anyway.

Parking her car outside the guardhouse, Lillian, with a knife concealed in her purse, simply followed a visiting family through the gate.

Once inside, it was easy to find Jessica's room. Looking for a redhead, Lillian did not believe what she saw. It really was her mother, but her hair was white. She was sitting in a wheelchair, looking out the window.

Lillian was shocked at how old her mother looked. She then realized how many years it had been since she had last seen her.

Now fearless, Lillian walked boldly toward Jessica, fully intending to kill her.

Jessica did not recognize her.

In that moment, instead of hatred, Lillian felt nothing. Lillian turned and walked out of the nursing home, leaving her feelings behind. Some months later, Letty told Lillian that Jessica had died. When Lillian asked Letty why she had not been notified at the time of death, Letty said that Jessica's doctor told her that "Jessica wanted it that way."

The next I heard from Lillian, she seemed so calm and collected, I sensed that she was almost well. I thought she didn't need me as she did before. It made me sad.

I stopped hearing from her and picked up my own life.

Lillian was still afraid that some of the people in her past would find her. She didn't understand what I was going through in my life. Years later, she remembered Dr. Kluft telling her, upon her release from the hospital, that the toughest task had been weaning her away from me! I wonder why he never told me. I wanted so much to help, and he shut me out. I felt rejected. I missed her so much. I missed all of the friendships that I had built with her other personalities. I realized, at last, that my near obsession with Lillian prevented me from grieving over each one as they became part of her. Oh, how I had loved them! The practical side of me rejoiced with each integration, but I had buried my emotional attachment and busied myself with whomever remained.

For Lillian's part, she felt abandoned and uneasy coping with life as a whole person outside the confines of the hospital. A subtle but unspoken estrangement settled over us. She stopped notifying me of her address changes. My notes were returned, stamped "Moved, no Forwarding Address." She convinced herself that I didn't care. My heart ached for both of us.

I found out that Lillian was on the road with Jimmy. Most of the time, they were living out of his truck, sometimes staying at motels when they could afford it. Contacting Jim's parents, I found out that they were now living with Pap and Grandma.

I bought a house (which wasn't easy for a single woman to do) and lived alone for five years. I was happy and content. When I met Bill, a retired minister, we fell in love and were married. He became fascinated with my anecdotes about Amy, Esther and all the others, and wanted to meet Lillian and Jimmy.

Now postcards came from California, Florida, New York, Texas and elsewhere. Lillian and Jimmy were happy just being together – no home, no furniture, very little money.

Lillian was one and alive!

Lillian and Jimmy eventually bought a newer mobile home and settled in Ohio near Pap and Grandma. Keith and Evan lived nearby.

Then came Lillian's letter saying that she was home from the hospital following heart bypass surgery. Six bypasses! She gave a new address but no telephone number. As fast as I could make arrangements, I went to see her. Although several years had intervened, it was as if we had never been apart. Our love was still there. We lived states apart, she in Ohio and me in Virginia, but I went to visit her often. My desire to write a book about Lillian was rekindled, and she agreed to my telling our story. She gave me her 26 journals as a starting place.

Six months later, Lillian's bypasses had produced heavy scarring, and she was hospitalized again at Christmas. But this time, things were different. Bill and I were by her side as well as Jimmy, Keith, Evan, and his wife and child. Lillian required angioplasty twice. All of the overdoses by her different personalities resulted in cancer. The doctors found myelofibrosis, a leukemic-type blood problem. The prognosis: terminal. Five to 14 years. But that diagnosis was worsened by her severe diabetes and her heart condition.

I retired from my job to devote myself full time to my new husband and to my precious Lillian.

Although Lillian suffered two heart attacks in the next year, I was able to bring her to my home in Virginia twice.

One day Lillian wanted me to see and appreciate her "treasure." She pulled a worn piece of paper from her wallet. That precious paper had been lovingly folded, read and refolded so many times, that little holes appeared at the junctures of the creases. Though she memorized it years earlier, she carried it with her at all times.

Do not stand at my grave and weep,
I am not there. I do not sleep,
I am a thousand winds that blow,
I am the diamond glints on snow,
I am the sunlight on ripened grain,
I am the gentle autumn rain,
When you awake in the morning's hush,
I am the swift uplifting rush of quiet birds in circled flight,
I am the soft stars that shine at night,
Do not stand at my grave and cry,
I am not there. I did not die.

Mary Elizabeth Frye

I was at Lillian and Jimmy's when she was given the information that she was near her end of life. We had taken her to the doctor's to have fluid drawn from her lungs. I spent several days with her, trying to be of help in preparing her for death. I had never been exposed to how to prepare or help someone accept death. But Lillian seemed to know just what we needed to do. She, Jimmy and I selected her outfit: plaid skirt, white blouse and her beautiful jacket. I offered her a selection of my earrings, and she chose a pair. The three of us lovingly placed all on "her" side of the closet. Oh, yes, she wanted the pair of slippers that my mother, "Grandma Baker," made for her.

As always, we talked and talked. Jimmy had to go to work, but we just talked. No tears, no sadness from her. She gave me her 26 diaries, the five shoeboxes of letters and her precious artifacts.

One day Dr. Kluft telephoned her. When she hung up, she told me he called her, but when she didn't talk to him, he finally told her he had to hang up. I think Jimmy had called Dr. Kluft, but Lillian didn't know what to say.

Lillian, Jimmy and I did all we could do to prepare us for Lillian's end of life.

I drove the long way back to Virginia. I had no contact with Rosalind or Letty.

Jimmy called me often to keep me updated with what was going on. My husband, Rev. Bill, prepared her service, and I made a list of Lillian's favorite hymns to play on the funeral-home organ.

Lillian passed on October 8, 1997.

Lillian had no idea how much she meant to me. I had learned to love her as Lucy, Julie and Amy, as Jackie, Rachel Ann, Mary, Lee and all the others. It was very heady being needed by so many. Lillian's therapy of 10 years had given her 10 more years of life.

Bill and I made the long trip back to Ohio and straight to the funeral home. As I was taking my last loving look at my dear niece, I said, "Jimmy, those are not the earrings she chose." Jimmy responded, "Letty wanted her earrings used. Oh, it's a different blouse." Rosalind had chosen a different one.

I felt pushed aside. I still had not seen Letty or Rosalind. I went to check the organ out. As usual, the funeral-home organ was pretty much out of sight. So I guess I began to feel that I was right where I belonged – out of sight. I had no conversations of any consequence really with anyone. I just stayed "in my place." I don't know for sure where Lillian is buried. I would guess beside James.

Bill and I drove home the next day. At least we had each other.

This is my true and honest account of Lillian's life.

JBR

***

Part 3

Epilogue
A Librarian's Dilemma

The Setting: A public library in a small Midwestern town. The librarian has just received a shipment of books. At the top of the pile, a copy of *Lillian* catches her eye.

The book piqued my interest when the new supply arrived, so I took it home and read it. Now, which shelf does it belong on? Where do I file it? Part 1 suggests the HISTORY section. Does it go there? No, that doesn't seem right.

Maybe in the MYSTERY section. The whole idea seems very mysterious, but there is so much more. No, not there.

Hmm, it made me cry. I laughed, and sometimes I had to put the book aside.

Maybe it's a NOVEL.

No. It's a true story.

Maybe in the PSYCHIATRY or PSYCHOLOGY section? No. That's too technical.

BIOGRAPHY? Story about one person? No. That's not right. AUTOBIOGRAPHY? Story about one's self? No. This is a story about two people.

A DIARY? It's not just a diary. She could only communicate with her other selves via her diaries. Nope. It's much, much more.

No shelf for diaries anyway.

RELIGION? No.

Maybe a LOVE STORY. Maybe two love stories: one between her and her husband, and one that came from the trust and loyalty of her aunt.

Let me think.

EDUCATION? Maybe it's a book for teachers, counselors, principals, psychologists, psychiatrists, clergy and parents.

Oh, that girl who comes in here looking for something, the one who does not respond when I speak her name; the one whose hair always needs to be brushed and whose dress needs washing. Should I suggest it to her?

All need to read it.

Oh, oh, oh, I get it! I know what to do. I will order 10 more copies and put one on each shelf!

– JBR

In Lillian's Own Words

In 1994, three years before Lillian's death, she wrote:

Multiple personality disorder, often referred to as MPD, is a severe dissociative disorder involving a disturbance of memory and identity. It is not moods or pretenses. It is all real, painfully real.

In 1976, I saw a doctor who said I was "one of those rare patients" who had this condition.

Dr. Eugene Bliss wrote in 1980 that approximately 200 cases had been reported. In 1984, the number was over 2,000. In September of that same year, Richard Kluft, M.D., polled a group of 70 physicians attending a seminar he was giving, and among the 70 doctors, they pinpointed another 267 previously unreported MPD patients under treatment.

In 1985, 6,000 MPD patients were under treatment, showing MPD to be considerably more prevalent than had been thought. The numbers are growing.

During the early years, after being told I was a "multiple," I experienced conflicting emotions. Initially, I felt relief because it explained to me and my family the inexplicable and helped me make some sense out of our chaotic lives.

However, the relief quickly became denial. Nobody believed me. I did not believe myself. I became silent.

So many silent years that I have no knowledge of have simply come and gone. I thought I had amnesia. Sometimes I knew I had lost time; sometimes I did not know. Time eluded me. I forgot my childhood, but I thought everyone did.

When I was first confronted by a psychiatrist in a hospital after a suicide attempt, he told me that I was a victim. I objected vehemently. I did not recall any abuse. Later I learned why I could not recall it: I wasn't there. Other "selves" were the ones who took the abuse.

MPD patients have usually been subjected to sadistic and bizarre abuse. I was told that the pain being inflicted on me was love, all the while being told, 'I will take care of you.'

I had acid burns from drain cleaner, cigarette burns and knife wounds. I did not feel the pain until I became me.

When I entered therapy, I was unaware of other personalities. After being diagnosed, I was told of their actions. They were not all aware of each other. I sometimes found myself in another state, even in another country. I could not see what was happening.

At times, as a child, I could see another little girl, as if I were standing outside myself watching.

There are "multiples" whose personalities have been "out" long enough and consistently enough to lead their own lives and to develop their own interests. Some of the personalities create the fantasy of caring parents, stating their intent to go home when they are no longer needed.

It is difficult to imagine, let alone overcome, circumstances that are so horrifying that a child is unable to retain her/his own personhood.

I saw a knitted baby blanket that grew from time to time, but I did not knit, crochet or do needlepoint. I tried to paint some, but things would strangely appear on the canvas that I didn't put there. I always gave away items I found and had supposedly made until my husband insisted they be kept. I felt uncomfortable being complimented for things I didn't even know how to make and couldn't account for. How did I explain this to myself?? By ignoring it or forgetting it?

Where am I now? All my time is mine. Not lost.

There are tears by the bucket for the lost years I now remember, along with the feelings. I don't automatically know how to cope with everything at once. But I'm staying one person. There are frustrations, glaring mistakes, faltering steps, and once in a while, success. I am relearning.

My husband and children continue to stand by me. I know now how much they love me.

Childhood abuse is just beginning to command the attention it needs. Much remains to be done. If my story helps even one child victim of abuse, my life will have been valuable.

Lillian Mason
(1939-1997)

An Important Message from Jean Baker Reynolds and Frank Alabiso, Ph.D.

At 93, I am now in my old age. It's time to complete what I have left undone.

I wrote the first version of Lillian's story in the years between 1976 and 1997. It sat in my closet for more than two decades.

I remembered how much comfort Lillian experienced from Dr. Alabiso's letter following James' tragic death.

Recognizing my age and Dr. Alabiso's generosity, I decided that I would just call him as a courtesy. When he learned of my wish to dispose of my closet full of boxes, he agreed to drive from New York to Virginia to retrieve them.

Dr. Alabiso has joined me in bringing this book to its readers.

As for me, I was privileged to be Lillian's friend and Aunt Jean. I now place all in the good and capable hands of Dr. Frank Alabiso. He will do what is right. And thankfully, I will rest from it.

Jean Baker Reynolds

***

The telling of Lillian's story represents her final triumph over multiple personality disorder. However, those afflicted with the disorder continue to be underserved.

The most recently published statistics by the American Psychiatric Association estimate the number of individuals in the United States suffering from dissociative identity disorder at 450,000.

There are no statistics that estimate the incidences of suicide among these individuals. Nor is there a way to estimate how many of these patients go untreated, given that many psychologists and psychiatrists continue to question whether MPD actually exists.

In many ways, these patients have been forgotten.

Lillian shines a light on an overlooked need for help.

Although controversial from the point of view of standard psychiatric practice, Jean's willingness to enter the world of multiplicity highlights the healing power of a therapeutic relationship.

The qualities of wisdom, patience, acceptance, empathy, kindness and belief in the patient that characterized Jean, Lillian's husband, Dr. Milton Robinson, Dr. Richard Kluft, Rev. Chris Hobgood, Ralph Zannoni, B.S., and Dr. Lynda Reed are not taught in graduate schools.

And yet, they are the qualities of those who were able to restore the spirit of a personality that was fragmented by trauma.

Frank Alabiso, Ph.D.

Sources of Help

*A listing of child protective services agencies by state and U.S. territory can be found at: U.S. Department of Health and Human Services (https://www.hhs.gov). Readers inspired to report child abuse are referred to the sources of help listed there.

Ingram Content Group UK Ltd.
Milton Keynes UK
UKHW022056230523
422235UK00004B/73